The Art of
SPEAKING
MADE SIMPLE

Revised Edition

The Art of
SPEAKING
MADE SIMPLE

Revised Edition

BY

WILLIAM R. GONDIN, Ph.D.

Associate Professor, The City College of The City University of New York

AND

EDWARD W. MAMMEN, Ph.D.

Associate Professor, The Bernard M. Baruch College
of The City University of New York

MADE SIMPLE BOOKS
DOUBLEDAY & COMPANY, INC.
GARDEN CITY, NEW YORK

EDWARD W. MAMMEN, Ph.D.

Co-author of:
The Spoken Word in Life and Art
Voice and Diction Handbook

Author of:
The Old Stock Company School of Acting
Turnipseed Jones

WILLIAM R. GONDIN, Ph.D.

Author of:
Prefaces to Inquiry

ABOUT THIS BOOK

The ability to speak well is one of the most valuable personal assets we can possess. Lack of that ability may be a serious personal handicap. Testimony of leaders in all walks of life has given these statements the ring of truisms. And rightly so . . .

In our social, business, and professional contacts, it is mainly by spoken words that we must communicate our ideas and attitudes. Whether we talk with strangers or acquaintances, it is largely by how we speak that others tend to form impressions of what we are "really like" deep-down-in beneath the facade of physical appearance.

This book is written to help individuals who wish to make the most of their resources as speakers, and who want to give the task the earnest attention it warrants.

Those who have a general interest in the subject may appropriately follow the order in which the chapters appear. The first six form a natural study sequence from *social conversation* and *business interviews* through to *public speaking, parliamentary procedure,* and *group discussion.* Later chapters cover fundamentals of *voice, pronunciation,* and *articulation,* which are important on any speaking occasion.

Readers who have a specialized interest in particular areas of speech, however, may turn to almost any chapter and find that understanding of the text does not necessarily depend on prior reading of other chapters, although appropriate cross-references appear in each.

Thus, the reader with a problem of *foreign accent* may turn directly to the account of its correction in Chapter X where he will find specific recommendations as to how he should also approach the more general treatments of voice, pronunciation, and articulation, in preceding chapters.

Likewise, in the account of certain types of *formal discussion* in Chapter VI the specialized reader will find frequent reference to points of parliamentary procedure in Chapter V. This is because the latter is in fact *a simplified manual of parliamentary law,* complete with a two-page table of motions, and designed to cover any point of procedure likely to arise in most business meetings.

All readers may therefore start their study of this book at the points of their own greatest interest, and each will find the route he has chosen fully posted.

Note: Since this book was first published, many years have passed, occasioning updating. The core of the book remains the same.

—WILLIAM R. GONDIN
—EDWARD W. MAMMEN

CONTENTS

CHAPTER I

CONVERSATION
What Is Conversation? 19
Conversational Weak Spots and Strong
    Points 19
Topics for Conversation 20
    Common Misconceptions . . . 20
    What to Talk About 20
    What Not to Talk About . . . 21
    Discovering and Developing Topics . 21
    Is It Topic Trouble? 22
Adjusting to the Other Fellow . . . 22
    Adjusting to Strangers 23
    Speaking to Children and Older
        People 23
Attitudes 24
    Good Attitudes 24
    Faulty Attitudes 25
Getting Conversation Started . . . 26
    Introductions 26
    Starting the Conversation . . . 27

After the Introduction 27
Keeping the Conversation Going . . 27
    Listening 28
    Your Contributions 28
    Transitions 28
    Trouble 29
    End of Conversation 29
On the Telephone 29
Faults 30
    Pet Words 30
    Superfluous Words and Phrases . . 30
    Vogue Words 30
    Too Much Slang 30
    Affectations 30
    Exaggerating 30
    Telling Personal Experiences
        Awkwardly 30
    Forgetting Names 31
Practice 31

CHAPTER II

INTERVIEWS
I. Applying for a Position 33
General Preparation 33
    Analyzing the Company . . . 34
        Present Status; Organization; Prod-
        ucts, Services; Personnel . . . 34
    Analyzing the Job 34
    Personal Data and Inventory . . . 34
        Education; Experience; Special skills;
        References 34
    Information about Interview Procedures 35

Applying for the Interview . . . 35
Special Preparations 36
    Mechanical Details 36
    Questions to Prepare For . . . 36
    Special Questions 36
        The opportunity-to-talk; The problem
        question; The judgment question . 36
        The getting-a-slant-on-you question 37
        The trick question; Practice . . 37
The Interview Itself 37
II. Interviewing the Applicant . . . 38

9

Preparation for the Interview . . . 39
  Job Analysis 39
  Rating the Applicant 39
  Rating Sheet 39
  Place for the Interview 40
  Scheduling the Interview . . . 40
  The Plan of the Interview . . . 40
III. The Sales Interview 42
  The Good Salesperson 42
    Knowing Needs and Wants . . . 42
    Knowing the Product 42

Knowing the Competition . . . 42
*Knowing How to Win Consumer Ac-
  ceptance* 42
Steps in Selling 43
  The Pre-approach 43
  The Approach 43
  The Presentation 44
  Overcoming Objections . . . 45
  The Close 45
Common Faults In Selling . . . 46

CHAPTER III

SPEAKING IN PUBLIC
  Feeling at Ease 47
  Basic Concepts 48
  Beginners' Faults 50
  Visual Factors 50
    Posture 51
    Movement 51
    Gesture 51
    Eye-contact 52
    Visual Aids 52
    Notes 52
    Dress 52
  Types of Delivery 52
    The Impromptu Talk 52
    The Memorized Speech . . . 53
    The Written Out and Read Speech . 53

The Extemporaneous Speech . . 54
Choosing a Subject 54
  Subject Which Suits You . . . 54
  Subject Which Suits Your Audience . 55
  Subject Which Suits the Occasion . 55
  *Subject Which Suits Your Time
    Allowance* 55
Deciding on the Response You Want . 56
  The General Purpose 56
  The Specific Purpose 57
Analyzing the Audience 58
Radio and TV 59
  Introduction—Special Problems . 59
  Camera and Microphone . . . 60
  Preparation 60
  Eye Focusing in Television . . . 60

CHAPTER IV

SPEECH COMPOSITION
  Elements of Composition 61
    The Body 61
    The Introduction 64
    The Conclusion 66

Types of Composition 67
  Narration 67
  Exposition 70
  Argumentation 73
Composition as Feeling for Form . . 77

CHAPTER V

PARLIAMENTARY PROCEDURE
Basic Definitions 79
Rules of Order 79
The Chair 80
Rising to be Recognized . . . 81
Having the Floor 82
Making and Seconding Motions . . 82
The Order of Business 83
1. The Call to Order 83
2. The Minutes 83
3. Reports 84
4. General Orders 84
5. Unfinished Business 85
6. New Business 85
7. Adjournment 86
Explanation of the Table of Motions . 86
Column 1—Precedence . . . 86
Column 2—Authority to Interrupt . 86

Column 3—Need for a Second . . 87
Column 4—Debatability . . . 87
Column 5—Amendability . . . 87
Column 6—Required Votes . . . 87
Column 7—Renewability . . . 87
Table of Motions 88
Column 8—Special Notes . . . 90
Column 9—Page References . . 90
Use of the Table of Motions . . . 90
The Classes of Motions 90
Subsidiary Motions 90
Motions Regulating Debate . . . 92
Motions Postponing Consideration . 92
Privileged Motions 94
"Incidental" Motions 96
Main Motions 100
Review Motions 101

CHAPTER VI

DISCUSSION TECHNIQUES
Parliamentary Discussion . . . 104
Formal and Informal Procedure . . 104
Parliamentary Strategy . . . 105
Organizing a Parliamentary Group . 107
Constitutions, Bylaws, and Rules . . 111
Program Forms of Discussion . . . 112
Platform Debates 112
Oxford style 112
Oregon style 114
Symposia 116
Forums 116

Informal Group Discussion . . . 117
Discussion as Group Thinking . . 117
Requirements for Cooperative
Discussion 118
Pointers on Agenda 119
Clarification of the Question . . 120
Surveying the Facts of the Problem . 120
Diagnosing Possible Causes.
Suggesting Possible Solutions . . 121
Evaluation 122
Summarizing 122

CHAPTER VII

DEVELOPING YOUR VOICE
Principles of Practice 123
Ear Training 123
Analyzing Your Voice 124
Basic Concepts in Developing Your Voice 125
Free the Voice 125

Concentrate on Meaning . . . 125
Let Emotion Help You . . . 125
The Voice Mechanism 126
Phonation—The Production of the Basic
Tone 127
Good Phonation 127

Achieving Relaxation 128
Toning Sluggish, Lax Muscles . . 128
Faulty Phonation 129
Controlled Breathing 130
Effective Methods of Breath Control . 130
Pitch 132
Changes in Pitch 132
The Habitual Pitch Level . . . 132
The Optimum Pitch Level . . . 132
Varied Pitch Levels 132
Intonation 133
Inflections 134

Volume 134
To Strengthen a Weak Voice . . . 135
Quality 136
To Focus the Tone 136
To Develop Nasal Resonance . . 136
Faulty Nasal Resonance 136
To Correct Nasality 136
To Develop Oral Resonance . . 137
To Develop Throat Resonance . . 137
Rate 138
Phrasing 138

CHAPTER VIII

PRONUNCIATION
Acceptable American Pronunciation . . 140
The Dictionary 140
How to Use a Dictionary . . . 141
A Note on the Pronunciation Lists . . 141
Pronunciation Key 142
Vowels 142
Consonants 142
Syllables 142
Accent 142
Common Mistakes in Pronunciation . . 142
Spelling Pronunciations . . . 142
Reversing the Order of Sounds . . 144
Added Sounds 144
Sounds Left Out 144
Substitution of One Sound for Another . 145
Confusing Words with Similar Spelling 145
Accenting the Wrong Syllable . . 145
Affectations 146

Helps Toward Better Pronunciation . . 147
Influence of Part of Speech on Pro-
    nunciation 147
Words We Read but Seldom Say . . 147
Choice of Pronunciation . . . 148
Foreign Words and Phrases . . . 149
Latin Words and Phrases . . . 149
French Words and Phrases . . . 150
Food and Restaurant Words . . 150
Military Words 150
Words from the Arts . . . 151
Political Words and Phrases . . 151
Social and General Words . . 151
German Words and Phrases . . . 151
Italian Words 152
Names of Persons and Places . . . 152
Names of Persons 152
American Place Names 153
Foreign Place Names 153

CHAPTER IX

ARTICULATION
Preliminary Explanations 155
How Articulation Can Be Improved . 155
The Organs of Speech 156
The Importance of Listening . . 158

Vowels and Diphthongs 158
Definitions 158
The Special Role of Vowels in Speech . 159
Vowel Production 159
The Extreme Vowels 159

The Front Vowels . . . . 163 | The T and D Sounds . . . 169
The Low Vowels . . . . 164 | The L Sound 170
The Back Vowels . . . . 164 | The Sibilants 171
The Central Vowels . . . . 165 | *The Linguo-dentals* . . . 173
Distortions . . . . . 167 | *The R Sound* 173
The Consonants . . . . 168 | General Articulation Faults . . . 174
Definition . . . . . 168 | *Omissions* 174
The Alveolars . . . . 168 | *Additions* 175
The N Sound . . . . 169 | *Over-Articulation* 175

CHAPTER X

FOREIGN ACCENT | Consonants 182
A Healthy Approach . . . . 177 | *The Alveolars—T, D, N, L, S, Z, etc.* . 182
Stress . . . . . . 177 | *TH* 182
Accent . . . . . 177 | *R* 182
Secondary Accent . . . 177 | *W and V* 182
Unstressed Syllables . . 178 | *Y and J (DZH)* 182
Stress in Speech . . . 178 | Cognate Confusion 183
Strong and Weak Forms . . 178 | *Voiced and Voiceless Sounds* . . 183
Linking Syllables . . . . 178 | *Pointers on P, T, K, B, D, G* . . 184
Linking Words . . . . 179 | *The Endings -d and -ed* . . . 185
Falling and Rising Inflections . . 179 | *The Endings -s and -es* . . . 185
Vowels and Diphthongs . . . 180 | NG Clicks and Confusion . . . 185
Production of Vowels . . . 180 | *Correcting the Substitution of N for NG* 185
Production of Diphthongs . . 181 | *Correcting the NG Click* . . . 185
Length of Vowels and Diphthongs . 181 | Consonant Combinations . . . 187

ANSWERS 188
INDEX 189

ILLUSTRATIONS

Fig. 1. Diagram of the Vocal Bands During Breathing and Phonation 126

Fig. 2. Diagram Showing Front of Larynx . 130

Fig. 3, 4. Diagrams Showing the Chest, Lungs, Diaphragm, and Abdominal Wall in Inhalation and Exhalation .   .   . 131

Fig. 5. Diagram of the Speech Tract .   . 157

Fig. 6, 7. Enunciating the EE Sound .   . 160

Fig. 8, 9. Enunciating the A Sound .   . 160

Fig. 10, 11. Enunciating the AW Sound . 161

Fig. 12, 13. Enunciating the OO Sound . 161

Fig. 14. Tongue Position Diagram .   . 162

Fig. 15. Lip Contour Diagram .   .   . 162

Fig. 16. Front Part of Tongue Position Diagram for Vowels 163

Fig. 17. Lower Part of Tongue Position Diagram for Vowels 164

Fig. 18. Back Part of Tongue Position Diagram for Vowels 165

Fig. 19. Center Part of Tongue Position Diagram for Vowels 165

Fig. 20. Vowel Chart 166

Fig. 21. Vowel Exercise Illustration .   . 167

Fig. 22. Good "T" Articulation .   .   . 170

Fig. 23. Dentalized "T" Articulation .   . 170

Fig. 24. Alveolars and Linguo-dentals . 182

The Art of
SPEAKING
MADE SIMPLE

Revised Edition

CHAPTER I

CONVERSATION

Good conversation is fun. It can make an evening pass as pleasantly as the theatre, movies or television.

Conversation also has more serious values. It links people together—family, business associates, friends. It is perhaps the most important single factor in better human relations.

Good conversation aids us in that much criticised American drive to "get ahead"; but it also helps us to achieve that relaxation, that freedom from worry and care, that peace of mind and soul which we all desire.

Yet many of us, when we plan a party, spend much time preparing food and games but do not give conversation a thought. Although it is bound to be an important part of the evening in any case, we seldom plan for it. We invite guests without considering whether they will have mutual interests to talk about. In introducing those who are meeting each other for the first time we fail to mention things they have in common that can set them off on a pleasurable conversation. And we fail to prepare ourselves to take the lead, if necessary, with a topic we can count on everybody being interested in.

Even in business interviews we may prepare for everything except the very core of the matter. We may come with shoes shined, clothing pressed, fingernails manicured—but vague about what we are going to say.

Many of us are not merely unprepared—we dread conversation itself.

Some of us are shy about meeting strangers; some of us shun working on committees; some of us avoid *any* conversational situation.

Where conversation is avoided it is probably because we feel inadequate in talking to others. We are afraid of repeating the mistakes we made at our first dinner party, or at our first job interview.

Those who find themselves shying from conversation would do well to examine this feeling of inadequacy and do something to remedy it.

The two most important first steps are: understanding what conversation is, and analyzing our conversation to decide what our specific weaknesses are.

WHAT IS CONVERSATION?

Conversation, in part, is self expression. It provides us opportunities for asserting our individuality, telling the world just how we feel, or "letting off steam." Talk of this sort is pleasurable and valuable. It is like tinkering with a hot-rod, or breeding tropical fish, or puttering around with painting or novel-writing. It serves as a sort of safety-valve and comes easily to almost everybody.

However, when conversation is entered into merely to "get something off your chest" it makes very bad conversation. It is too one-sided. No number of monologues ever adds up to *real conversation*. When everyone wants to shoot baskets, the ball doesn't get passed around enough for a good game.

At its best, conversation means the pooling of information, the sharing of interests, the bringing together of ideas.

Conversation is a two-way thing, involving give and take, action and reaction. Indeed it is a many-way thing—the communication of many ideas among many people.

CONVERSATIONAL WEAK SPOTS AND STRONG POINTS

If you find yourself shying away from conversation, analyze your experiences in recent conversational situations. Ask yourself such questions as:

Did I find it difficult to pick a *topic* for conversation? Did I cause embarrassment by talking on some tabooed topic?

Was adjusting to persons my problem? Did I get tongue-tied in the presence of certain individuals, or of certain *types* of individuals? Did I fail to give proper deference to older or more distinguished persons?

Was my general *attitude* at fault in dealing with people? Was I dogmatic, condescending, argumentative? Did I *adjust* well to the attitudes of *others*? To their *changes* in attitude?

Did I have trouble *starting* a conversation? Getting *others* to start?

Did I fail to keep a conversation *going*? Did I let it bog down? Could I have moved more smoothly from one topic to *another*? Was I clumsy in ending a conversation?

Was it some *mechanical* fault that made me ill at ease? Was it mispronunciation, forgetting names, overuse of slang?

On the basis of your analysis, give special study to sections of this chapter which most apply to you. Take up one area at a time and follow the suggestions for practice at the close of the chapter.

Prepare carefully for the more formal conversational situation. If you are to go into a business conference or an interview, become as well informed as you can about its subject. If you are to meet some new people, try to learn as much as you can about them. Even in casual meetings you can do this much planning—you can think **before you speak.**

But do not prepare and rehearse phrases to use on a specific occasion, for this is futile. You can never anticipate the exact turn a conversation will take. In using this chapter, moreover, you must not expect it to ease you over your very next conversational hurdle and all hurdles thereafter. No chapter, or book for that matter, can tell you what to say when your former college roommate arrives unannounced with lots of luggage planning to spend three weeks with you. But armed with some principles, and some previous practice of these, you ought to be able to greet her or him and discourage the plan with more poise than apoplexy.

During the coming week take careful note of your conversations and their characteristics. What were your weak spots, your strong points? At the end of the week, decide what you need most to improve upon.

Each successive week, for a month or two, sit down at approximately the same time and repeat the process. Pick a time when your schedule isn't likely to be broken or interrupted.

TOPICS FOR CONVERSATION

Common Misconceptions. If your difficulty seems to be **finding suitable topics,** your real problem may be thinking about topics in the wrong way. You may have some misconceptions concerning the things people talk about.

One common misconception is that only the very unusual event is worth talking about. You ransack your mind for some preposterous coincidence, some tremendous achievement, some shattering experience, some hilarious situation.

Vastly exciting and amusing events do occur in this world, of course, and people enjoy hearing and telling about them.

But many an agreeable evening has been spent in small talk about the ordinary happenings and problems of everyday living—getting the children off to school, whether tomato plants should be staked or not, good places to spend the weekend.

So if you have never had quintuplets nor explored the upper Amazon, nor been forced at the point of a gun to prepare breakfast for four bank robbers, you need not remain silent. However simple the life you lead, it provides plenty of material for conversation.

Another misconception is that a topic must be literary, or abstruse, or very learned.

People do talk about the special theory of relativity, gambits in chess, and atomic fission, to be sure. But more often, they talk about life and love, and food and drink, and the weather. So do not feel that only topics you have studied for months are suitable for conversation.

What to Talk About. As a matter of fact, almost any topic is suitable for conversation.

You can talk about basketball or badminton, knitting or carpentry, crime or punishment, tea or astrophysics or door-to-door selling, the stock market or a new chain store, or shoes, or ships, or sealing-wax, or cabbages, or kings.

You can discuss books, plays, movies, television programs, news events, national policies, or local problems.

You can swap stories, anecdotes, observations, opinions. You can recall some idea from a magazine article, a newspaper column, a sermon. And **your reaction** to the idea may be more important to the conversation than the topic itself.

For one purpose of conversation is to enable other persons to compare their thoughts with yours. Ask a person how he or she feels about a subject; if there are disagreements, remember that minor differences of opinion are intriguing.

Conversation is a friendly art with a double pleasure—the warmth of sharing similar beliefs, and the stimulation of discovering differences.

So don't hesitate to express agreement, for fear of being thought unoriginal; and don't hesitate to express disagreement, for fear of being considered contrary.

If you can't praise a play or concert others liked, don't think you must stay silent about it. If you think reporters are a nuisance at international conferences, say so. But remember to voice your dissent in such a friendly way that the conversation can continue. If you force your opinion as if you had a mission to convert others, you will not be contributing to the conversation, but stopping it.

Air your prejudices, too, if you want, provided you show by words or your tone that you know them to be prejudices; and provided, of course, that they are not offensive. If you can't stand calorie-counting, or amateur psychoanalysis, don't hold back. On the other hand avoid becoming known as a person who "can't stand" things. It matters very little to anyone that you "can't stand roses." And not at all to the rose.

Some persons like to make challenging statements. To an admirer of Toscanini, they'll say, "Don't you think he plays everything too fast?" Such remarks may provoke stimulating discussion; they may also provoke discord. The challenge must be carefully handled, and perhaps you had better leave it till you are very sure of yourself and your company.

Before offering a topic, be sure you know something about it. This doesn't mean your knowledge must be encyclopedic. But be sure you are familiar with it. If you have had only a week-end of skiing you had better not tell how to execute a stem-Christy. There may be an expert present, and you will be much safer describing your first reactions to skiing, your first fall.

What Not to Talk About. The wide variety of topics available to you is proved by the small number of topics to be avoided.

Discussing personal matters in general company is inconsiderate. So also is embarrassing your family or friends by describing their faults to strangers. Unless you aim to be an untouchable, you had better not reveal plots of books or movies or plays to those who haven't yet enjoyed them. Your chances of being invited again are slight if upon being introduced you promptly launch into a shady story.

Having only *one* topic for conversation is as bad as having none. We have all suffered from bores who could only "talk shop" or who would never let anyone forget their aches and pains, or who chattered incessantly about the brilliance of their children.

If you think the variety of your topics is limited, set about finding some new ones.

Discovering and Developing Topics. You read newspapers daily, probably subscribe to a magazine or two; you listen to radio programs or watch television; you hear stories from friends; you go to church and hear sermons; you attend the theatre; you have a multitude of interesting experiences with customers, salespeople, colleagues, your family.

These are storehouses of topics for conversation.

Are you neglecting them? Do you use reading simply as a time-filler? Is the newspaper only something to look at while you ride from home to office and back? Do you listen without really paying much attention? Do you say, "That was a good speech," and promptly forget it? Do you hurry so busily and thoughtlessly from moment to moment that you never let your experiences sink in, become meaningful?

If so, begin to make use of these storehouses.

When you come across a likely item in the newspaper, make a mental note of it. Circle it in pencil. Better still, cut the item out.

Fix in mind an idea you read in a magazine: "Americans are perfectionists. They have a naive faith that there is a best way of doing things, and they're going to keep on trying till they find it."

Remember the pungent phrase from the speech or sermon: "Every man is an unrepeatable experiment."

Out of such materials, **build your own storehouse of topics.** If your memory is not good enough to store such bits, keep a notebook or a card-file.

Develop this material, moreover, while it is still fresh in mind. Talk an idea over with family and friends. It may seem quite a different, certainly a fuller, one when you have examined and explored its possibilities.

Read up on topics that particularly interest you. The *Readers' Guide to Periodical Literature,* which you can get at public libraries, will help you to find articles on the subject. Make this reading active. And for every hour you spend reading, set aside some time afterwards for thinking about what you've read.

If you keep on discovering and developing topics in these ways, you will never be at a loss for conversational topics.

Is It Topic Trouble? One possibility remains —that you haven't really got topic trouble at all. There may have been topics you could do well with, only you were too shy to speak up when they were mentioned.

You may have set your sights too high. You may have talked very well without realizing it.

Or you may have wrong goals. You may have been comparing yourself with someone who is a good conversationalist, but in a style not suited to you.

If that is the case start afresh. At the next occasion where you can do so, sit in, but only as a listener.

Use your silence. Listen carefully. Practice listening. Be able to report afterwards, to yourself, or to others, what topics were covered and how.

Compare the participants, their successes and failures. Evaluate their techniques.

At another time, though still making no direct contributions, ask questions. Try to draw people out. And evaluate what you hear.

At still another time use only single-statement contributions and questions. Evaluate the performances of others. Evaluate your own.

On the next occasion let yourself go. See how you do.

You may be very proud of the result.

Practice Exercise No. 2

Jot down a list of possible topics from your past reading and listening. Make a separate list of topics you have heard discussed in groups you were with during the week.

Do any topics occur on both lists?

Could you have used any other of the topics from the first list?

If so, why didn't you?

ADJUSTING TO THE OTHER FELLOW

One may be able to talk about a great many topics, or at considerable length on some topic, and yet not be adept at conversation. One may tell some very good stories connected with the topic and yet provoke groans and boredom instead of laughter and interest.

For good conversation involves *two, three,* or *more* persons, not just one. It demands recognition of the knowledge and interests of the *other fellow,* of the *group.*

The good conversationalist tries to find topics the others *also* are interested in and *also* know something about.

The good conversationalist, as far as he can, avoids the wrong topics—those that will have little appeal for the others or that may embarrass them.

The good conversationalist *slants* his contributions to his listeners, much as a magazine such as *Esquire* or *Seventeen* slants its stories and articles to the particular group of readers it seeks to serve.

If you meet a designer who has worked on the Cuisinart, which you have recently purchased, you can tell him so, you can praise the appliance, or ask him about problems in designing it. But you wouldn't begin with a recital of defects you have found in it or with your notions of how he should have designed it.

Try to *stimulate* talking. Like Falstaff, be not only witty in yourself, "but the cause that wit is in other men." Try not to hinder the interchange of ideas. Try to keep the conversation moving. Try to keep it pleasant.

With old friends, this is no problem. We know their likes and dislikes. We enjoy talking about the same things. We feel at ease with them, even during long silences. If we didn't, we wouldn't be old friends.

But with strangers, difficulties arise. Discovering their interests may take effort and time. We may even have grown shy of meeting and talking with strangers generally.

Are those your problems? If so, let us see what you can do to make meeting and talking with strangers easier and more pleasurable.

Adjusting to Strangers. When you know that you are going to meet strangers at some function, try to find out something about them from mutual friends. Inquire about their occupations and interests.

When you go into a strange home, be observant. Look for clues that will help you to know the people who live there a bit better. What pictures, books, magazines do they live with? Do they read *Time* and *The New Yorker*? Or do they enjoy magazines you never heard of before then? If you don't like their taste in interior decoration, cross those topics off your list. Look for things you can praise or that suggest a mutual interest.

At a large party, survey the several groups before you join one. Try to spot a likely-looking one, one whose members at least *look* as if they might have something in common with you.

When you join a group, listen for a while for hints about the speakers' personalities before making contributions yourself. It is better to hold back a bit than to blunder. (If what you hear doesn't interest you, wander off to another group. And listen there for a while before joining in. Be sensitive to the level of the conversation.)

Pay attention to the remarks made by the host or hostess in introducing you to the stranger. For example, with "Mr. Carr has just returned from the Middle East" as a lead, you can comment that the Middle East is much in the news these days, and you can ask him about his mission, or his opinion on recent events there. Or you can merely express pleasure in the opportunity to hear about that place at first hand. In a few moments you will probably know considerably more about him.

Volunteer information about yourself. Mention what you do, or happen to have been doing just before you met him. This will probably lead him to tell you something about himself.

Ask *personal*, but *not too personal*, questions. Obviously, one doesn't ask a person's salary. But if one's host is with Bethlehem Steel, you can certainly ask of a guest, "Are you with Bethlehem too?" If he is, you can express interest or go on to further questions. If he isn't he'll probably say what his work really is, and you can go on from there.

The stranger's first few remarks should give you clues to his interest. If he says, "This rain is certainly good for crops," you know that his interests are different from one who says, "If we have any more rain, the shops may as well close up."

The other fellow may be more ill at ease than you. Help him out. Talk about small matters to put him at ease.

Be on the alert for changes in mood and be ready to shift with them. Notice the other fellow's facial expressions, his hand movements, his stance. When does he perk up? When does he look vague or uninterested?

With strangers, especially, shun the argumentative approach, the challenging statement. Avoid politics and religion. You probably won't get far with such topics, and your host will certainly not thank you.

Speaking to Children and Older People. Perhaps the most important thing in conversation is to apply the "golden rule": when talking with others, no matter what their status or age, treat them as you would like to be treated . . . with respect. Whether very old or very young, eight or eighty, fourteen or forty, male or female, mechanic or executive, people are interested in talking about things that affect them: from the rising cost of rents and housing, to the best place to buy fresh vegetables, to the presidential elections or the Middle East crisis, to their favorite sport, book, game, movie, or television program. When talking to or about children, avoid patronizing words such as *tots, youngsters, kiddies,* or *tykes.* Similarly, when talking to or about older people, avoid the words *oldsters, old folks,* and other stereotypical and condescending expressions.

ATTITUDES

A group of college students, asked what bothered them most in conversation, answered that it wasn't the topic, or the people as such, but rather the *attitudes* of people. They found it easy to talk with the *friendly* person, difficult to talk with the *dogmatic* person.

Is it your own attitude that you're uncertain about? Is your worry, not *what* you say, but *how* you say it? Do you think you might improve your attitudes, but don't know quite what to aim at?

Below are two lists, one of attitudes generally considered good in conversation, one of faulty attitudes. Run over both. If you think you have some of the good attitudes, strengthen and develop them. If you're afraid you have faulty attitudes, change them.

Good Attitudes

Be interested. Be interested in what's going on, in what's being talked about; in the other fellow, and in what he's doing.

Be interested, not just in the one person you know very well, but in *all* the persons in the group. Let your gaze move from eye to eye. Pick out the person who hasn't said much, who looks ill at ease, and make a special point of talking to *her.*

Be friendly. Conversation withers if you are critical of the persons present, or are caustic about their contributions, or show, by your expression, that you don't think much of them.

Don't be so misled as to ape the trading-of-insults that goes on among professional comedians. Their feuds are carefully concocted by their gag writers, to spice up what might otherwise be a dull script.

Be cheerful, good-humored. Smile. Make it an interested, friendly smile. Show your good feelings in the way you say things.

Leave your tragic mask at home. Don't try to get people to gather round by exhibiting what a hurt, misunderstood soul you are.

Be animated, and yet relaxed. You're alive, so let your face and gestures show it. Time enough for immobility when rigor mortis sets in. (Of course, if on a particular occasion you don't feel up to being animated, beg off.)

But good conversation also has a certain calmness, a feeling of relaxation about it. It isn't work, strained and effortful. It is a play-activity, a refreshing *rest* from work.

Be flexible. Topics change, and people, and moods. The good conversationalist changes with them. Tenacity is a quality we admire in a bulldog, and rigidity in a ramrod. But neither of these qualities has a place in conversation.

Be tactful. Follow that old adage, think *before* you speak. Think *first,* not *afterwards.* That is the essence of tactfulness.

If your neighbor's son has been expelled from school, stay far away from the topic of college requirements when chatting with him, or any talk about the irresponsibility of youth.

We can't help wounding people at times because we do not know all their sensitive spots. But we should try not to wound through mere thoughtlessness.

Be courteous. One could make a presentable case for the idea that good conversation is good manners. This does not mean merely remembering to say "Please," when asking for something, or thanking one's host for a pleasant evening upon leaving.

It does mean having a general attitude of consideration for others.

True, so famous a conversationalist as Dr. Johnson was notorious for his colossal rudeness. But the prodigious Samuel was much more a monologist than a conversationalist. People swallowed his insults for the sake of his enthralling discourses.

Quote Dr. Johnson's definition of *oats,* if you will: "food for horses in England, for people in Scotland." But do so only if there are no Scots present.

Faulty Attitudes

Don't be dogmatic. Avoid the sweeping generalization, such as "All politicians are corrupt." Lord Acton took care to say, "All power *tends* to corrupt."

Moderate your statements. Avoid *all* and *always.* Swing over to *some* and *sometimes.* Use *a few, many, a great many, occasionally, infrequently,* whichever you think is warranted. Be careful too not to say *golfers* when you really mean *the golfers I happen to have met during my three-day stay at Oceanside.*

Learn the face-saving and argument-avoiding uses of: *perhaps; do you think; last week I heard someone say that; maybe I'm wrong, but.*

More important, avoid using a dogmatic *tone.* Some people manage to say, "It looks like snow," as if they were government meteorologists and infallible, to boot. Conversely, outrageous exaggerations can be gotten away with if you say them lightly and with a twinkle. "Fashion is spinach," didn't anger the couturiers overly—and perhaps turned them for a season or two to broccoli.

Don't be condescending. An attitude of being superior to everything and everybody will soon leave you in splendid isolation. There are better amusements than sitting alone looking down one's nose.

Don't be argumentative. Almost everybody likes a good fight—in the prize ring or the political arena. But almost no one is overjoyed to discover a battler in the living room.

Save your strength for fighting the good fight where it will do some good—in the courts or at the polls.

Take the chip off your shoulder when you're going into company. The company will have a better time, and so will you. Do not argue for argument's sake. When you disagree, be, in Robert Louis Stevenson's phrase, an "amicable adversary."

Don't be lifeless. The other fellow expects to get some response from you to his witticism. Don't let him carry the entire burden of the talking.

Moreover, make your responses something more than monosyllables. Conversation is a game which requires at least two players, and no game is fun if one player is half-hearted about it.

Don't be insincere. Praise people, but don't overpraise them. Don't gush, don't be fulsome. And praise the right thing. If your hostess serves excellent food on acceptable, but undistinguished china, praise the food, not the plates.

Don't be egocentric. Express your opinions, certainly; state your reactions; but without giving the impression that you think the universe revolves about you. Don't talk in such a way that your topics can be described as "the Pyrenees and me," "inflation and me," "the Taj Mahal and me," "the Supreme Court and me," "the decimal point and me" etc.

Don't aim to be "the life of the party." We admire the wonderful story-teller, the brilliant wit, the character whose infectious humor keeps the party convulsed with laughter. But we shouldn't let our admiration lead us into thinking that our every remark must be a joke, that the chief goal of conversation is laughter. Good-humor is as important as humor, and good conversation can be serious as well as jovial.

If you wish, practice story-telling, read magazines such as the *New Yorker* for their humor, commit to memory prize bits of wit. These will help your conversation; and you'll have many chuckles as you read, say, Sydney Smith's "Bishop —— deserves to be preached to death by wild curates," or "he was very agreeable, but spoke too lightly, I thought, of veal soup."

But you will do better to try to find your own strengths in conversation. And you may discover yourself accounted the best conversationalist in town because you *listen* better than anyone else.

Finally, don't be a mumbler. Speak clearly. Speak up. Before a remark can be understood, before a question can be answered, before a joke can be laughed at, it must be heard, and it must be intelligible.

GETTING CONVERSATION STARTED

Some people get off to a bad start in conversation by becoming confused during introductions. These are often the same people who don't help their guests much in introducing them.

And there are those who sail briskly through the introduction stage, and then come to a dead halt.

Let's examine these two phases of getting started in conversation:

Introductions. The principles underlying introductions are not difficult. Memorize them by practicing them. Have members of your family act out various roles.

In most cases, introduce the man to the woman (defined here as a female of at least eighteen): "Mrs. Smith, may I present Mr. Jones?" (The only exceptions are that a woman is introduced to the President of the United States, royalty, or a high church dignitary.)

Girls under eighteen are introduced to the other person, whether man or woman. "Mr. Thomas, my daughter Jane."

In general, in introducing people of the same sex, the younger person is introduced to the older, and the less to the more distinguished person.

The wording of the introduction may take any one of several forms.

The most formal is the one first cited: "May I present ——"

The most typical is the mere saying of the two names: "Mrs. Clark, Mrs. Brown," the first name spoken with a rising inflection, the second with a falling inflection. In introducing a man to a woman, the woman's name is said first: "Mrs. Clark, Mr. Taft."

Other forms: "Mr. Black, may I present you to Ms. Cary?" or "Mr. Black, I should like to present you to Ms. Cary."

"Ms. Blane, I'd like to introduce you to ——"

"Mrs. Clements, do you know Mrs. Fisher?"

"Mrs. Clements, you know Mrs. Fisher, don't you?"

"Mr. Huggard, have you met Miss Jebb?" (But not, "Miss Jebb, have you met Mr. Huggard?")

In introducing the members of one's family socially, omit such titles as *Mr.* and *Mrs.* (In business, these titles are retained.) "Mr. Tarr, I should like to introduce you to my sister."

A woman introduces her husband to friends as "Harry"; to acquaintances as "my husband."

Introduce your son's wife to friends as "Jack's wife, Ann"; to acquaintances as "my daughter-in-law, Mary." For other in-laws, use: "This is my father-in-law, John," "This is my wife's brother, Sam," "This is my sister Ellen's husband, Tom."

Children are always introduced to adults. "Ms. Smith, this is Johnny, our son."

To introduce yourself, say: "I am Fred Nash," "I am Ethel Farragut."

In introducing one person to a group, introduce him to all at a small party; if the party is large, to one or two people and rely on these to make him acquainted with others.

In replying to an introduction, simply smile, or say, "How do you do?" or "How do you do, Ms. Swift?"

But if a friend calls with a stranger, saying, "I've brought Mr. Ford, who is staying with us," you should say, "I'm glad you did, Tom." Then, to the stranger, "I'm glad to see you, Mr. Ford."

Practice Exercise No. 3

The Smiths have just settled down in Corinth: The family consists of: Mr. Smith, his wife, their married son, Richard, their daughter Ellen, 20, their other daughter Ruth, 16, and Richard's wife, Helen.

The day after they've moved in, there arrive in quick succession three callers: Mrs. Brown, a church-worker; Mrs. Early, of the town's Welcome Committee; and

Colonel Black, a friend of Mr. Smith's from his college years, but not known to the rest of the Smith family.

Assume you are one of the Smiths, that you answered the door for the first of the callers, and that you must introduce the rest of the family and also the other callers. Have members of your own family take various roles.

Starting the Conversation. The above are the forms of introduction. But the host, or whoever does the introducing, should also mention some fact, tell something about either or both the persons introduced, that will help to start them off in conversation. Say: "Mrs. Green is a tax consultant in the city," and "Mr. Green grows the best roses in town," or "Mr. Fitch is with the local bank" or "Mr. Fitch does a great deal of sailing."

A play, recently produced on Broadway, reached there only because, some years previous, a host, upon introducing a playwright and a director, launched them in conversation with this remark: "You two ought to have something in common because you both have red hair and you both look discouraged."

Even at a large party, the attentive host will try to remain a few minutes with newly introduced guests to see that they are started off in conversation.

After the Introduction. If you're uncertain about the other person's name, be sure to get it straight. This is insurance against the arrival of a friend to whom you will have to introduce the new acquaintance.

If the name is unusual, you may comment on this, or ask about the spelling, for some people are very proud of their names. But be cautious here. If the name is far out-of-the-way, perhaps you'd better not show that you think it unusual at all. Osbert Thwistletick has probably suffered enough from his name already, without your comment.

A remark about the surroundings is a standard starter, and a good one. "It's a lovely party, isn't it?" will do; and so will pleasant comments about the house or the other guests.

Keep to light, casual topics for a while: the party, the house, the guests, mentioned above; the occasion, the weather, the food, the difficulty of managing the egg nog, the hors d'oeuvre, the napkin. . . .

Let more serious topics develop later.

Keep the *tone* light at the beginning. A banker and an economics professor, upon being introduced, each adopted a bantering tone. "You're one of those fellows who tell us poor bankers what to think and do." "Well, you seem to like it. You're always stealing our best professors away to work for you." Several more smiling interchanges, and they settled down to serious talk of the state of the nation.

Asking the other fellow about himself and his work or interests, or volunteering information about yourself, are, as has been suggested, excellent starters. "Do you come from this part of the country?" "Have you lived here long?" Or, if the host has mentioned his being an engineer, you can well ask whether he is a civil, electrical or chemical engineer. But don't be too personal.

And in volunteering information, be sure merely to mention what you do or what you're interested in. Don't launch into a five minute description of your entire working-day routine.

Finding a mutually satisfactory topic to talk about, and the right tone, may take time and effort.

Sometimes two people click immediately. They spy one another across a crowded room, head for each other and, somehow or other, are soon immersed in exchanging hints on the cultivation of mushrooms.

But sometimes half-a-dozen or more topics will be attempted and none will strike a spark. If this happens, don't give up. Keep trying. Bearing in mind what you know of the other fellow, the group, keep throwing out the best ideas you can. All of a sudden, there it will be—the thing that two of you, or all of you, can have a very good time talking about.

KEEPING THE CONVERSATION GOING

There are many factors involved in keeping a conversation going, not the least being that the participants are willing to go on talking.

Here are a few suggestions to help you.

Listening. Listen to what is being said. Don't let the talk flow over and past you like water over a stone. Focus on the ideas, focus sharply.

Listen actively. Let yourself react to what is said. Think about it. Feel about it. Show your reaction. Nod, smile. Don't be a jellyfish, floating passively with the tide.

Try to listen so well that you will be able to tell afterwards fairly accurately what was said.

Keep your eye on the ball, on the topic or the aspect of it that is being discussed *now*. Don't think ahead to what may be said two minutes from now. This may help you endure a boring speech. But conversation requires alertness. You don't want to come to, suddenly, to find everyone waiting for you to answer a question you haven't heard. That's stopping the conversation, not keeping it going.

Don't interrupt. Listen politely to the other fellow. Give him his say. Don't be so anxious to cut in with your idea that you disconcert the person talking. Learn to listen so well that you can tell when he *is* coming to the end of his contribution, so that you can come in with yours as a fellow contributor, not an intruder. Then you will have had your say, and you will have been a pleasant companion too.

Your Contributions. Your contributions may be of almost any sort: forthright statements of fact, questions, expressions of opinion, mild disagreement, comments refining what has already been said to something that you think is closer to the truth.

But make sure that in your contribution, as in your listening, you are on the ball. Don't hark back to foreign sports cars, when the group has left that topic ten minutes ago and is now discussing hot rods. And don't spend your time planning what to say when they get round to the Stanley Steamer. The planned bright remark usually sounds dragged in.

Try to make your contributions more than monosyllables. *Yes, no, perhaps,* are not stimulating. Give your fellow-talkers something to work on. On the other hand, don't deliver orations, long discourses. Be crisp. Let your remark have a beginning and an end. You may have a lot to say on the topic. But the other fellow may have a few worthwhile ideas too. Give him a chance.

Remember the point made at the beginning of this chapter: Conversation means give-and-take. The long contribution may stifle talk. The too-short one does little to help.

Transitions. The time comes when the best of topics seems to be exhausted. Interest wanes, contributions lag. That's the time to turn to a *new* topic.

One way to make the transition is to let the old topic die. Miss Frost says the last word on Florida oranges. Silence. Then, out of nowhere, "I met an interesting character last week. He grows worms." And you're off to interesting characters, worms or odd occupations.

Another way is to pick up the last bit of talk on the old topic and shift by one or more steps to something new. When no one has anything to add on different types of mortgages you may remark, "Mortgages don't come into plays much any more, do they? In the old days no self-respecting drama could do without one. The suspense was terrific, everybody wondering whether the old six-percenter was going to be paid off or not in the last act. But nowadays it's bigamy, and psychoneurotics . . ." So there you are, right in the middle of modern drama. Or bigamy. Or psychoanalysis.

A third way is to shift suddenly and sharply, making no pretense that you're doing anything else. "Well, we've about finished Hemingway, haven't we? If nobody has any objection, I'd like to ask about that picture over there. It's interested me ever since I came. . . ." Or more simply, "To change the subject. . . ."

Try not to change the subject unwittingly. If the topic is wonder drugs, and someone is telling how her Aunt Martha was cured, don't latch onto the *Aunt* part and give your Aunt Emma's recipe for elderberry wine. If you must talk about aunts, restrict yourself to those who have taken experimental medicines and lived.

And don't shift too soon. While the topic still seems to interest the others, don't let your waning interest lead you into pushing them around. Make a polite comment or two, or sit silent and try to look interested. A few coins of patience must sometimes be paid for the delight of good conversation.

Trouble. Sooner or later we all make a *faux pas*. In the excitement of talking, we momentarily forget the tragedy that has happened to some member of the group. Before we know it we have blundered, said something that hurts.

The way out depends on the individual situation. If you've blundered badly, and know the people well, perhaps you'd better say, "I'm sorry, Jane," and move on to another topic. But if you've only veered close to danger, then do your best to veer swiftly away. Do not make a scene by profuse apologies, and try not to become flustered. By staying poised yourself, you help the other person do the same.

When it's the other person who has blundered, do your bit to help. Become interested in the safe topic which she happens to think of, and talk about that. If she becomes flustered, supply one of your own.

End of Conversation. There are times when conversation is out of place. The game of bridge doesn't require conversation, and some players prefer silence during the play, except for the bidding. We go to the theatre to hear the play, not a neighbor's comments. (A converse suggests itself here: If you have friends in for the evening, ask if they'd like to see a particular television program, before you condemn them to a watch-night of silence.)

And the best of conversations must end. Start to go before the others look at their watches, don't dawdle over collecting the coats, avoid starting new conversations at the door, pay your respects briefly, and leave.

Ending a conversation is also a way of keeping one going—the next one, the one you hope you'll be invited for.

ON THE TELEPHONE

The telephone companies rightly publicize the value of "the voice with a smile." To the caller at the other end it conveys the same friendly interest that a guest in your home feels as you give him your smiling, warm attention. Don't let the impersonality of the instrument betray you into dead-pan talking. Use a pleasant and friendly conversational tone.

Speak clearly, precisely, and energetically on the phone. Open the mouth for the vowels, produce the consonants firmly. (See the Chapter on ARTICULATION.) The telephone is not a high-fidelity instrument, and *Smith* may sound like *Fish* if you slur or mumble.

Talk unhurriedly. If you talk too fast, you will only have to repeat.

Speak directly into the phone, your lips half an inch away from the mouthpiece.

To introduce yourself on the phone, simply say, "This is John Brown," or "Good morning, Mr. Jones. John Brown calling." If the one who answers is not the person you want, say "May I speak to Mr. Jones? This is John Brown." If you're calling on a business matter and don't want any particular person, begin with your business: "The Furniture department, please," or "Will you please take an order for ——?" If you think you've got the wrong number, don't ask sharply, "Who is this?" or "What number is this?" Say courteously, "I beg your pardon, but is this 684-1099?"

In answering a call at your office, give your name, or your department and name, or the name of your firm and your name, whichever is most suitable. At home, answer either with your name, or "Hello," letting your caller introduce himself. The latter is probably preferable, for a man's home is his castle, and one does not announce one's name to everyone who rings the doorbell. Avoid "This is John Brown's residence," for it sounds pretentious, as if you were acting the part of a butler. Use a phrase of this sort only if you are asked to answer a phone while in the home or office of a friend or associate.

Finally, answer calls promptly and let your conversation be as brief as the situation permits. The telephone allows only two to talk at a time. By humoring a long-winded acquaintance you may be discourteous to a friend who is trying to call you. For good telephone conversation, adopt that other motto of the phone companies: "Phone as you would be phoned to."

FAULTS

The major faults in our conversation are, of course, the violation of any of its underlying principles, such as talking on topics which are taboo, or conversing without regard for the other fellow.

But there are also several mechanical faults which we should avoid. These result from carelessness, allowing ourselves to slip into a conversational rut, not thinking seriously about conversational techniques, not criticizing our own conversational efforts.

Do you have any of the faults below? If so, try to eliminate them by adopting the suggestions for correction.

Pet Words. A common fault is to have pet words and to use them whether or not suitable or wholly inappropriate.

Some people call all things they like or want to praise *terrific* or *fabulous*. They describe all things they dislike or consider unsatisfactory as *ghastly*, or *weird*, or *dull*, or *putrid*. Sometimes an overheard conversation seems to consist largely of *lousy*, *wonderful*, and *cool*.

Obviously, a mountain is not *cute*; and there are more precise words for describing people, places, and books than *ghastly*.

The correction lies in learning to use those other words. Eliminate the pet words from your conversation for a while. Try to use terms which fit what you are describing. Refine your evaluations. Praise and blame with discrimination. Think first: Is it *excellent, good, fair, poor, completely lacking in merit*? Learn to use *admirable, deficient, awesome, spurious*. Build your vocabulary. Then, if you wish, say *cute* or *ghastly*, but use them properly.

Superfluous Words and Phrases. Other persons add *naturally*, or *really*, or *actually*, or *literally* to most of their remarks. "Naturally, I told him to go, and naturally, he ——." Also over-used are: *frankly, to tell the truth, so to speak, you see, you know, if you see what I mean, do you get the point*.

Eliminate such unnecessary words and phrases.

Vogue Words. Still other persons load their talk with the fashionable words and phrases of the moment. They do not *dislike* things, they are *allergic* to them. At present, *lifestyle, you know, gimmick, low-profile, hopefully, instant, can't miss, sensitive, existential crisis, real experience, connects, bottom line* are over-used and abused, when not misused.

Too Much Slang. There's nothing wrong with slang itself. Even the college professor uses it, though he may confine himself to old forms now considered "acceptable." But much newly coined slang hardly lasts for a year.

Avoid too much slang. Use it occasionally and sparingly when you think it will lend vigor and color to your talking.

Affectations. Occasionally, people sprinkle conversations with *bête noire, accouchement, fin de siècle, amour*, etc. Avoid using too many foreign words and phrases.

Also occasionally, we meet affectation with a reverse twist. The well-education person decides to be "one of the masses," inserting *Guys and Dolls* expressions into otherwise very grammatical sentences. Such an attempt is as futile as the result is ludicrous.

In conversation, don't feel that the addition of a few, too-well-chosen words will make you something different from what you are.

Exaggerating. You must have heard a would-be wit proclaim his story beforehand as "the funniest story I ever heard," only to look crestfallen when the company didn't laugh quite as hard as he expected. Or you've heard an enthusiast describe the wonders of a gadget, and then have to retreat when some more objective user listed its limitations.

Avoid embarrassment by avoiding exaggeration.

Your story may go over better if you introduce it with "I heard a funny story about that the other night."

Telling Personal Experiences Awkwardly. An interesting personal experience can be ruined by too much dialogue, and by too much "So he said," "So I said," "And she said," "And they said." There's more apparatus here than story.

An interesting personal experience can be ruined by too much detail: "I went into this barber shop—it was the one on the corner of State Street and Knott—1516 the number was—closed up five years ago—anyway, I went into this barber shop—I had a dark blue suit on——." It's going to be a long while before anything happens in this story.

Good stories can be ruined by vagueness of detail: "Well, it seems there was this man and he went into this store and he asked for one of those, those what-d'ye-call-'ems. . . ." This man doesn't seem to know what "this" story is about.

Make up your mind what the point of your personal experience is. Gives names or not as you please. Mention only the details that count, but be specific about those. Use dialogue sparingly, to advance the story or to reveal character.

Listen to good story-tellers to improve your technique. And read stories for the help they can give. There's a very good one which begins: "Once upon a time there were three bears, a father bear, a mother bear, and a baby bear." A wonderful opening, for with fewer than twenty words, you're right into the story.

Forgetting Names. People like to have their egos bolstered. To remember the other fellow's name is to please him, to praise him by showing him that he's worth remembering. Knowing the names of his constituents is the politician's stock-in-trade.

By forgetting the other fellow's name you hurt him. You are acknowledging that you have forgotten an essential portion of his identity. Such forgetfulness is, therefore, a conversational fault which should be remedied.

If you forget names, it is probably because you *do* nothing about remembering them. Or perhaps you are so excited and confused during introductions that you never consciously hear a name to remember.

To help yourself overcome this handicap:

Before attending a function where you know that you will meet strangers, say to yourself that this time you're going to remember names. During introductions, fix the idea of remembering names in your mind. Help yourself by re-peating the name, "How do you do, Miss Finch." If you are uncertain about the name, ask to have it repeated. During the conversation, use the name once or twice. In such ways you can fix the name in your memory.

There are several systems for remembering names. You can assist your memory by associating the name in some way with the person. Pick an outstanding characteristic of the person: red hair—Mrs. Carroll; explorer—Mr. Stark. Or select some group of personal characteristics: small woman with large, blue eyes—Miss Janes. Another system is to use the name itself as a link. For Mr. Penn, say "Sylvania," silently to yourself, for Mr. Cotter, add a silent "pin." Some people use numbering systems, 1—Clark, 2—Firestone. Others try to find a key word beginning with the same letter as the name: Bergenthal—berry.

Try out these systems, and select the one you find most helpful. Or combine two systems; or develop one of your own. The possible weaknesses of the association systems are that you may remember the key better than the name, or, worse, that you may not remember the key.

However, *using* names and *concentrating* on remembering them are probably as efficient as any system. And you can strengthen your memory by reviewing names after you have met three or four persons.

Practice

There are very few practice *exercises* for conversation. One can rehearse the telling of a story. One can practice introductions.

The best *practice* for conversation is conversation itself.

Practice at home with your family. If you feel your weakness is topics, talk about the play you have all seen (or the movie, or the television program). Try to keep the conversation going for a good while. Build conversations out of the events of the day as given in your evening newspaper. Bring half a dozen possible topics to the dinner table.

Practice with your friends. Invite a few over

for the evening. In planning the evening don't let it be all bridge or some other game. Reserve part of the evening for conversation. If you feel that an innate friendliness is one of your strengths, and want to develop it, concentrate on an attitude of friendly interest in the talk of the others for that evening.

Practice with strangers. Try to put the principles you have been reading about here into practice. Be on the alert for hints that will help you. Adjust to the other fellow. Try to talk. Be an alive, an interested listener and talker.

Most important of all, seek out conversation. Look for the situations in which conversations will develop. Cultivate a healthy, positive attitude toward meeting friends and strangers. Each opportunity to talk will provide practice. And as you improve, you will know more and more the stimulation and relaxation that good conversation offers.

CHAPTER II

INTERVIEWS

The interview is a business or business-like conversation. Usually it is between *two* persons. However, an applicant for a training program may be interviewed by a *panel* of executives; and a *family* or *group* may consult a lawyer, an investment counselor, a psychiatrist, or a social worker.

The interview has some characteristics in common with social conversation. It, too, is a give-and-take situation. The participants should know what they are talking about, should adjust to the other fellow, should be interested, friendly, and tactful, and should avoid such faults as "pet" words, exaggeration, or excessive slang.

But the interview also differs from social conversation in several important respects:

The interview is a serious conversation with a specific purpose. One participant tries to *persuade* or *motivate* the other, to *learn facts* from him, or to *give* him *information*. We do not request an interview for the mere *pleasure* of talking. We seek out the other person because we want a job, need help on some problem, or want to sell him some product or service or idea.

The interview usually looks toward a *decision*. We get the job or make the sale, or we do not. Information is given to induce a decision, or at least to serve a specific use.

In an interview, one participant is *always* in a *superior position*. Dependent upon the laws of supply and demand, the employer or the applicant, the buyer or the seller, may be in that superior position. But he should not abuse his privilege, for market conditions may change. In any case, an interview stands a better chance of success if each participant has a strong sense of his *responsibilities* to the other.

Other points about the interview are that it is initiated by one of the participants, that a time and place are set and that it usually has a time limit.

Finally, the interview has much less *flexibility* than the social conversation. The participants may talk about other things than the purpose of their meeting, of course, but they should not wander too long or too far. They must get down to the *business* of their conversation.

This chapter covers the two types of interview most likely to interest the general reader— **the employment interview and the sales interview.** In a book of this general nature we cannot treat specialized techniques such as those of the psychiatrist or case worker.

I. APPLYING FOR A POSITION

When applying for a position, you are engaging in what is essentially a sales interview. The goods you are selling are you, your skills and abilities.

Though the thought in your mind may be, "Am *I* going to get the job?" you will probably be more successful if you try to show the employer what you can do for *him*.

Keep this in mind while *preparing* for the employment interview, and during the interview itself.

GENERAL PREPARATION

First analyze the company or companies that might possibly employ you and the jobs you might possibly obtain. Having decided on the position or positions you would like to obtain and the companies to which you would like to apply, prepare a personal data sheet and an inventory of your qualifications. Find out, if possible, with whom you will have the interview and what form the interview is apt to take.

Analyzing the Company. A company analysis will enable you to weed out unlikely prospects, or concerns where you think you would not fit in or be happy. It should also help during your interview, if you are asked the almost inevitable question, "Why do you want to work for *us?*"

Try to include in your analysis as much as you can of the following data about the company:

Present Status. How old is it? How large? Is it financially stable, gaining, or declining? What are its business policies? What distinguishes it from other companies in its field?

Organization. How is it organized? Where are its plant(s), office(s), subdivisions located? Who are its executives?

Products, Services. What products and/or services does it offer? Are these high-, medium-, or low-priced, or does the company attempt to blanket the field? What competition do these products have? How are these products and services regarded by users?

Personnel. How many people does it employ? What are its induction procedures? Does it provide in-service training? What are its policies on salaries, advancement, benefits? How high is employee morale?

The above information can be obtained from:

Booklets and brochures, which can be secured by writing the company. Annual reports may also be available.

Trade journals and business magazines, available in your library.

Who's Who's, business directories, registers, guides, and catalogues, and financial services, available in your library. (See E. T. Coman, Jr., *Sources of Business Information,* published by Prentice-Hall.)

Financial sections of metropolitan newspapers.

Interviews with friends, or with employees of the company. An inspection of the plant may also be possible.

Analyzing the Job. The employer may think you better fitted for a position other than the one you apply for. Also, if there are no openings in your specialty, he may ask you to take another job temporarily.

Prepare a job analysis which answers the following questions:

1. What **education** and/or **special training** is required?

2. What **experience** is necessary or helpful?

3. What **personality traits** are essential? Does one work mostly with things, with people, or about equally with both?

4. What are the **duties** of the position? What skills, abilities, and aptitudes does it call for? What disadvantages does it have? Does it promise a career? Is it a dead-end?

The Dictionary of Occupational Titles and its supplementary volumes, entitled Job Descriptions, are available to you from the United States Government Printing Office, at a small cost. You will find them helpful in answering these questions.

Personal Data and Inventory. Prepare a personal data sheet, a résumé of factual material about yourself, and have it handy for reference. Keep it up-to-date. Some modification of this should be sent along with your letter of application. The sheet will also be useful in filling out application forms. Refer to it before an interview, to refresh your memory of names and dates. The following suggested items are drawn from application forms:

Name, address, telephone, social security number. Health for the past three years.

Place and date of birth, citizenship status.

Military service: rank, dates, and type of discharge.

Education: grammar, high school, college, graduate school, or other (including special or technical school); location; years attended, major course; dates of graduation; date left if not graduated; type of diploma or degree; present school attendance; special honors and activities.

Experience: previous employers, addresses, dates of employment, positions and salaries, reasons for leaving.

Special skills: business machines, technical skills (including typing and steno speed if applicable), professional licenses, knowledge of foreign languages (reading and writing ability).

References: names, addresses, and telephone numbers of at least three persons, not relatives (and not members of the firm to which you are applying), who know you socially or in business; their occupations and the number of years they have known you.

Recreational interests and hobbies.

Also work out an **inventory** of your assets (and liabilities). Answering honestly the questions below will help you to decide between jobs as well as prepare you for the interview:

What sort of work do I find most interesting? Which kinds do I dislike? e.g., contacting people, working with my hands, working on ideas, writing, experimental work, outdoor work, talking before groups, giving orders, following instructions.

What special skills or aptitudes do I have?

What is the most outstanding accomplishment of my business career? Of my social life? What other business or social accomplishments am I proud of?

What activities have I taken part in, socially or in school, that will help me in business?

What is my aim in life?

Information about Interview Procedures. If you can, secure from friends or acquaintances information about the interview procedures of the company to which you are applying. Ask whether employment agencies are used, whether preliminary interviews are scheduled or not, how long an interview you may expect. You may even be able to learn something about the characteristics of the interviewer.

APPLYING FOR THE INTERVIEW

A letter of application should be in two parts: a personal data sheet, and the letter itself. The following form is suggested as a basis for your data sheet:

Name ....   Age ....
Address ....
Telephone number .   Height and Weight .
Education ....
    ....
Experience ....
    ....
Additional information (or Special knowledge); including languages or machine operation) ....
References ....

If you are a veteran, you should add this to the list in the upper right hand corner. The *experience* section should include *descriptions* of the types of work you have done. A section on *Activities* may be included; and you may also wish to indicate your willingness to travel, or to move to another section of the country. The data sheet you send need not include all the items contained in the form you prepared for your own use. Include only those facts which you consider relevant to the job for which you are applying. Be sure to obtain the consent of the persons whose names you are using for reference.

The *application letter* itself is a special sort of *sales* letter; in it you are trying to sell your services. It seeks to arouse the employer's *attention* and *interest,* to make him feel that he *wants* what you can do, to convince him that he will be *satisfied* by your performance, and it asks for the specific *action* of an interview. The data sheet is drawn upon only for material which you wish to highlight.

Your letter will be read, moreover, not only for its contents, but also as an evidence of the sort of person you are. Therefore, spend time and thought on its construction. Make rough drafts, and be willing to re-write. Let your final copy be careful in arrangement, vocabulary, spelling, and punctuation.

Thinking of your letter as having three parts will be a useful guide. Let the first part answer the employer's question: "What does this person want of me?" The second part (one or two paragraphs) should answer his: "What does he have to offer my business? Does he offer enough to warrant my hiring him?" The third part should answer his question: "What am I expected to do?"

Good openings would be:

"For the past two years I have been interested in electronics, and I should like to work for your company."

"Dr. Arthur L. Jones, of Science High School, suggested that I write you concerning a laboratory position in your firm."

"I wish to apply for the position of Junior Accountant, advertised in today's *Star-Journal.*"

Good sentences for the second part would be:

"At Macron's, I developed a new unit control system designed to save space, time, and effort by better organization of work-flow. This was based on intensive examination of company practices."

"My present employer, Mr. Johnson, will tell you that he has found me an able and interested worker."

"I plan to continue my studies at night."

Good closings would be:

"If you have an opening for a full-time book-keeper, I would appreciate the opportunity of a personal interview."

"I would prefer to work in training or personnel. If my qualifications interest you, I shall appreciate an interview at your convenience."

"I will be free for an interview at any time you suggest. A stamped, self-addressed envelope is enclosed for your convenience."

Letters of application should be typed, unless you are answering an advertisement which requests longhand.

(Further help in English and the application letter will be found in *English Made Simple,* a companion volume in the "Made Simple" series.)

If you answer an advertisement by telephone, state the position for which you are applying, give your name (spelling it out if necessary), address and phone number. Mention your chief qualifications briefly, if these are requested, and jot down carefully the time and place of the interview. Speak slowly, carefully, and with a smile.

SPECIAL PREPARATIONS

Mechanical Details. Be ready for a brief test on skills related to the job, such as typewriting speed and accuracy, or folding and enclosing letters.

From your personal data sheet, refresh your memory on names and dates. Pay particular attention to the *Education* and *Experience* sections.

Samples of your work and skill, such as charts or direct-mail advertising letters, are effective arguments. If you have these, prepare a few neatly for presentation.

Some firms ask for a 500-word statement on your history and capabilities. Prepare such a document if you wish. Or prepare an outline, and leave the writing till you know precisely what form the company desires.

Questions to Prepare For. Certain *stock* questions crop up again and again in interviews. Know your answers to the following:

Why are you interested in advertising (selling, teaching)?

Why are you interested in copy (selling tractors, teaching kindergarten, i.e., a subdivision of the larger field)?

When did you first think of —— as a career?

Why do you want to work for us?

What is your strongest qualification for this job?

What are your goals in life?

What accomplishment(s) are you proud(est) of?

Have you ever been fired? Why?

Are you willing to start at a lower position? At a lower salary? At the bottom?

What is your background? Education?

What were the best courses you ever took?

Were they the courses you did best in?

How long would you plan to stay with us?

What are your hobbies? Amusements? What do you do for recreation?

What have you read recently?

Special Questions. Certain *special* questions or devices may also be used:

The opportunity-to-talk. The interviewer may hold off questioning you and say "Just tell me about yourself." It is a good idea to decide in advance what you will stress if given such an opening.

The problem question. "You've told us how you would train a high school senior. Now supposing you had to train a group of middle-aged, casual workers? How would you go about that?"

The judgment question. The interviewer hands you a company product, a business form, or a photograph and asks: "What do you think of this?" Here, as in the problem question, the interviewer is as much interested in the way you answer as in the answer itself. Don't beat about the bush, try not to falter. Quickly make a decision and express it forthrightly, clearly, and simply.

The getting-a-slant-on-you question. "How did you like your previous employers?" "Which of these two jobs would you prefer?" "What position would be your first choice? Why? Which would be your second choice? Why? Your third choice? Why? Your fourth? Why?" Obviously such questions are intended to get you to reveal your personality.

The trick question. There is a story that a radio network, in filling an important executive position, asked all applicants: "Supposing there were 100 applicants for this job. What rank would you give yourself among the 100?" Most of the highly competent persons applying, apparently feeling that modesty was a virtue, put themselves in second or third place. But the job, it is said, went to the individual who answered, "First." Those who had to stick to their old jobs could comfort themselves with the thought that they really wouldn't want to work for a firm which used such trick questions.

Practice. You will feel more at ease in your interview if you rehearse beforehand. With friends or some member of your family, act out employment interviews. Use several jobs, several situations, as a frame-work, and play the part of both interviewer and interviewee. Criticize each other. If possible, have an audience of one or two to criticize you both.

As the final item of preparation, decide *exactly* what salary you will *ask* for and the *minimum* amount you will accept.

THE INTERVIEW ITSELF

For the interview itself, dress neatly. Avoid overdoing as much as you would avoid being slovenly. Moreover, dress fittingly. A stock clerk doesn't wear the same sort of clothes as a junior executive, and a section manager doesn't dress like a model.

Before setting out, make sure you know the full name (and spelling) and title of the interviewer. (When you arrive check on the pronunciation with the receptionist.)

Make an early start for your appointment, planning to arrive at least a quarter hour before. Look the neighborhood, the building, and the office over. A walk around the block beforehand will be better for your nerves than a last-minute, pell-mell rush.

Leave hat and coat in the reception room, if people are doing this. But if this outer room is too busy and public, carry them in with you. (If there's no rack in the room to which you are sent, beware. The interviewer may be using this as a test. Perhaps you had better then say simply: "Where would you like me to put my things?")

As you walk in, try to be confident and relaxed. Say to yourself that your appeal is going to be a positive one: you are there to show the interviewer what you can do for him, not to *plead* for a job.

Your greeting should be friendly and dignified, a simple "How do you do?" Wait to see if the interviewer extends his or her hand for you to shake.

Stand till you are asked to sit; then sit tall and attentive and yet relaxed. If there are letters on the interviewer's desk, don't let your eyes stray towards them. You don't want to be considered a snoop.

Your interviewer may begin with some casual comment, such as one about the weather, to help put you at ease. Respond in kind, keeping the tone casual.

The getting-down-to-business question will come soon thereafter. If it's of the "tell me about yourself" type, then you know you have the floor for some minutes. Develop the selling points you have planned to stress. Talk freely, but watch your interviewer so that you will know if he wants to interrupt to ask about some detail, or if he is interested in some special aspect of your work.

If the opening is of the "stock" question type, then you can expect the interviewer to feed you a series of questions. Be specific in your answers, and crisp. Be neither glib nor monosyllabic in your replies.

The interviewer is interested not only in information. He is watching and rating you on your bearing, manners, tact, command of English, responsiveness, alertness, powers of observation, powers of analysis, frankness, initiative, common sense, and sense of humor. Therefore:

Be healthily and objectively confident. Avoid appearing shy or smug or arrogant. Do not brag, "I can do anything"; do not offer to do "anything you'd be willing to let me do."

Be specific, concrete. Don't say: "I handled a large payroll." Say: "I was responsible for preparing and distributing paychecks to 1,400 employees."

Speak up. Use a clear, strong voice, full sentences, good articulation, acceptable pronunciations. Avoid slurring and slang. This is a business conversation, not a bull session.

Stay alert and observant. The employer wants people who know what is going on about them.

Show initiative. If the interviewer doesn't mention the possibilities for advancement (and he may refrain deliberately), be sure to ask. But do so in a manner that shows you realize that new employees rarely are promoted to vice-president the first year.

Be responsive, interested. React. But let your reaction also be an adjustment to this other personality. If he shows you something of the company's of which he is obviously proud, let him know that you understand and appreciate his enthusiasm.

Don't be so awed that you are afraid to smile. On the other hand, don't be facetious and flip.

Finally, though you are trying to show yourself at your best, **be natural.** Don't try to be somebody else, to act a part, "to talk a good line." A skilled interviewer will quickly spot artificiality.

Some interviewers will do most of the talking. Do not be lulled into inattention by this. You are being tested even though you say very little, for the interviewer will be watching your every reaction. Be an interested, alert listener.

Sales firms, or concerns in other fields where aggressiveness is thought to be an asset, will sometimes keep applicants waiting, or make them appear several times. Show firmness without losing your temper. Show that you can be patient as well as aggressive.

Other testing devices may also be employed.

A prospective camp counselor, applying in January, and arriving cold and chilled at the camp-owner's home, was greeted by the host and his wife in summer-camp clothes. They told him they were testing some summer games and sat down on the floor for the testing. The applicant sensibly sat down too and played the game as enthusiastically as his hosts.

Sometimes you will encounter an inept interviewer, who will conduct other business at the same time or leave you for periods of time. Be patient, meanwhile making up your mind whether you want to work there, whether this is merely a temporary crisis in an otherwise normal workday.

When you sense that the interviewer has asked a last question, rise, say thank you, and go. You may ask if he wishes any more information, but don't dawdle over your leave-taking. If you notice the interviewer glancing at his watch, you will know that you have already overstayed.

Unless you are hired immediately or flatly refused employment, it is a good idea to write a follow-up, thank-you note a few days after the interview. Breathe life into it by mentioning something about the plant or the interview that impressed or interested you. Such a letter may be the added ounce of weight that swings the balance in your favor.

A final point: Tell the truth in your interview. A lie may tempt you with seeming advantages. But such advantages are offset by risks. Jobs can be lost, as well as gained, by lying. And sometimes jobs or advanced positions have been forfeited months or years later because a routine check uncovered an unfortunate bit of wishful thinking.

II. INTERVIEWING THE APPLICANT

In the interview, the employer's task is to find the *right person* for the job he has to offer. If he has to fill several fairly similar positions, he tries to fit the person into the *right job*. He must know the facts about the job, learn the relevant facts about the applicant, then match the one set of facts against the other. This tells him whether to hire, to rule out, or to list the applicant for future consideration.

The employer has a responsibility to the applicant. He must explain the nature of the job carefully, so that the applicant may decide whether the job is the right one for him. The employer who wishes to maintain a low rate of turnover will refrain from overselling the position.

A third function of the interviewer is to "sell" the company. Even if he must turn the applicant down, he sees to it that the latter leaves with a friendly feeling toward the company and its goods and services.

PREPARATION FOR THE INTERVIEW

Job Analysis. Making a good analysis of the job he is offering helps the employer in choosing between applicants. The analysis should include a description of the *general daily* duties of the job, its *responsibilities,* and its *specific* duties. The last include the precise operations the worker performs and the materials, machinery, and tools he uses.

From this analysis a list of *specifications* is drawn up: the mental, physical, and personality requirements; education, both formal and special; and skill. The last includes type and amount of experience and the degree of precision required, and the amount of time needed for training a beginner to master the skill.

The analysis and list of specifications are based on descriptions by employees and supervisors, time and motion studies, and the *Job Descriptions* volumes published by the United States Government.

Rating the Applicant. In evaluating applicants, the interviewer will find a *rating sheet* helpful. It focuses attention on the qualities considered necessary for the position, and helps to assure that they will be covered.

Items often seen on rating sheets include:

General knowledge, special knowledge, interest in field, skills.

Appearance, bearing, manners.

Delivery, voice, pronunciation, enunciation, choice of words.

Likeableness, sincerity, animation.

Initiative, drive, decisiveness.

Emotional maturity, emotional fitness.

Organizing ability, observation, insight.

Using the above list as a guide, the interviewer should prepare a rating sheet suited to his own needs. He may prepare a *general* sheet, or a series of special sheets, to cover specific positions, containing from ten to fifteen qualities to be rated. Too short a list will prove inadequate; too long a list will prove cumbersome. The interviewer should exclude from the rating sheet qualities such as honesty, loyalty, cooperation, whose rating requires longer and more intimate observation than a single interview allows.

Rating Sheet
Form A

	Very poor	Poor	Average	Good	Excellent
Self-Confidence					
Emotional Fitness					
Observation					

A Simple Form for a Rating Sheet (Partial)

Rating Sheet
Form B

1. INSIGHT INTO SITUATIONS AND JUDGMENT

Muddled thinker	Slow reaction to situations	Recognizes main from secondary points	Alert mind and keen judgment	Exceptional insight and analysis

2. CHOICE OF WORDS

Excellent choice of words and good grammar	Descriptive and clear expression	Satisfactory vocabulary	Gropes for proper words	Uses poor English and improper meaning

3. SPEECH DELIVERY

Unpleasant quality	Adequate quality	Pleasant voice quality		Excellent delivery; clear enunciation

A More Elaborate Form for a Rating Sheet (Partial)

(Adapted with permission from the Rating Form for Applicants for Store Service, Baruch School of Business.)

In Rating Sheet Form B the specific descriptive phrases are helpful. Four or five columns may be used. The movement of the highest ratings from side to side tends to avoid a mechanical vertical column check.

Place for the Interview. The interview is best held in a quiet, private, and business-like room, with the telephone temporarily disconnected. There should be a comfortable waiting-room adjoining.

Scheduling the Interview. Ample time should be allowed for the interview. If the number of applicants is large, brief preliminary interviews will serve to weed out the unlikeliest candidates. Time should also be allowed for writing up a report on each applicant after his interview.

Schedule the interviews so that they will not be interrupted by other business; and always *keep* the appointment.

The Plan of the Interview. The interviewer will decide for himself, beforehand, which of the three chief types of interview to use:

Asking a series of questions (the most usual type)

Letting the applicant do most of the talking

Doing most of the talking himself.

In the first method, the questions are of two types: simple, "stock" questions, designed to elicit information and give a broad picture of the applicant's personality; and more difficult "problem" or "judgment" questions, designed to probe more deeply. (Examples are given in the preceding section, **Applying for a Position.**)

If the interviewer gives the applicant fairly free rein, he will probably wish to interject questions from time to time. Since these will be unprepared, the interviewer should avoid negative questions ("Didn't you —"); questions which require only *yes* or *no* for answer ("Did you leave of your own accord?"); and questions which imply the answer ("You liked the work, of course?").

If the interviewer does most of the talking, he must be prepared to be a very acute observer of reactions.

In all cases, the interviewer must plan to:

Establish *rapport* with the applicant, i.e., be friendly enough to win his confidence.

Check orally on at least some of the items covering education and experience in the applicant's letter or application form.

Test the applicant's skills.

Arrive at some estimate of the applicant's personality.

Explain to the applicant the duties and responsibilities and possible disadvantages of the job (twenty-six weeks on the road), and supply information about salary, promotion, vacations, benefits, and company policy.

The employer or interviewer wants to get as *true* a picture of *each* applicant as he possibly can. He also wants to treat all the applicants *equally fairly* and *objectively*.

The following suggestions will help the interviewer to get closer to the truth about the applicant and to make his judgments as between applicants more reliable.

Use opening remarks to ease tensions and create a wholesome atmosphere. Use digressions for the same purposes and also to round out the picture, to help you discover what sort of person he is. But keep your opening remarks brief; don't let the digressions become the substance of the conversation. Keep control of the interview.

Separate facts from inferences. During the interview, concentrate on fact-finding. Build your picture of the applicant slowly, and out of *all* the facts you can obtain by listening and observing. You may miss pertinent facts if you draw inferences too soon; the crucial fact may not appear till late in the interview. Follow leads, of course, and hunches. But don't come to conclusions till the interview is over. Hold up the final decision till all the interviews are completed.

Let your attitudes be in line with your basic functions. You are a judge, a friendly judge—not a critic, who tells the applicant what he ought to be; nor a district attorney or detective, looking for incriminating evidence. Nor are you, except when you describe the position, a teacher. Philosophize a bit, if you want, but remember that your homely wisdom is gratuitous and largely for your own enjoyment.

Take the applicant's point of view from time to time. It will help you to judge your own techniques. But don't give him leads that will tell him the sort of response you expect.

Since you must base many of your judgments on the responses you elicit, **use questions which will stimulate him to talk, and allow him to qualify and explain his answers.** Listen attentively, interjecting an interested "Yes?" or "Mmm—mmm," when you want him to go on. Maintaining silence after he has made a contribution will practically force him to continue. If you talk a lot yourself, let your monologue be interesting, not soporific.

Don't let your interviews become stereotyped. Vary their form, covering all the points, but covering them in a different order or in different ways. Otherwise, at the end of a half-dozen identical interviews, you will only be going through the motions. You won't get adequate responses from the applicants, and your own perceptions will be blurred.

Watch word-meanings. Make sure you and the applicant are talking about the same thing. The words *industrial engineer* and *machinist* have many meanings. You will get a true picture of the applicant's experience only if you have him describe his specific skills.

Don't let your general impression of a person bias your ratings on details. Conversely, don't let a single detail, such as a physical characteristic, influence your total judgment. A pleasant smile may betoken a happy disposition; but it may also be a fortunate cast of countenance, an accident of birth.

Try to avoid "stereotyping" the applicant. Try to see the *individual*. Not all musicians have long hair; not all Harvard graduates speak with a Boston accent. Avoid ethnic stereotyping and the belief that anyone named Jane is plain. Also avoid your pet prejudices. You may believe in long walks and eight hours' sleep. But there may be a place in your organization for someone who is indifferent to walking or who sleeps six or nine hours a night.

Go slow with the man who "talks a good line." Remember the old expression, "the empty vessel makes the greatest sound." The applicant who makes a glittering first impression calls for careful testing. You must dig beneath the surface to see the true worth of the ore.

And to close with the close, be especially alert

during the last few moments. In the easing of tension, in the off-guard comment, in the good-bye and the walk toward the door, there may be significant clues to personality.

III. THE SALES INTERVIEW

Salesmanship has been defined as "the art of providing products that won't come back to customers who will."[1] It has also been called the act of persuading someone to buy what he would not otherwise have bought.

Both definitions have value. Taken together, they stress that a salesman sells customer satisfaction, that he must always think of future sales as well as the present one, that to be successful he must have know-how.

THE GOOD SALESPERSON

A good salesperson knows the needs of the public and which of those needs the products will satisfy. He or she knows how the line satisfies those needs better than the products of the competition.

Knowing Needs and Wants. The basic human needs can be grouped fairly simply. Normally, we tend to do things which will bring us: physical well-being; success and achievement; recognition and approval; a sense of belonging, of being loved and wanted; security and peace of mind; and a feeling of adventure, of living zestfully.

Out of these basic human needs, molded and shaped by our background, training, personality, and present surroundings, come our individual wants. We want a beautiful home, or recreation and amusement, or a college education for our children. We work and we spend our earnings to achieve these goals.

A good salesperson must be a convincing man or woman. It is the function of the good salesperson to help people achieve their goals, spend time and effort devising how best to appeal to the customers' needs. He or she stresses the nutritiousness and tastiness of the food; the economy, speed, ease-of-handling, and safety of

[1] George S. Jones, Jr., "Opportunities in Selling," U.S. Dept. of Commerce, Washington, D.C., 1948.

the car; the allure of the perfume; the excitement and relaxation of travel; the fun and profit of working at home; the satisfaction of owning your own home; etc.

When needs go unrecognized, the good salesperson points them out, as in selling special types of insurance. Sometimes he or she may even be said to "create" the feeling of a need. In that way, the luxuries of yesterday become the necessities of today.

Knowing the Product. The good salesman knows his product. He knows its uses and how it should not be used. He knows how and of what materials it is made, and why.

He knows its points of superiority, whether they be strength, or simplicity, or appearance or long-life. He also knows its disadvantages. With the customer who complains of difficulty in parking the car, he doesn't suggest the model with the greatest overall length.

He knows how his product should be cared-for, adjusted, cleaned; how simple repairs may be made; and when it is safer to call in the repairman.

He knows its price, why that price has been set, and the terms and conditions of sale.

He samples his product, tries it out, asks friends to give it a trial. He takes it apart, re-assembles it, studies the instruction book and accompanying descriptive materials.

He knows and does these things *himself,* so that he can answer questions himself. If he must refer to the manager for the answer, he makes sure that he remembers the answer.

Knowing the Competition. All, or almost all, that the salesman knows about his own product, he knows about his competition. He can compare them right down the line.

The good salesman knows the *exclusive* features of his product, those which *no* competitor enjoys. He knows where his product is superior. And when his product is shaded in some respect, he knows how this disadvantage is balanced, or outweighed, or compensated for, by other superiorities.

Knowing How to Win Consumer Acceptance. The good salesman knows the *attitudes* that will help persuade the customer to accept his viewpoint. He is friendly and respectful, confident and positive. He is enthusiastic, though never obnoxiously so. His good spirits should seem to derive from enjoyment in his work and pleasure in pleasing a customer.

He shows that he is grateful for the opportunity of serving, and that he will appreciate future business. He gives full information and offers advice tactfully.

He knows that he cannot sell to every customer. He welcomes those who just "look around," and he maintains his friendly attitude even during an interview that he realizes will end in no sale. The not-quite-convinced customer of today may be the completely convinced customer of tomorrow.

He is ethical. He realizes that both high-pressure and low-pressure selling are wasteful and result in lowered standards of living.

He knows, too, the *faulty attitudes* that will hinder him in winning acceptance of his viewpoint. He avoids being indifferent, inattentive, unwilling to help, ungrateful, and discourteous.

He doesn't try to force his own judgment of what is best on the customer. He recognizes the customer's right to choose.

Moreover, he personalizes his selling. He plans each interview carefully. In his planning he adapts each step to the individual.

STEPS IN SELLING

There are five steps in planned selling: the pre-approach, the approach, the presentation, overcoming objections, and the close.

The Pre-approach. This is the step in which the salesman goes prospecting for prospects. Its keynote is constant alertness.

The alert retail salesman knows the specials for the day. He tries to build a core of steady customers by letting them know, in advance, about sales on items in which they have a special interest. He displays his stock in an attractive, attention-getting way. On the floor, he is ever-watchful for the potential customer. He doesn't park his rear against the back counter and devote himself to chit-chat with other salespersons. As he comes forward to serve a customer, he makes a preliminary analysis of the customer's appearance and actions.

The alert manufacturer's representative keeps in constant contact with dealers and purchasing agents. He strives for complete coverage. He works to please and keep his own customers. He explores to see if he can possibly capture some of his rivals' domains.

The alert realtor, or appliance salesman, or insurance agent keeps building his list of prospects. For material he draws upon present users, relatives and friends and their friends, acquaintances in clubs and social groups, the businessmen who serve him, and news items and listings. He also tries to attract prospects by demonstrations, exhibits and contests. He makes himself known to his neighbors by doing community service.

He takes careful notes on whatever he can learn about these prospects; their personal characteristics; their likes and dislikes; their estimated income, members of the family, whether they are home-owners, etc. From his notes, he decides whether they have a need for his services, which of them can afford a purchase, and whether other salesmen have an inside track. Where the prospect is an employee, he finds out whether he has the authority to buy for his company.

His ratings enable him to select the better prospects for immediate action and to eliminate deadwood or unlikely candidates. He keeps a tickler file on those prospects who are not available now, but who might be approached some weeks or months later.

The astute salesman does not attempt to build his list by obviously spurious means, like the roofer who, every three months, blankets the community with postcards reading: "While working near your home recently, I noticed that your roof needs repairs."

The Approach. Here, the salesman establishes contact with the prospect, obtains further information about his needs, and confirms what leads he already has. He aims to establish a pleasant and positive contact and to attract attention and interest. He tries to obtain the information efficiently, unobtrusively and accurately, making it clear that his purpose is to serve.

The retail salesman greets his prospect cordially and promptly. He regards all prospects as customers. If the prospect is looking at the merchandise, the salesman makes some pertinent remark about it: "This is a special for today." "This is a new design by Fowler." Only to those who look bewildered does he say: "May I help you?"

Through observation, trial questions, and the response to his opening, the retailer tries to discover what types of merchandise the customer is interested in and at what prices. He notices the appearance of the customer, remembering, however, that the well-to-do may dress plainly, or the poorly dressed person may be an enthusiast who spends every cent on rare books or tropical fish. If a second customer approaches, he greets him promptly with: "Good morning. I'll be with you shortly." But he doesn't leave his first customer unless she has great difficulty making a choice, and then only if he secures her permission.

If a representative makes his first contact by phone, he says with a smiling voice: "This is Arthur Jones. I'd like to speak to Mr. Barton." (Not, apprehensively, "Do you think Mr. —er —Barton has time enough to speak to me?") His request for an interview is direct, honest, and brief.

If this contact is made by letter, the tone is simple and vigorous and stresses the service angle. The flashy letter, "Don't read beyond the first paragraph unless you ——," may not be read beyond the first sentence.

When keeping the appointment, do more than announce yourself to the receptionist. Ask her a simple question, such as the correct spelling or pronunciation of your prospect's name. Be very pleasant and courteous here. It will pay to make a favorable impression. Receptionists and secretaries can be important helps or hindrances in your present or future sales efforts.

If you drop in without appointment, try to pick a time when your prospect will not be too busy. But if he is, don't become impatient. Request a definite appointment at some future time.

The actual contact with your prospect may begin with discreet praise of him or his company, with some brief casual comment, or a direct plunge—some attention-getting, "headline" statement: "Mr. Barton, you're interested in the safety record of your employees." You will have prepared these and the sentences immediately following carefully, remembering that you are appealing to his needs and wants and also confirming your knowledge of them. You attempt to show him what a disadvantage he is at in not having these wants and needs satisfied. Thus, the auto insurance salesman, approaching a prospect who carries $25–50,000 liability insurance, will stress the larger amounts recently awarded in accidents.

Avoid any resemblance to the "Help me through college" line. Direct your appeal toward a need which your product can satisfy. And stick to business. Your prospect may be active in civic affairs; but if you let him infer from your opening that you seek his aid in combatting juvenile delinquency, he will be annoyed when you switch to selling machinery.

The Presentation. This step, whether short or long, is the one toward which all your preparation has been heading. For here you show how your product or service *satisfies*. You turn your prospect from wanting a product to wanting your brand of that product.

The *major* ingredients of success here are:

Be confident. Believe in your product or service. Otherwise how can you expect your prospect to believe in it?

Be clear. Use a vocabulary adapted to the level of your listener: technical, if he is professional; simple, if he is a layman. Use short sentences. Restate points in several ways. Take up one thing at a time. Demonstrate before you describe. Think of your presentation as akin to the first paragraph of a good newspaper story, covering *who, where, when, how* and *why*.

Be as complete as is necessary for the particular prospect. If he can afford only $16,000 for a house, it is foolish to show him $25,000 homes. If he is already half-sold, you may anger him by covering points on which he already agrees with you. Being complete, however, implies anticipating objections he may bring up.

The following special points will be helpful:

During the presentation, strengthen the prospect's sense of need by referring back to points made during the approach.

Pave the way for a final *Yes* by asking questions which will bring a Yes-response. "That's a heavy loss to incur, isn't it?"

Though, in general, assortments should be full, it is sometimes helpful to limit your items to those from which a choice is *most* likely to be made. The retailer, in dealing with children or a person who can't make up his mind, should whisk out of sight items which get a frown. By a series of choices he can whittle the possibilities down to a final choice between two or three.

When you demonstrate, let the article sell itself. Or rather, get the prospect to try it out and by so doing let him sell it to himself. Point out only distinctive features: "A very handsome set, at $25." "Our most popular set, $18."

People like to talk. Get your prospect to do so. He may talk himself into buying. And while he is talking, listen. He may disclose a need, a want, that you hadn't suspected. Conversely, if you do all of the talking, you will learn little about your customer, and may even talk yourself out of the sale.

Be prepared to shift ground. Your analysis may be faulty. Or your customer may think he knows what he wants until he sees the article, and then change his mind.

Avoid disparaging remarks about competitors. Your prospect may think highly of their product, and consider yours only on the basis of price or special services offered.

Be objective about your product. "All our pianos have a fine tone," may suggest to the prospective purchaser that you are lacking in discrimination.

Overcoming Objections. Objections may arise at any point during the interview. When they do, meet them in one of the following ways:

If the objection is a serious one, use the "Yes, but ——" technique. Agree with the prospect, and even praise him for his perspicacity: "That's a very good question," "I'm glad you brought that up." Then show him how the disadvantage he has mentioned is counterbalanced or outweighed. The price is high, but the article has

extra sturdiness, and promises fewer repair bills and longer life. Or balance the price against other features—greater safety or ease of operation.

If a strong objection is raised on a minor point, concede the point and do something about it. Offer extra service, replace or change a part, make a special concession or price. The new arm rest, cost $2, may sell the used car, price $1,095.

If the objection is too formidable, don't argue with the prospect. If the icebox won't fit, it won't fit. Shift to another article or offering.

If the objection is trivial, ignore it for the time being. The comment may only be a random one, soon forgotten or overcome during the general presentation. Deal with it only if it is repeated.

Deny an objection only when the customer is obviously misinformed. "We thought that for a long while, but recent research has shown that . . ." Be cautious and tactful in your denial, and use the objection as an opportunity to educate the customer. "The manufacturer advises that a carving-knife be honed both before and after using."

Never try to overcome a legitimate objection by seeming to deny it. If the customer mentions a feature of some other brand, don't tell her that in all your twenty years of selling you've never heard of that brand. Similarly, avoid the cliché: "We don't have any call for that." This may be interpreted as a lame excuse for your own lack of alertness, or as a snub. The writer was once told this when asking for a 15-gallon fish tank, and the words had hardly been spoken when another customer came in and called out loudly, "Got any 15-gallon tanks?" It is much better to say: "We don't have that in stock right now, but I'll be glad to order it for you."

Be brief. Don't magnify the objection by spending much time on it.

Remember, the best way to overcome objections is by anticipating them.

The Close. The customer has reached his lowest level of resistance and is ready to buy. He needs just a little push to get him to sign on the dotted line. How does the salesman give that last little push?

Be sure to ask the customer to buy. Take the initiative, or the sale may be lost.

Ask him to buy when his interest is strongest. The article he comes back to, the one he looks back at while examining something else, obviously interests him. Judge his interest by the tone of his questions, the look in his eye.

Offer a series of minor choices. Blue or gray, disability waiver or not, this accessory or that?

Ask questions or make comments which suggest that the article is already sold. "Would you like delivery next week?" Have the order form on the desk and fill out part of it when you think he is really interested. If he isn't, he'll stop you soon enough; if he is, you'll have closed the sale.

Use a trial close. "If you bought this . . ." "Just let us deliver this to your home and . . ." The trial close may become the real close.

Summarize your arguments, with stress on the chief points of appeal. "Mr. Barton, we've agreed on point 1, that you . . . We've agreed on point 2, that we . . ."

If the facts warrant, dramatize the advantage of buying now. "Prices will rise on the first of the month." "We have only one of this type left." But remember that misrepresentation on this score is one of the easiest ways to lose a customer.

Use a reverse twist, so to speak. Suggest that perhaps the article is not the one the customer wants. "Are you sure . . . ?" This should be used, of course, only when you are quite sure that he *does* want it.

Get the pen into the customer's hand indirectly. Ease the asking for the signature by having him write something else, for example, the full name of a beneficiary.

If a sale is impossible, make your close an opening for a next time. "I'll call again in three months."

COMMON FAULTS IN SELLING

A variety of faults and what to do about them have been covered throughout this section. But certain faults are altogether *too common*, and deserve renewed attention:

Not emphasizing needs and wants enough. You make the sale only when the prospect knows his need, feels it strongly, feels that your product satisfies his needs.

Emphasizing price exclusively. Price is important, of course, but sales are not made on the basis of price alone. The person had a reason for buying a car before he started shopping around. Try to find that reason, and address your chief appeal to it.

Failing to show an adequate assortment. You must give the prospect a chance to choose the one thing that is right for him.

Neglecting to explain the use and care of the article you sell. For example, why risk having your customer get angry at your washing-machine because you've neglected to tell him that it has a sand trap which requires regular cleaning.

Forgetting that suggestion may sell. Not all towns are taken by storm or a frontal attack. Call the prospect's attention to something. "This nail polish remover leaves the nails perfectly clean." Of course, suggestion selling is more than the stock "*And* something else?"

Overcoming objections in an objectionable way, or not being alert enough to them. Prepare to meet the challenge of the objection whenever it arises.

Not taking the initiative in closing the sale. What is the point of doing everything except sell the item or the service? A salesman's job is to sell, and the last step is as important as the first.

CHAPTER III

SPEAKING IN PUBLIC

All of us have gone to a meeting, not expecting to do anything more than listen, only to have the program chairman tell us on arrival that he expected us to "say a few words." Perhaps you are reading this book because you were not then satisfied with your performance. This chapter is designed to help you to do better on such occasions. It discusses certain general problems of talking on your feet, such as feeling at ease and using gestures; and certain preliminary matters, such as choosing a subject and analyzing the audience. The following chapter takes up the composition of the speech itself.

FEELING AT EASE

How to *feel at ease* before an audience. That is the chief problem for most people when they take up speaking in public.

"How can I get rid of stage fright?" they ask. And their manner shows that they think of it as some dread disease for which they hopefully seek a wonder-drug.

Actually, the nervousness you feel in making a speech is quite normal. The runner is nervous before his race, the student before his examinations. You would expect to feel nervous when applying for a new job or asking the boss for a raise. Why not then in addressing an audience?

For in speaking in public, as in these other situations, we are going to be tested, criticized, judged.

"But," you may say, "the professional speaker doesn't feel stage fright. He's wonderfully at ease."

To which the reply is, "Nonsense." Ask any professional public speaker or actor, and he will tell you that he still feels nervous before a speech or a performance. "I'm petrified," some

will tell you, "I don't dare eat anything for hours beforehand."

The explanation is that the professional speaker *seems* to be at ease, even though he does feel stage fright. He has had so much experience before audiences that he gets over his fear very quickly, usually at the moment he starts to speak. He has studied this problem and has found ways of reducing excess tension. He has probably even learned how to make use of it.

The problem of feeling at ease, then, is not to cure a disease called stage fright, but to control tension. It has two aspects: To keep tension from mounting into a panic fear reaction; and to put to good use the extra energy which is normal in a stirred-up state of the body.

Always be well prepared. This is probably the most important single rule for feeling at ease.

Being well prepared means thinking, talking, reading about the subject matter of your talk, organizing and revising what you want to say, and then practicing it—several times.

Start your preparation at least a week in advance. Take three or four days for your preliminary work, set aside one day for organizing your ideas, then allow a day or two for ironing out rough spots and trying out your talk on your family or anyone willing to listen.

Don't try to cut down on this schedule. Take more time if you like. Hasty, last-minute planning is bound to be sketchy and may lead to confusion and greater nervousness. The speeches for which many politicians became famous frequently took their staffs weeks to prepare.

Say to yourself: "I am not alone." Comfort yourself with the thought that in feeling nervous about your speech you are like everyone else. Demosthenes and Daniel Webster and William Jennings Bryan were nervous about their speeches—and so is the speaker who sits waiting on the platform beside you.

Say to yourself: "This is part of the game." Keeping one's teeth in good condition means going to the dentist regularly. In many jobs, a worker must face dangerous situations.

If a public speaker is ever to gain the satisfaction of getting his ideas across to an audience or of moving people to do something, he must be willing to pay the price. Part of the price is this ordeal of feeling nervous.

Think of your audience as individuals, friendly individuals. Beginning speakers sometimes think of the audience as a ravenous monster, waiting to pick to pieces everything they do or say.

Actually, the audience is composed of individuals. Some will be interested, some apathetic. But unless you are advocating some violent change that they fear means the destruction of what they treasure, most of them will feel friendly towards you.

Therefore, talk to individuals in your audience. Pick out the most friendly, most interested face. That's the person you want first to talk to. Then look for another interested person. Talk to him—or her. By the time you've finished talking to half-a-dozen friendly-looking people scattered throughout the group, you'll feel this is indeed a pleasant audience; and you'll find yourself having a good time talking to them.

Concentrate on what you have to say. Beginning speakers tend to exaggerate the importance of trivialities. They may worry about clothing or nervously twist hands or wristwatch or shove hands in and out of pockets. Each imagines that some slip of the tongue has ruined the speech.

If this is your tendency, remember that the audience has come to hear what you have to say. Concentrate on that.

Should a plane pass close by while you're in the middle of a sentence, stop and smile and make a remark about the noise if you wish. But the moment quiet returns, get back to your speech.

Relieve your excess tension—use your extra energy. The shaky knees, the palpitating heart, the clammy hands you are so conscious of are merely evidences of the changes your body is making to prepare you better for your task. Don't fear these changes. Accept them. Try to make good use of them.

Relieve excess tension while waiting to speak by saying to yourself, "Relax." Sit back comfortably in your chair. Take deep, slow breaths. When you are introduced, walk slowly to the platform or to the speaker's desk. Take your time about beginning. Wait for silence and attention.

Use up some of your extra energy by consciously moving muscles. If you can do so without being observed, clench and unclench your hands several times. Take a drink of water. Make your walk to the platform firm as well as deliberate. Nod to the chairman and the audience. Open your mouth wide and begin talking in a loud, clear, vigorous voice.

REMEMBER: if you *welcome* your *nervousness,* you will soon find, like the professional, that your extra energy is a source of *greater expressiveness* and *strength.*

Put your best self forward. If you are one of those who ask themselves, "Will I do a good job?" do everything you can to insure that the answer will be "yes."

Look your best (fresh hair-cut, shoes shined). Arrive early, so that you can adjust to your physical surroundings. Then think of past successes you have had involving relations with other people.

Finally, remember that there will aways be a next time. Of course, this speech means a lot to you. But its success or failure is not a calamity. The chances are that the sun will rise tomorrow, no matter what mistakes you make.

Do your best, but also keep a proper perspective. If your best is really good, perhaps you will have started yourself on a career of making speeches that will be *really* important—to others as well as yourself.

BASIC CONCEPTS

Public speaking is enlarged conversation. There is little difference between talking to one person, to ten persons, or to a hundred. You must talk louder; but the talking that goes on around your dinner table does not differ in essence from the talking that goes on at a meeting. The only real difference is that at a meeting the speaker is allowed to talk for a longer time without interruption.

Therefore, think of your speech as a conversation with the audience.

Talk *with* the persons you see in front of you. Talk *to* them. But never, never talk *at* them.

It is helpful, too, in preparing and practicing your speech, to think of it as a *discussion* with people you know. Imagine that they have asked you an important question and you are doing your best to answer. As you do so, they put other questions to you, and you try to answer these. You explain, tell stories to illustrate what you mean, and cite statistics. Or someone objects, and you offer counter-arguments, and produce facts to back them up. Finally, you sum up everything you've said with a "There, that's it. That's what I've been saying."

Thought of and prepared in these ways, your address will be *good talking*.

Public speaking is purposeful communication. You talk to an audience for a specific purpose. You want them to feel, to think, to do something.

Therefore, during your speech, concentrate on this objective. Keep your eye on the ball.

Don't let yourself be distracted by late-comers or noises. Don't let your talking become mechanical. Don't let your attention wander, your manner become absent-minded. If you do, you will not be communicating.

Think what you are saying while you are saying it. Think it *hard*.

Then the audience will know that you mean what you say and will listen.

A good speaker is lively, interested, enthusiastic, vital. He feels alive; he sees his audience as living people. He is interested in his topic and considers it vital to such people.

So he speaks of it with enthusiasm. That's the best way to interest an audience.

A good speaker is earnest. He doesn't talk for talk's sake, to show off his clothes, or his smile, or his diction, or his voice. He doesn't turn on the charm when he stands up only to switch it off as he sits down.

He has something he thinks worth saying and he says it. He is earnest.

A good speaker has a sense of responsibility. He has a sense of responsibility to his *listeners*. He realizes that if he talks for five minutes to a hundred listeners he is taking five hundred minutes out of people's lives. He tries to say something that will be worth that precious time.

He has a sense of responsibility to *others on the program*. If he has been allotted five minutes, he does not take ten. He takes care not to squeeze others off the program, or force them to hurry. They, too, may have something worthwhile to say.

He has a sense of responsibility to his *subject*. He doesn't bite off more than he can chew. He doesn't spread it thin.

The good speaker has a sense of leadership. He stands up tall, as a leader should.

He talks eye to eye as a leader should.

He speaks responsibly and with authority, as a leader should.

He is positive, friendly, straightforward.

The good speaker keeps his head. He doesn't let his enthusiasm carry him too far. He doesn't become a zealot.

He doesn't let his confidence become over-confidence.

He doesn't let himself get intoxicated with the sense of power that comes with being in the public eye.

He tries to be balanced, sane.

He keeps his sense of humor.

To the beginning speaker: Be yourself. Say what *you* think, not what some columnist or newscaster thinks.

Study other speakers, but don't ape them.

Recognize and admire the fine qualities of experienced speakers. But don't feel that these are necessarily the qualities you must have. You must develop your own potentialities, work out your own style, discover what will make *you* an effective speaker.

Therefore, another word to the beginning speaker: Know yourself. Do not indulge in wishful thinking about your speaking ability.

Learn to accept criticism and to profit by it. After each performance, analyze it. Ask trusted friends about it. Try to form some objective estimate of its worth.

Discover your weaknesses; don't cover them up. Do something to correct them.

Discover your strengths. Emphasize them, develop them.

BEGINNERS' FAULTS

Here are several of the more common beginners' faults. If you have some, try to eliminate them.

The "er" or "and-er" habit. All of us will say an "er" if we are tired, or can't collect our thoughts, or if we've been reading or doing mechanical tasks too long. But "er" 's sprinkled throughout a speech make it tedious.

TO CORRECT: With a sweep-hand watch in front of you describe the room you are in as if to a radio audience. Try to talk for forty-five seconds without an "er." Have someone check you, if you don't hear the "er" 's yourself. If you slip, start over for another forty-five second try.

Describe what you see out of a window in the same way. Talk of some news event in the same way.

The apologetic opening, the apologetic tone. Only the best speakers can afford to apologize, and they only do it when a busy schedule actually hasn't left them enough time to prepare.

The audience will regard your apologetic opening as a routine; or, if you are too convincing, will start looking for faults.

If you haven't had enough time to prepare, if you don't know much about the subject, get out of the assignment as best you can. Let someone better equipped do the talking.

Being a copycat. Don't take your speech from, or copy the style of, the Sunday Magazine section of your newspaper or the *Readers' Digest*. Their articles are intended for a reading audience. Their style will sound artificial coming from your lips.

Build your own talks. If a magazine article interests you, read other articles on the same subject, take notes, add your own ideas and observations. Then prepare your speech in your own words.

Fidgeting, jiggling, playing with things. Beginners sometimes drain off their extra energy by nervous playing with coins, buttons, keys, pencils, pens, notes. In doing so, they distract the audience's attention.

Don't carry small objects with you to the platform. When you're there, concentrate on your message and use up your extra energy in *vigorous* talking.

Lack of audience contact. Beginners may tend to talk only to themselves or to the front row. Public speaking is *enlarged* conversation, it is communication to *others*.

TO CORRECT: Talk to the person in the *last* row *first*; then talk to the persons close to you.

Jargon. Professional persons tend to use a jargon which is intelligible only to other professionals.

EXAMPLE

"Familial societality is already a settled question biologically, structured in our inherited bodies and physiology . . ." (from *Social Casework*, quoted as a horrible example by Jacques Barzun in the December, 1953, *Atlantic*).

Beginners sometimes seem to feel that they will make an impression if they talk over the heads of the audience in such jargon. They will do much better if they use plain, everyday language and say (interpreting the above): "Family life is born and bred in us."

Meaningless words and phrases.

AVOID: *"something or other," "and so forth," "exact same thing," "all that sort of thing," "this here thing," "that there place."*

BE SPECIFIC. Name names. Say exactly what you mean.

ALSO AVOID: *"Before I begin I should like to state . . . ," "I could talk on this for hours," "I haven't time to discuss this fully but . . . ," "I'll have to leave this for another time," "I hope I'm not boring you with this, but . . ."*

Those phrases are useless and irritating. Prepare your talk well so that you won't be tempted to fall back on them.

VISUAL FACTORS

An audience *sees* a speaker before it *hears* him. It also *forms an opinion* of him before he says a word. "Timid," or "aggressive," it may say to itself, or "How poised!"

Whether these judgments are valid or not, they are nevertheless made. The speaker must consider how he *looks* to the audience.

Visual factors are important for still another reason: the phenomenon of *empathy*. We tend to feel-ourselves-into what we see. We wind up with the pitcher, suffer with the movie heroine. The fidgeting speaker makes his audience nervous. If he is poised, they will relax too. And they will have confidence in the confident speaker.

Posture. A good posture combines both the command "Attention!" and the command "At ease!" The speaker will then suggest to the audience that he is both alert and poised.

For good posture in talking to an audience:

Keep your heels fairly close together, toes turned out somewhat. Heels may be on a line, or one foot may be a bit to one side and in front of the other.

The weight of the body should be on the balls of the feet. If one foot is in front, the rear foot takes the weight, the front foot serving as extra balancing point.

Stand tall. Keep stomach in, chest high, chin in.

Do with your arms and hands whatever is easy for you and looks graceful and natural to the onlooker. Let them hang easily at your sides; fold them across your chest; or put them behind your back. During the course of your speech do not hesitate to slip one hand into a pocket.

The question, "What shall I do with my hands?" is a psychological rather than a physical one. The answer is: "Concentrate on what you are saying, and the audience will not notice your hands."

If there is a speaker's stand, you may grasp it or rest one arm upon it. But do not lean over it, or drape yourself upon it, as though it were a prop to hold you up.

If there is a desk, place your notes upon it if you wish. But then stand clear of it. Avoid slumping over stand or desk, or using them as you would a crutch.

In general, avoid stiffness and exaggeration.

Strive for naturalness and alertness. Make sure that your basic posture is one from which you may move or gesture with ease.

Practice Exercise No. 4

Try out several of the arm-and-hand positions suggested, to see which suits you.

Practice Exercise No. 5

Try a heels-on-line stance, a one-foot-in-front stance. Shift your body weight with no foot movement; shift your foot position and your body weight with a minimum of movement.

Movement. Begin your talk standing *at*, or *near, stage center*.

Thereafter, *move* your position only with a *purpose*. Move forward to emphasize a point, to bring it closer to the audience.

Move to another part of the platform, or change the way you're facing, when you have finished with one point and are taking up the next.

Avoid the extremes both of standing stock-still and of pacing back and forth.

Practice Exercise No. 6

Practice suitable posture and movement for: "So much for the political aspects of this question. Now let's take up the economic aspects." Test the result before a full-length mirror.

Gesture. Gestures, that is, *movements* of the *hands, body,* or *face,* should be meaningful.

The good gesture illustrates or emphasizes what is said, strengthening and clarifying it. A speaker may:

Count off points on his fingers,

Point with full arm extended to some object or in some direction,

Outline with his hands and arms contrasting sizes or shapes,

Let his face mimic an emotion, a grimace,

Simulate some action, such as throwing a ball, with his entire body.

Some general suggestions about gesture: Don't think of a gesture as being just a hand gesture. Get the whole arm, the whole body into it.

Let the gesture precede the word by a fraction of a second.

Don't be half-hearted in your gesturing. Carry the gesture through to the end.

The amount of gesture you use will depend on your personal preference. Today, because of our conversational style of talking, and because of microphones, speakers tend to use fewer gestures than formerly. But do not let this style-preference push you into giving up gestures altogether.

Gestures can be powerful aids to good talking. When you practice your speeches, practice appropriate accompanying gestures. After you have tested them, decide whether you will use them or not.

But avoid making showy gestures for their own sake. Let the test of the gesture be that it is decisive, significant and unostentatious. Also avoid nervous mannerisms.

Practice Exercise No. 7

Work out and practice appropriate gestures for:
a. contrasting a tiny tot with a basketball pivot-man.
b. "I demand to be heard!"
c. "When I see the flag of our nation flying there . . ."
d. "Oh! But he was a tight-fisted hand at the grindstone, Scrooge!"
e. "You know what a quonset hut looks like."

Eye-contact. In conversation, we all tend to look at the person we are talking to. Yet in talking to an audience, many beginners make the mistake of looking at everything *but* the persons they are addressing.

Looking at the *eyes* of the *audience* makes people feel that you are interested in them. It also gives you more assurance. Let your eyes sweep around from person to person, section to section, forward and back, side to side.

You need not keep eye-contact constantly; but do not neglect this excellent method of establishing and maintaining rapport with your audience.

If you plan to read a quotation during the speech, do not keep your eyes glued to the page. Take in a half-dozen or more words of the text, then look up at the audience as you say them.

Visual Aids. The charts, diagrams or pictures you use should be large enough to be seen and understood from all parts of the auditorium.

If they are hung on the wall, stand to one side as you discuss them. If you yourself hold them, keep them in front of you or to one side. In either case, know the charts so well that you do not have to pore over them to explain them. The charts are for the audience's benefit, not yours.

Elaborate blackboard drawings should be prepared in advance. Simple ones may be sketched quickly during the talk, but practice this so that you can sketch from one side and talk at the same time.

Distribute materials for the audience to look at only if you have enough copies or samples for everybody. To pass around a single copy only causes confusion and distraction.

Notes. There is little use bringing scratchpad scribblings to the platform with you.

Prepare a clean set of notes, preferably on small, numbered cards, which can be read easily, held unobtrusively in the hand, and kept in order.

Use key words, phrases, or brief sentences. Quotations should be copied out in their entirety, preferably typewritten, and double-spaced. If you plan to read from a book, use a large and obvious marker for your place. Neither you nor your audience will enjoy your search for an unmarked page.

Dress. The most important thing about your clothes is that they be appropriate to the occasion. The afternoon and the dinner dress, the business suit and the sport jacket, each has its proper function and sphere.

The next most important thing is that your grooming be neat. Rumpled or tight clothing, and bright-colored or distractingly patterned materials should be avoided, as well as jangling or light-reflecting chains and bracelets whether worn by men or women.

TYPES OF DELIVERY

There are four ways of delivering a talk. A speech may be: impromptu, memorized, written and read, prepared in content and structure but not in wording. The last way is called the "extemporaneous" speech.

1. The impromptu talk is the one delivered without preparation.

Beginners sometimes make the mistake of attempting this type of delivery. They feel they will talk better if they leave everything to "the inspiration of the moment."

The difficulty is that the moment for talking inevitably arrives but the inspiration seldom does.

Only the most accomplished speakers can handle the impromptu talk well. They have made so many prepared speeches that they can readily draw upon this store of experience to make some apt remarks. As Daniel Webster supposedly told the lady who asked how he could ever reply to Hayne so magnificently on the spur of the moment: "Madam, I had been preparing for that speech all my life long."

If, through some chance, you are suddenly called upon to rise and "say a few words," as quickly as possible select some simple message appropriate to the occasion and the audience. This need be merely, "Occasions like this are always inspiring," or "Harry Smith has been one of the best secretaries we've ever had," or even "Honesty is the best policy."

Then, rise and:

State this message,

Say it in another way,

Tell a story, or give a few examples, to illustrate your message,

Re-state your message in still another way, trying to say it even more strongly than before.

Then, sit down.

You will have said your "few words" and, having kept them to a few, you will have said them well.

2. The memorized speech is also sometimes attempted by beginners. They write out their thoughts and commit them to memory for fear that they will forget what they want to say.

Unfortunately, stage fright affects the memory. Though you may be able to go on for a long time you are apt to break down. You may then be able to continue by going over silently what you have already said, but this makes a sorry spectacle.

Memorizing an entire speech is not recommended for beginners.

3. The speech which is written out word for word and then read is encountered fairly frequently today. Statesmen and scientists make use of it because every word may be reported, and even the slightest mistake may call forth severe criticism. Television and radio stations almost always require it because in any break or silence the unseen audience may switch to another station.

Yet this type of delivery involves difficulties and dangers which make it unsuitable for the beginners. Written style is so much more formal than oral style, that unless great care is taken to avoid it, such a speech will sound more like a schoolbookish composition than a talk. Furthermore, most people today have so little experience in reading aloud that they are likely to do a dull, amateurish job.

Winston Churchill, who was magnificent at this type of delivery, prepared for it very carefully. He dictated his first draft, had his speech typed as *sentences* rather than as paragraphs, and corrected his typescript. Then he made a *recording*, and *listened* to the playback for analysis and self-criticism before he delivered the speech.

Though Mr. Churchill's speeches were memorable for much more than delivery and though they *read* as well as they *sounded*, his methods of preparation offer fruitful suggestions for a speech of this sort.

If you must write out and read a speech: Try for an oral, rather than a written, style. Keep your vocabulary simple; use a conversational, person-to-person approach.

The following is a good example of written style:

"After a regular course of legal education, which lasted five years, the students dispersed themselves through the provinces, in search of fortune and honours; nor could they want an inexhaustible supply of business in a great empire, already corrupted by the multiplicity of laws."

But for speaking purposes, one might better say:

"Students attended law school for five years. After graduating, the young lawyers scattered through the provinces to seek their fortunes. They couldn't have wanted for business. There were so many laws that—well, you might even say that the great empire had been corrupted by its laws." (For help on vocabulary and levels of usage, see the companion volume in this series, *English Made Simple*.)

While writing your speech, test your sentences by saying them out loud. Can you say them easily? If they sound stiff, long, or involved, shorten and simplify them, trying for a conversational effect.

When you have finished your writing, **practice your speech aloud several times,** both alone and before family or friends. Keep your tone conversational, and know the speech well enough so that you can look directly at your audience a good part of the time.

You can develop your ability to maintain audience contact in this way:

Look down at your manuscript for the first half-dozen or so words.

Look up at your audience before you actually say those words.

Go back to your manuscript only as you are finishing saying what you have previously read.

4. **The "extemporaneous" speech—the type prepared in content and structure, but not in wording**—is probably the most popular today. One hears it at almost every function where public speaking takes place.

In this type of delivery the main idea of the speech, its structure and materials, and perhaps two or three sentences are carefully selected and prepared beforehand. But the major portion of what is to be said, the words and sentences that the audience will hear, are left for the speaking situation itself.

This type of delivery is also best for training. It requires talking on your feet, and so is better than the written-and-read speech. It involves memorizing (or jotting down on some cards) only a few of the chief ideas, and so incurs less risk of forgetting than the completely memorized talk. It involves careful preparation, and so is more inviting to "inspiration" than the blank brain of the impromptu speech.

It provides the opportunity, moreover, for the spontaneity and flexibility which are the essence of speech.

In preparing for an "extemporaneous" speech: Choose the subject and decide on the specific purpose of your talk.

Gather your materials by thinking about your subject and reading up on it if necessary.

Organize your materials in a flexible outline.

If you prepare notes, use key words and phrases set down in large print letters on small cards.

Practice delivering your speech, trying to change the wording each time. Some key sentences will emerge that you will want to keep. It is a good idea to decide on, write down and memorize your opening and closing sentences.

Having been through this experience several times, and having criticized your speeches *after* you have made them, you will have gone a long way in developing your speaking ability. (For further details on composing a speech, see the next chapter.)

CHOOSING A SUBJECT

The program chairman may tell you what he wants you to talk about. You may know specifically what you must do in your speech: praise an associate who is retiring, nominate someone for office, or describe your firm's booth at a coming exhibit.

But, sometimes, the program chairman is vague, or the meeting is a routine one, and you must choose your subject yourself. That problem need not present difficulties. Once you have mastered a few simple principles, you should be able to decide easily what to talk about even at short notice.

The best choice is a subject which suits you, your audience, the occasion, and the length of time you have been allowed.

Choose a subject which suits you. You will talk best on a subject you know well, or in which you are deeply interested.

Remember, when you are talking you are an *authority*. You ought to know more about your subject than any member of your audience. This should be true if only because you are presenting your personal viewpoint and experience.

Therefore, consider as possible subjects:

Your job

Your hobby, or your interests

Your past experiences

Your beliefs and convictions

Some field of knowledge you've studied

Some idea or process you'd like to explain

Some issue you've discussed with friends

Some project you're interested in

Some desire, or hope, or wish of yours

Something you've read that you'd like to give your reactions to.

EXAMPLE

Such a list might be: accounting; golf; baseball; gardening; trip across the continent; hitchhiking; better schools; sales taxes; tax laws; how to prepare your income tax; how to buy a used car; safer cars; safer driving; shopping centers; war and peace; the mature mind; better reading habits.

Practice Exercise No. 8

List ten subjects about which you think you have enough information to deliver a talk. List ten propositions which you would enthusiastically defend or attack.

Choose a subject which suits your audience. Audiences will listen more readily if your subject is one they too are interested in.

They are likely to be most interested in subjects which vitally concern them and are timely.

Certain subjects would appeal to parents but not to youngsters; others to youngsters but not to parents; others to both groups. Suburban businessmen might well be interested in parking problems, in meeting the competition of a branch store which a large city firm is going to establish in their midst, or in a "pet" charity.

Therefore, always think over what you know, or can find out, about your audience. Ask yourself the following questions:

What are they likely to be interested in as *individuals*?

What are they likely to be interested in as an *organized group*, that is, as health workers, engineers, members of a social club.

What are they likely to expect me to talk about?

Practice Exercise No. 9

Jot down subjects you think might interest the groups mentioned above: health workers, engineers, members of a social club.

Practice Exercise No. 10

Go over the two lists you made in the preceding section (ten subjects about which you think you have enough information to deliver a talk, ten propositions which you would enthusiastically either defend or attack). From these, select subjects you think would interest: a. a group of Boy Scouts, b. the Ladies' Aid or Women's Guild of your church, c. a group of tourists visiting your city, school, or plant.

Choose a subject which suits the occasion. The demands of the occasion are so obvious that they would hardly seem to need mention. The Memorial Day Program demands a tribute to the dead and the ideals for which they gave their lives. The annual business meeting calls for reports on the year's activities and perhaps a look at plans for the future.

Yet all of us have been bored or annoyed by the speaker who disregarded this principle. He was so wrapped up in his own interests or wanted so badly to get something off his chest that he completely forgot the occasion. At a graduation ceremony a prominent doctor got very little applause for his excellent paper on "Diseases of the Liver." And at the initiation of new members into a society, a defeated candidate for office probably lost all chance of ever being elected by attacking the successful candidates and the election methods.

Keep your subject within the spirit of the occasion.

Practice Exercise No. 11

What subjects would be suitable for: a. a Christmas party, b. the laying of a cornerstone, c. the fiftieth anniversary of a club, a business organization or a college?

Choose a subject which suits your time allowance. That is to say, be sure your subject is one you can discuss *adequately* in the two, five, ten, twenty or thirty minutes allotted you.

A talk on the "Causes of the American Revolution" can hardly be crammed into four minutes. But do not feel that you must give up this subject because you cannot treat it fully.

Narrow a broad subject, or limit yourself to some aspect of it. In this case, "The Stamp Act," "The Boston Tea Party," or "The Sons of Liberty" are certainly relevant subjects which could be treated in a short time.

Conversely, if you merely must congratulate some team-workers on the success of their charity fund drive, don't take half an hour at it.

Practice Exercise No. 12

Assume that "Democracy at the Crossroads" is the theme of an hour-long radio program. List four subjects which might be discussed by as many speakers under this general heading.

Sometimes all four of the above factors will be of about equal importance in the choice of a subject. Sometimes one, such as the occasion, will be the most important.

Finally, if you are given a specific topic and find, after some thought, that you are not interested in it, suggest another topic that you feel would be more suitable, or refuse the invitation politely. There are times when it is better to remain silent than to speak.

Practice Exercise No. 13

Assume that you are program chairman for the opening of a Youth Center in your town. The program committee has decided to include three short talks on the general theme of "Youth Today." What would you suggest as three subjects under this head?

Practice Exercise No. 14

A famous explorer returns from a trip. If he were as good a speaker as he is an explorer, how might he vary the subjects of a series of talks to fit: a. an explorers' club, b. a garden club, c. a junior-high school assembly program, d. a re-union of his college classmates, e. a group of meteorologists?

Practice Exercise No. 15

Take the original lists of subjects you made out for yourself and see how you might adapt them to fit the various situations mentioned in this section.

DECIDING ON THE RESPONSE YOU WANT

The speaker delivers his speech in order to get a response, a reaction, from his audience.

You will make a better speech, have a better chance of getting the response you want, if you define clearly beforehand both the *general* and the *specific purpose* of your talk.

The General Purpose. On the basis of the general purposes for which they are made, speeches tend to fall into four categories. Keeping your subject in mind, decide into which of the following your speech falls. Do you wish:

To interest or amuse the audience. This is the general purpose of many after-dinner speeches, the chairman's or toastmaster's introductions, the preliminary talks before the main speech of the evening, the professional comedian's contribution, the popular travel or "culture" lecture, and indeed of many so-called "educational" talks.

In such cases speakers rely mainly on stories, anecdotes, and humor. Some introduce touches of wit or excitement.

It is successful when it whiles away the time, when it keeps the audience, for a brief space, interested or amused.

To inform or teach the audience. This is the purpose of the classroom lecture, the business report, the training talk given to new or old employees by a manager or supervisor, the paper delivered at a convention by one specialist to other specialists, the "popular" lecture given by a scientist or expert to the general public.

This type of speech, besides being interesting or even amusing, conveys information. It discusses, explains, or describes events or ideas, or teaches the audience how to do something. It strives for clarity and simplicity. It often uses audio-visual aids—charts, graphs, film-strips, recordings, movies.

It is successful when the members of the audience, besides being interested or even amused, leave the auditorium with more knowledge, understanding or skill than they had upon entering; and when at least some of the listeners remember the content of the speech long enough to put it to use.

To stimulate or impress. This is the purpose of many sermons, of the inspirational talk to salesmen or other businessmen, of the pep talk to athletes between halves, or to workers in some cause at a rally, and of speeches made at "occasions": Fourth of July and other holiday programs, memorial services, anniversaries, graduation and commencement exercises, reunions, induction and inauguration ceremonies, and other festive or solemn celebrations.

This type of speech does not attempt to change people's beliefs, or get them to do something. Rather its general purpose is to strengthen existing beliefs, to get the auditors to do better or more vigorously things which, at the time, they are doing only adequately or even half-heartedly. This is the speech which seeks to substitute earnest effort for lip-service.

As such, it tends more to emotion than to logic, and may contain little or no information. It is frequently accompanied by other stimulants to the emotions: food, flowers, decorations, music, costumes, flags, lighting effects, processions, rituals.

It is successful when the audience leaves feeling ennobled, exalted, stronger in its faith, eager to fight the good fight.

To convince or persuade. This is the general purpose of the speeches made by the courtroom lawyer, the candidate for office, the salesman, the legislator proposing a bill, the crusader, the reformer, the pleader for a cause, the scientist offering a new theory, the ordinary citizen getting up at a town meeting or public hearing to argue for something he says will benefit the community.

This type of speech seeks to change an audience's beliefs, to get them to take some specific action. Its appeal may be entirely intellectual and logical, or it may be strongly emotional. It organizes its arguments, backs up these arguments with facts and statistics, and frequently utilizes the methods of the stimulating and impressive speech.

It is successful, of course, when beliefs are changed, when, to some degree, the audience is more persuaded to do as you ask.

Obviously, a speech whose general purpose is to amuse will differ considerably in materials, tone, language, and structure from one intended to teach. Both will differ from speeches to stimulate or to convince. Knowing the methods and limitations of each will be a decided help in preparing your talks. (Examples of how narration, exposition, and argumentation are used in any type of speech are given in the next chapter.)

Practice Exercise No. 16

On the subject of the weather, think of possible speeches you might make whose general purposes would be to interest, teach, impress, persuade.

Practice Exercise No. 17

What were the general purposes of the twenty subjects on your original lists? Could you also deliver other speeches on the same subjects, but with different general purposes?

The Specific Purpose. The next step is to phrase as concisely as possible the *specific purpose* of your talk.

Think of the specific purpose variously as the main idea or central thought of your speech; the point you wish to make; what you want your audience to carry away with them; the special angle in your approach.

Boiling down your subject in this way will help you to concentrate your efforts, to eliminate related but distracting details.

Make sure your specific purpose contains one thought and one thought alone, is simple, easily understood, easily remembered, and calculated to arouse interest.

It may be phrased either as a **sentence** or a **question,** or the sentence may be **implied.**

EXAMPLES

Vote for Thomas Brown for Town Clerk!
A high fidelity set will increase your enjoyment of music.
How does one cut a one-seam skirt?
It's about time Colford had a woman Mayor.
(My specific purpose is to teach a group of Sea Scouts): How to Tie a Bowline.

Avoid the **vague,** the **complex,** the **lengthy,** the **indefinite.**

EXAMPLES

Some thoughts on Mexico
How to start a store
Lincoln as a young man gave little promise of his later greatness, but when we consider his background we can readily see . . .

Practice Exercise No. 18

What is wrong with the following specific purposes:
a. The Washington Monument
b. Hints for a long distance call
c. Savings banks, and investment funds, and stocks and bonds, and loans
d. I want you to think about taxation
Try to improve the statement of these specific purposes.

Practice Exercise No. 19

For a general audience, which of the following is the best specific purpose?
a. Christmas and New Year's
b. How to conduct an audit of a commercial bank branch
c. I'd like to help you save a life

Practice Exercise No. 20

Assume you have to speak at 1. a party at a senior citizens' club, 2. an assembly program at a senior high school, 3. a meeting of members of a theatrical union, 4. a political rally. Which of the following subjects might be suitable? a. Careers, b. Children's fears, c. Communism, d. Events in the news, e. Arbitration, f. Television, g. The spoken versus the written word, h. Basketball.

Choose good specific-purpose sentences for those subjects you consider suitable. In these situations what subjects would you choose to speak on? What would be your specific-purpose sentences?

ANALYZING THE AUDIENCE

Once you have picked a subject which you think will interest a particular audience, *analyze* your *prospective listeners* and determine how the speech as a whole can best be *adapted* to them.

A speech in favor of lower real estate taxes might conceivably be made both to a group of tenants and a group of landlords. But it could not be the same speech, with the same approach and arguments. What won applause in the one case might call forth hisses in the other.

A speech must be "pitched" to its particular audience.

Before you make a talk, decide how the answers to the following questions will affect your speech:

Will the audience be a general or a specialized one? A specialized audience, such as a group of doctors, requires slanting of the subject to its peculiar interests. The general audience needs a broader appeal.

What will be the probable size of the audience? With a small audience one can be more informal than with a large crowd.

What will be the age-range of my listeners? How far back the experience of your listeners goes will affect your choice of material. With people over sixty, a mere reference to the depression of the Thirties will elicit an immediate personal response. But for teen-agers, those painful years will be known only at second-hand.

Will the audience be male, female, or mixed? Material suitable for one sex might not be suitable for the other or for a mixed audience.

What is the educational and cultural background of the audience? It is as much a mistake to talk over the heads of the audience as to underestimate their capacities.

What social, political and economic prejudices are my listeners likely to have? Try to find out beforehand the economic level of your audience, the sort of clubs they belong to, their social position. Liberal or conservative, management or labor, homeowner or apartment-renter—each tends to have firmly-held beliefs. The skillful speaker avoids arousing needless hostility. In his arguments, he tries to show that his proposal ties in with principles they cherish.

What do they know about my subject? To cover in detail facts they already know will only bore them. To assume they have knowledge which they do not actually possess will leave them bewildered.

What will their attitude be toward my subject? Some members of your audience will be interested in your subject; others will be indifferent or apathetic; others, still, if your specific purpose is to persuade, will be hostile. You should try to determine which of these attitudes predominates. Adapt your speech chiefly to this predominant attitude with, of course, appreciation of the other attitudes.

The interested audience needs only to have its interest maintained. Perhaps the chief fault here is to talk too long.

The apathetic audience must have its attention caught, its interest aroused and held. A strong opening, the early stressing of what the audience may hope to gain from listening, and the steady, forward movement of your ideas are your best tools. (See *The Introduction* in the next chapter.)

The hostile audience is, of course, the most difficult to handle. Many skilled speakers follow the practice of delaying, for a considerable time, any direct mention of their specific purpose. They show themselves to be friendly, modest, and good-humored. By their fair-mindedness they let it be known that they expect the audience to be as fair. They explore all the common ground they have with the audience, they return to points of agreement, before venturing into areas of possible disagreement. In other words, they hope that if the audience gives a series of "Yes" responses, it will be less disposed to say "No."

What are they likely to know about me? If the audience knows little about you, you may tell them some of your past accomplishments. But do so modestly. Whether they know you little or well, avoid the pitfall of boasting. Let the audience learn your worth from the competent way you handle your subject.

Answering the above questions should not be difficult when you are to speak in your local community. The important thing is to adapt your speech to your audience, even though you know its members very well.

When you talk outside your community, your basic answers will come from the person or committee that invited you, supplemented by such information as you can gather from friends, associates, books. Professional lecturers often visit a town beforehand, to look it over, talk with townspeople—the butcher, the banker, the farmer, the millhand—to get their views, test their reactions. Borrow this technique if you can, for it helps to show an audience that you know something of them and their special problems.

Keep on the alert, moreover, ready to change your adaptation to the audience up to the last moment. An important event on the afternoon of your talk may change the temper of your audience; the weather may dampen their spirits; or a preceding speaker may say something which you think will influence the audience against the opening you had planned.

Finally, watch the reactions of your audience, as you talk, particularly with regard to the special adaptations you have made for them. If you do not get a favorable response, take another tack.

Practice Exercise No. 21

Select several subjects you might conceivably talk on and determine how you might adapt them to fit the interests and firmly held beliefs of audiences drawn from the following:

a. Rotary Club, b. Elks, c. Taxpayers' Union, d. Knights of Columbus, e. Masons, f. Christian Endeavor, g. Zionist Organization of America, h. 4-H, i. Hi-Y, j. a country club, k. an electrical workers' union, l. a social fraternity, m. the National Association for the Advancement of the Colored People, n. the National Association of Manufacturers, o. Young Republicans, p. Young Democrats.

RADIO AND TV

Introduction—Special Problems. Talking on radio and television presents problems. On radio, your audience cannot see you, and yet you want them to think of you as a pleasant, warm, and cordial person. Also on radio and sometimes on television, you cannot see your audience and get no immediate response from them. You have in front of you only a mechanical instrument: the microphone.

If you let your gaze and thoughts concentrate on the microphone, you may find it difficult to feel in direct communication with live listeners.

Therefore, as you talk, think of your listeners. Forget the surrounding studio equipment. This will help prevent you from sounding flat and expressionless. Think of your speech as a conversation with just one or two other persons.

Talk *to*, talk *with* these persons, not *at* them. Though your speech has been well prepared, keep the tone of active, spirited conversation. Let the next be an idea that has just popped into your head. Pause as if to find the right word. Think "because" or "not at all" or "in short" before appropriate sentences. Give your audience the illusion that what you are saying, you are saying for the first time.

Camera and Microphone. If you are appearing on a panel show, talk to the people on the panel, not to the camera. Or if there is a live audience, speak to the audience (unless otherwise directed).

If you are wearing a microphone around your neck, try not to wriggle or move unnecessarily so that it brushes back and forth against your clothing and picks up "static."

If you have to use a hand-held microphone, hold it nine to twelve inches from your mouth and hold it steadily at a constant distance (sometimes, as a member of the audience, you will be handed a microphone). Don't wave it around. Keep it below chin level. If you hold the microphone too close, such letters as *b*, *p,* and *t* will make a popping sound.

Speech delivery is important in both radio and television. Your personal appearance is also important on television.

Preparation. If you know what the topic is you will be speaking about, be prepared to answer questions on your subject such as who, what, when, why, where, and how much. Be prepared by familiarity with the subject to answer questions spontaneously.

If there is a host, or if members of the audience ask questions, answer the questioner directly and simply. Don't ramble. If further clarification is needed, the host or questioner will ask for it. One other pitfall: don't be argumentative.

Eye Focusing in Television. When a question is asked, look at the person asking the question. When you answer, look at the person who asked the question or at the camera that is in use (indicated by a light). If the question requires a long answer, you probably should shift your gaze from time to time from the camera, to the host, and to the audience.

CHAPTER IV

SPEECH COMPOSITION

Public speaking, we have already said, is enlarged conversation. By thinking of it that way you may feel more at ease before your audience, and are likely to express yourself more naturally.

But public speaking is a very one-sided sort of conversation. Questions and their answers, pauses, examples, transitions, side-remarks—all are yours. So the way it is to go is up to you.

You are at the wheel, as it were. Expressions on the faces of your listeners may give you hints as to when to slow down and when to get along. But the route to follow is for you alone to decide.

You doubtless have heard the kind of public speaker who starts off:

"Well . . . uh . . . Let me see now. Before I begin, perhaps I had better explain . . . But it would probably be better if I first tell you what I have in mind. . . . It seems that . . . uh . . ."

Such a platform stumbler will wander from one point to another until he finally ends up:

"And so . . . uh . . . Oh, yes! There was one point I forgot to mention . . . But perhaps, on second thought, we had better skip it now . . . So . . . uh . . . Well, I guess that's about all I really have to say. . . ."

A speaker like that may have interesting things to say. But he certainly does not give that impression to his listeners.

To avoid anything of the kind, you should know in advance exactly what you are going to talk about. You may leave most of the wording, the pace, and some details of emphasis, to the spirit of the occasion. But you must decide well beforehand the main points you will cover and the order in which you will cover them.

ELEMENTS OF COMPOSITION

The composition of a speech may be divided into three main parts: Introduction, Body, and Conclusion.

A natural thought of most beginners is to start their planning with the first of these. But that is a mistake which can cost you much wasted time.

When the time to face your audience arrives, your first words will be introductory. But preparation is another matter. How you will eventually introduce your speech should largely depend on what its main content is to be. So it is best to work that out first.

The Body

If you have followed the advice of the preceding chapter, you will have agreed to speak only about something in which you are truly interested and on which you are well informed. The chances then are that you will have more ideas about points to cover than your speaking time will allow.

But do not try to decide what to include and what to leave out until you have jotted down all the likely ideas on separate slips of paper. Three-by-five file cards do very well for this purpose.

Then, spreading these cards or slips of paper out before you on a good broad surface, begin your process of elimination by considering the following:

How does each fit in with the particular approach you wish to make to your general theme? And how is it adapted to the particular audience you are to address?

Let us suppose you are speaking about your favorite sport. Do you wish to talk mainly about its fine points? Or mainly about its great players?

If the former, eliminate notes on the players which do not help to illustrate points of playing technique. If the latter, eliminate notes on technique which do not help to explain the qualities of the players.

Likewise, if the sport is an unusual one and the audience is unfamiliar with it, eliminate anything which assumes an advanced knowledge of its technique. But if the sport is a popular one and the audience consists largely of fans, discard points of elementary explanation.

Or let us suppose you are speaking about job opportunities in your field. Is your main interest in such opportunities in your own locality? Or do you wish to give an over-all view of them in the entire country?

If the former, eliminate references to situations elsewhere except in so far as they relate to the state of affairs locally. If the latter, do just the reverse.

Likewise, if the processes of your field are little known and your audience is generally unaware of them, there is no point in listing openings for senior technicians. But if its processes are well known to your listeners, you must again be careful to cut out whatever might be too elementary to hold their interest.

Next, sort out those cards which contain the most general points you thought of covering. You may find that you do not yet have some of your principal headings jotted down at all.

Suppose your talk is to be on the fine points of baseball. You may find that you have a note on the pitcher, Hank Haller, always sizing up the weaknesses of each individual batter. You may find that you have another note on how Lefty O'Leary surprised batters with sudden changes of pitching speed. But you may have no note covering the general strategy of pitching.

Adding such notes as needed, you will find yourself with a number of "high point" cards with entries like:

Fine points of pitching
Fine points of batting
Fine points of fielding, etc.

In what order should you organize these?

Generally, several possibilities will present themselves. There is no more reason why an explanation of the fine points of baseball should start with pitching than with batting or any other position. The choice may be a toss-up; or it may depend on some special slant of your own on the game.

Yet, once you have made your choice of a starting point, you cannot go on from it in just any order whatsoever. To proceed from batter to catcher, to second baseman, to outfielder, to pitcher, to shortstop, is literally "jumping all over the field."

If your listeners follow you on such meanderings, it will be in spite of your organization rather than because of it. So keep arranging and rearranging your separate notes until they bring out your ideas in an order which makes good sense.

As you do so, you may change your mind altogether as to what main headings to use. Or, you may combine some and sub-divide others. For example, those mentioned above may eventually shape up something like this:

A. *Pitching and Catching*
B. *Covering the Outfield*
C. *Covering the Infield*
D. *Batting and Running*

On another plan:

A. *Pitching and Batting*
B. *Fielding*
C. *Running and Covering the Bases*

On a still different plan:

A. *Playing Individual Positions*
B. *Teamwork*

In any event, these are only the *main* headings. You will next need to sort out the rest of your notes to group the more general remaining ones in the same way. Under the third heading in the first preceding arrangement, for example, you may have:

C. *Covering the Infield*

1. *Playing first base*
2. *Playing second base*
3. *Playing third base*
4. *Playing short stop*
5. *Covering home plate*

Another plan might be:

C. *Covering the Infield*

1. *Infielding hit balls*
2. *Covering runners on base*

But all this relates only to the larger framework of the Body of your talk. You will finally need to group all your usable remaining notes on specific points, according to how they fit into such a general scheme.

You might, for example, end up with an arrangement which starts something like this:

II. Body

   A. Pitching and Catching

      1. "On the mound"
        a. The need for control
          (1) Example of Cy Siskin
            (a) Could always "place 'em where he wanted 'em."
            (b) Once pitched 80 strikes in nine innings.
        b. "Headwork"
          (1) Example of Hank Haller
            (a) Pitched differently to every batter.
            (b) Always sized up their weaknesses.
          (2) Example of Lefty O'Leary
            (a) Changed pace when least expected to.
            (b) Got crucial third strike on Slugger Simons with a slow ball.

      2. "Behind home plate"
        a. Cooperating with the pitcher
          Etc., etc.

With your ideas thus jotted down on separate notes and spread out before you, you can rearrange them at will. You can see at a glance how all that you mean to say fits together in each possible presentation. And it is a simple matter to add points, take them out, or shuffle their order.

The platform stumbler who omits such written preparation tries to do this very same thing, as he says, "in his head." But he usually does it too little and too late—with his audience watching his embarrassment while he fumbles with "mental notes."

After you have become a seasoned speaker, you may well be able to cut some corners on this routine. For a given speaking assignment on a familiar theme, you may be able to jot down your notes directly. But then you will be drawing upon past experience.

Meanwhile do not be deceived into thinking that outlines are unnecessary. Any good artistic job appears to flow so smoothly and effortlessly that it *seems* to have been produced spontaneously. But that is only because the trials and errors of many false starts do not show in the finished product. The many discarded plaster models for a marble statue, the many discarded pencil sketches for a mural painting, the many tentative drafts of a poem, play, or novel—these are never seen in the seemingly inspired result. They have been washed away with that ninety percent of genius which is perspiration.

And the same is true of the art of speaking. Eloquence is rarely spontaneous. But you are much more likely to sound *as though* your speaking was the inspiration of the moment if you sweat out your problems of composition over your notes well before you get to the platform.

Practice Exercise No. 22

With the above suggestions on outlining in mind, analyze the texts of speeches you read in the newspaper. In the case of the body of each:

What are the main points?

What general plan of organization appears to have decided the speaker to present these points in the order he does? Is it a good order? What other arrangements would be as good, or possibly better?

How is each main point explained, illustrated, or developed by minor points, anecdotes, and other such material? Could different materials have been better used?

Try drafting the complete body outline of the most worthwhile of these speeches as it may well have been prepared by the speaker himself. Experiment with different re-arrangements of the same material and note how different the effect of the speech would have been on each plan.

So far as possible, try to do the same for speeches to which you actually listen.

In the preceding chapter you listed ten subjects for possible talks. Using the suggestions of this chapter, now prepare an outline for the main body of several of these talks. Save your work for additions to be made later.

The Introduction

After working out the main body of your speech, the next step is to plan its introduction, or beginning.

Your first need in this phase of the speech is to arouse your listeners' interest. Fascinating or important as your subject may seem to you, the audience may not at first take the same view. Until they start paying close attention to what you have to say, you will be up there talking to yourself. And there are few sounds more disturbing than the louder and louder shuffling of feet, the growing buzz of conversation, while you are trying to get your point across from the platform.

Interest will of course remain a problem throughout the entire course of your speech. But the moment when you first address your audience is your best single chance to do something about it. Even those members of the audience whose minds have already wandered to other matters, are likely to take notice when a different speaker is about to begin. That is the time, therefore, to make your most carefully considered attempt to get their attention.

One standard device is to select from your material some particularly striking instance or aspect of your theme. Choose one which points up its *human interest angle* in as vivid or dramatic form as possible.

When Frank Pace, Jr. was Secretary of the Army, he used this type of beginning in a speech before the National Wool Manufacturers Association (New York, N.Y., May 8, 1952):

On April 22nd, millions of Americans saw an atomic explosion on their television screens for the first time. The awesome sight of this explosion, coupled with the stepped-up tempo of our current experiments, has inspired fresh public speculation on the status of our atomic weapons program and raised many questions in the minds of the American people. How far have we progressed in our development of atomic weapons which are potent deterrents to those who might contemplate armed aggression against us? And how do those weapons affect the preparation of our Armed Forces to fight and win such a war if it should start?

I believe it is proper at this time for your Army to make a report to you . . .

This example also illustrates the device of connecting what you have to say with some current event which has already caught public attention. Thus, a speech on so different a theme as baseball might start off with comment on a coming or recent World Series. Or a speech on job opportunities might open with some recent statistics on employment trends, especially if the trend is down.

Humor is another standard device of introduction. A good joke has almost universal appeal. A weary audience appreciates the brief break of a good laugh even more than an attentive one.

Governor Adlai Stevenson was celebrated for his witticisms. When he was campaigning for the presidency at San Francisco (September 9, 1952), he began a foreign policy address:

I want to share with you, if I may, a letter from a California lady who knew my parents when they lived here fifty years ago. She writes that after Grover Cleveland was nominated for the Presidency in 1892 and my own grandfather was nominated for Vice President, she named her two kittens Grover Cleveland and Adlai Stevenson. Grover, she writes me, couldn't stand the excitement of the campaign and died before the election. But Adlai lived to be a very old cat.

And this, my friends, is obviously for me the most comforting incident of the campaign so far.

As your chairman said, because of my prior service here and because San Francisco is our window to the Far East, I wanted to talk and soberly tonight about foreign policy. . . .

Note how the anecdote used here ties in with the theme of political candidacy. A joke which is just another "funny story" and relates to nothing else that is said, may actually distract your audience's attention from your main subject.

Another thing to be careful about is the question of **propriety**. On a truly solemn occasion humor can strike a discordant note.

And different people draw the line on humor at different places. For such witticisms as Mr.

Stevenson's above, some people questioned whether he was "serious enough for a presidential candidate." So even a joke must be carefully considered beforehand by the speaker who plans to use it on a public platform.

Certain formalities of the speaking occasion should also be attended to in your opening. It is rude not to reply to a polite introduction. It is courteous somehow to acknowledge that it is to your immediate listeners that you are speaking rather than to the world in general.

Yet, a routine handling of these formalities may get a speaker off to a weak start:

My good friends, I am most unworthy of the too flattering introduction which your distinguished chairman has just given me. Nevertheless, I regard it as an honor and privilege indeed to address this splendid gathering on this great occasion . . .

Such stale generalities make us shudder. Especially when uttered mechanically, they lead us to expect the worst.

Experienced speakers, on the other hand, may use effective references to the speaking occasion as their means of first establishing contact with the audience.

When General Dwight Eisenhower spoke at his homecoming celebration at Abilene, Kansas (May 4, 1952) he started off with these words:

Governor Arn, Ladies and Gentlemen: We are of course experiencing today a Kansas shower, but I assure you there's not half as much water here today as there was in the English Channel eight years ago today. Moreover, in Kansas we can use this rain—it's okay by me.

Today I return to the home of my boyhood to join with friends and family in reunion, to see again familiar faces, to receive an inspiring welcome.

No man can experience these things without deep gratitude and humble thanksgiving for the benefits and kindness he has enjoyed. He realizes anew what he owes to those who guided him in his youth—who taught him—who gave him a share of their own spirit and heart and soul. For such things he strives through the years to repay dear ones and friends—yet he can never entirely erase the debt. He can only testify what he owes.

Here and now I have the opportunity to speak out . . .

This speech went on to review the major phases of our national policy. Yet it was effectively begun with these warm personal remarks intimately associating the speaker with his listeners. Some observers had thought the bad weather was going to "spoil the whole affair." But the speaker made it an opportunity to show his good humor, to reveal that he remembered what rain meant to the Kansas farmer, and incidentally to remind his audience of his part in the great events through which he first became well known to them.

There are times, of course, when a well-meaning chairman, *excessive* in introducing you, will give you so strong a *build-up* as actually to put you at a disadvantage. In such a case, it is best to put your relations with your audience back on a more reasonable basis by your own opening remarks. Note how the famous preacher Harry Emerson Fosdick did this at the outset of an address to the Economic Club of Detroit (May 19, 1952):

I warmly appreciate that far too generous introduction. I do not deserve it. But I am comforted by the remark of a friend of mine: "Flattery never hurts anybody unless he inhales." You see, Bill Gossett (the Chairman) and I have been friends for a long time, and I am affectionately devoted to him and to his wife—I married them—so that Bill is not prepared to speak objectively about me. He is an honest man, but I don't believe quite half of what he has just been saying; nevertheless, I warmly appreciate it.

Frankly, I have been apprehensive about speaking here today. I know nothing about running a business, and for me to talk about economics or politics or business administration would be nonsense. My only hope is that you have been talked to so much about your specialized problems that it may not be altogether unwelcome to have someone speak here about something else altogether. And there is something else which concerns us Americans: the moral situation in our country.

In one of our grammar schools the teacher asked the class one day, "What shape is the earth?" One small boy raised his hand and said, "My father says it's in the worst shape it ever was." I suspect it is . . .

This introduction combines qualities of both of the previous ones. It is warmly, even intimately personal. At the same time it reveals maturity of mind which can raise serious questions without being self-consciously solemn.

Such a beginning invites our attention no matter what the subject, because it commands respect for the speaker himself. A man like that, we instinctively feel, must have something worthwhile to say.

The final need of your introduction is to direct attention to the main body of your speech. Otherwise the interest it arouses in other matters may actually serve to defeat your real speaking purpose.

Reviewing each of the above examples of effective introduction, you will note how each also has a good **transition**, or carry-over, to the main theme.

Mr. Pace's reference to the television broadcast of an atomic bomb explosion at once raises questions of our defense measures against such bombs. And that is what he mainly meant to talk about.

Mr. Stevenson's reference to San Francisco as "our window to the Far East" opens directly on his theme of foreign policy.

Mr. Eisenhower takes his reunion with the friends of his youth as "an opportunity to speak out."

Dr. Fosdick's mention of the main business of his audience leads him to "hope" that they will find his very different theme "not altogether unwelcome." If that is too abrupt for some listeners, his small boy's answer about the "shape of the earth" completes the transition to questions of morality.

The very word, *introduction,* comes from two Latin words: *intro* meaning *into,* and *ducere* meaning *to lead.* It is literally a *leading into.* What it should lead is the audience's interest. But it should lead this interest into the main body of the speech which is to follow.

Practice Exercise No. 23

With the above explanations in mind, analyze the introductions of each of the speeches you have considered in the preceding exercise. In each case:

How do they arouse, or fail to arouse, interest? Is a single device used? Or a combination of devices? And how effectively?

Do they attend to formalities of the speaking occasion? How? Is the effect a loss or an increase in possible audience interest?

Do they tend to distract attention from the main theme? Or do they have effective transitions? And by what means do these transitions carry interest over to the main body of the speech?

Analyze in the same way speeches to which you actually listen.

For each speech for which you have already prepared a Body outline in the preceding exercise, now prepare an Introduction outline.

The Conclusion

If first impressions are the most striking, last impressions are often the most lasting.

Your very first words may determine what kind of a hearing your speech will get. But your very last words may decide how it will be remembered or acted upon by your listeners.

The experienced speaker is careful, therefore, to save some appropriate material from the body of his speech in order to clinch it effectively at the end. He would no more think of beginning a speech without knowing how he was going to finish it off than of building a house from incomplete plans.

The easiest type of conclusion is a **summary** of what has been said. It is reported that a certain backwoods spellbinder with very little formal education, when asked the secret of his success, replied:

"Well, Ah'll tell yuh, Fust Ah always tells 'em what Ah'm gonna tell 'em. Then Ah tells it to 'em. Then Ah tells 'em what Ah done tol' 'em."

"Tellin' 'em what you done tol' 'em," gives your listeners a final chance to reflect back and realize how all you have been saying finally stacks-up or ties-in together. This is most obviously necessary when your talk centers upon detailed technical information.

If the purpose of your speech is **inspirational**, however, a mere recapitulation may weaken its final effect. In that case you will find it more effective to end with a general restatement of your theme in strongly inspirational terms.

Here, for example, are the conclusions of two of the speeches from which introductions are quoted above.

General Dwight Eisenhower at Abilene, Kansas:

From this rostrum, looking back on the American record through these years, I gain personal inspiration and renewed devotion to America. There is nothing before us that can affright or defeat a people who, in one man's lifetime, have accomplished so much.

Ladies and gentlemen, I believe we can have peace with honor; reasonable security with national solvency. I believe in the United States of America."

Governor Adlai Stevenson at San Francisco:

Some may say to you that this is visionary stuff. To this I reply that history has shown again and again that the self-styled realists are the real visionaries—for their eyes are fixed on a past that cannot be recaptured. It was Woodrow Wilson, with his dream of the League of Nations, who was the truly practical man—not the Old Guard who fought him to the death. And in the fateful summer of 1940 it was the vision of a Churchill that saw beyond Dunkerque to victory.

I say that America has been called to greatness. The summons of the twentieth century is a summons to our vision, to our humanity, to our practicality. If these provide the common purpose of America and Asia, of our joint enterprise, of our progress together, we need have no fear for the future. Because it will belong to free men.

Neither of these endings reiterates the separate points of the preceding speeches. But both restate the spirit or inspirational message of what has been said.

Practice Exercise No. 24

With the above explanation in mind, analyze the conclusions of each of the speeches considered in the two preceding exercises.

So far as possible, do the same for speeches to which you actually listen.

For the speeches for which you have already prepared Body and Introduction outlines in the two preceding exercises, now prepare conclusion outlines.

TYPES OF COMPOSITION

Thus far we have taken up only the elements of speech composition. Introduction, Body, and Conclusion have each been discussed separately in general terms.

Now we shall illustrate in more detail, how all these elements need to be combined in types of speeches you may have occasion to make.

Narration

Everybody loves a good story. Almost any kind of a point can be made in story form. That is perhaps why **narration—story telling—**is one of the oldest and most popular forms of public address.

It also happens to be the easiest kind of speech to organize. And that makes it the best to start practicing on.

You might not think so to hear the way some people handle it:

A friend of mine told me the funniest story when he heard I was going to speak here tonight.

It seems that these two men (Question: Which "two men"?) were coming into a building at the same time . . .

Now wait a minute! I should have said in the first place (Why didn't he, then?) that the man who was going to the basement had just got off a Northbound bus. And the man who was going upstairs— he was the one who really found the briefcase— had just got off a Southbound bus . . . Or maybe it was the other way around . . . Oh, well, it really doesn't make any difference . . .

Anyway, as I said before (Did he?), they were both late and . . . etc., etc.

There is really no excuse for *scrambling* a narrative like this.

In other kinds of speeches, the problem of what order to follow is more difficult. To tell about the game of baseball *in general* you can start with pitching, batting, rules, personalities, or a dozen other possible points of departure. And each such starting point limits you in different ways as to how you can go on from there.

But events—real or imaginary—take place in time. They occur in succession. Clock and calendar can settle the elementary problems of order for you.

To tell the *story* of a *particular* baseball game should be a simple matter. From the opening pitch of the first inning to the last "out" of the final inning, each play follows the one before and precedes the one after. All you need do is follow the sequence of events.

Why, then, the difficulty which some people have with narration?

Perhaps the most common fault lies in how the **introduction** is handled.

The beginning of a narrative must, of course, serve the usual purpose of arousing interest. But like the first act of a play (which is just a story acted out) it must also **identify the characters** and **set the scene** for what is to follow.

Narrators who start off with unclear references to "these men" or "this girl" would do well to recall the technique of the first stories they probably ever heard:

"Once upon a time there was a boy named Jack who lived with his mother in a little cottage. His father was dead, and they were very poor . . ."

The subject matter of such old fairy tales may seem childish. But not the technique of their telling.

Their narrative beginnings give you at once a clear picture of recognizable individuals. There is never any danger thereafter that you will mistake Jack for the Giant, Mother Bear for Goldilocks, or Alladin for the Genie.

Most of these characters are pictured, moreover, against a *background* which is equally clear. Each indicates a certain atmosphere—simple poverty, forest wildness, oriental splendor—which gives added poignance to what is to happen.

The intended effect of a *mood* story—horror, mystery, adventure, or the comic—may depend almost entirely on striking the right note at the outset. But even the most straightforward sort of narrative usually needs some kind of preliminary explanation of circumstances before your listeners can fully appreciate the point of whatever else you are relating.

If you are telling about a baseball game, for example, you need to mention, as soon as possible, the names of the teams, the occasion, and perhaps some of the players in the line-up. Mention of the gate receipts and a spot description of the fans' excitement in the stands might also help to sound the intended key note.

Then you will be free to go ahead with the plays of the game in any needed detail. You will not have to backtrack for explanations. And you can be reasonably confident that your listeners are able to stay with you.

There is, of course, an *artful* way of beginning in the middle of a tale and then filling in the background later. Known as the **flash-back technique,** it is sometimes used by experienced story tellers to grip their audience's attention at once with a tantalizing foretaste of the later action.

On such a pattern, your account of a baseball game could start with the last half of the last inning. Interrupting at a crucial point, you could then review the previous innings, the previous games of the season or of other seasons, even the parallel sandlot experiences of the same players in childhood, before returning to the situation with which you had started.

But that is, essentially, a dramatic method. You can have lots of fun experimenting with it *after* you have had some experience with direct narration.

Perhaps the most common error in handling the **body** of a narrative is failure to focus attention on what is really significant.

Present in any form of speech composition, the problem of *focus* comes close to being the universal problem of all art. But in narrative it arises from the fact that, to be truly tellable, a tale must first be disentangled from a thousand and one trivial incidents which have no real bearing on its point.

Even the most exciting baseball game through which you ever sat must have had its comparatively dull stretches. In order to high-light main events, therefore, you need to give relatively brief treatment to relatively long periods of intervening time:

The first five innings of the game were quite uneventful. The few hits that were made were only pop-flies caught in the infield. And the few men who were walked never got past second base. Then, in the beginning of the sixth inning, Lefty slammed a line drive over the right field fence and the fans began to go wild . . .

Or:

The first several days we spent trolling those waters were as dull as any I have ever spent. No matter what kind of bait we tried, we got no action. There just didn't seem to be any more fish left in the sea. But we had no sooner let out our lines on the fourth day when Bob got a strike which nearly pulled the rod right out of his hands . . .

Note in each of these examples how much irrelevant routine is telescoped into a few terse sentences. Pop-flies caught in the infield, days of trolling and changing bait to no avail—it is pointless to go into detail on matters like these.

If you do so you only draw on your audience's reserve of interest. So never try to give a full, play-by-play or blow-by-blow account in any ordinary narrative. Always plan your material so that the time you give each part is in proportion to its importance.

Another helpful device is to organize the events you are narrating into several related groups or **phases.**

A familiar pattern in fiction runs somewhat as follows: An opening phase in which things are running smoothly. A phase of foreboding in which signs of trouble appear. A phase of complication in which things become worse and worse. A phase of climax in which matters come to a head. Then a final phase in which the problem is resolved.

There may, of course, be double climaxes, pessimistic tales which are grim from the very beginning, or other variations of pattern.

The important point is this: By organizing the events of your narrative into some such groupings, you will not only keep them more clearly in mind without looking at written notes, but you will also make it easier for your listeners to follow the thread of your story.

Psychologists have recognized that we grasp things better when we can perceive them in recognizable patterns. A number like *9481* is harder to keep in mind than the number *2468* which sticks in our memory because we see in it the familiar pattern of the table of two's.

But ever since ancient times, good story tellers have understood this principle well. Although they may not have written books about it as a technique, they have applied it in the **plots** of their tales.

Your vacation tour may not have been high drama. But if you are to tell a travel club's members about it, you might well group its several phases on a comparable plan or plot. For example:

    A. *Getting ready*
    B. *The route out*
    C. *Crossing the mountains*
    D. *Visiting the National Parks*
    E. *The route back*
    F. *Homecoming*

As for the **conclusion** of your narrative, the main thing is to make it short and simple.

The Greek slave, Aesop, always appended a moral to his fables. But there is reason to suspect that he did it as a deliberate dig at the intelligence of the Roman masters for whom he wrote. "All's well that ends well" may make a good title. But it makes a lame ending.

If you have really told your story effectively, it will point to its own conclusion. What you add may only detract from the final effect. So, unless there are the most urgent reasons to do otherwise, break it off sharply at the end.

Practice Exercise No. 25

If any of the speeches you analyzed for the three preceding exercises included narratives, review them now in the light of what has been discussed here. In each case:

Does the introduction serve to identify the characters and set the scene, as well as arouse interest?

Are the events organized in their proper time sequence? Are they grouped in appropriate phases?

Are flash-back methods used? If so, to what effect?

Does the conclusion allow the story to speak for itself?

So far as possible, analyze in the same way, narratives to which you actually listen.

Review in the same way any narratives you may have outlined for the three preceding exercises. If necessary, add new ones now which are narrative in form.

SUGGESTION

If you have young brothers or sisters, or if other children are available to you as an audience, arrange to "tell them stories" sometime.

If you can draw on your own experience or imagination for such tales, so much the better. If not, read up in some good children's books.

Do not try to follow the published stories exactly as they are written. The illustrated page may use quite different techniques than the speaker. So re-work the outline, as suggested above, to adapt them to your purpose.

In such a venture you will find audience analysis more important than you may at first suspect.

If your stories are the least bit "too old" for the group, they will promptly let you know they are bored by becoming restless. If your stories are the least bit "too young" for them they will be positively indignant. In particular they will not stand for anything they believe to be childish.

But if you can strike their level just right, you will have a rewarding experience.

Children are also more responsive than adults to the manner in which stories are told. If you are getting across to them, they will sit with mouth and eyes wide open. If not, they will act out their boredom. At every change of tone, pace, expression, wording, material, you will see the results at once.

Thus you will get valuable experience in the feel of the live speaking-situation. Especially if you lack practice in speaking to adult groups, you will find yourself a lot more at ease before youngsters. And you may well be able to carry that feeling of confidence over to adult occasions.

Exposition

Exposition is explaining—telling about, telling why, telling how.

It is what you seek when you consult your lawyer or broker, when you have a new tax form to fill out, when you want a better understanding of child psychology, business cycles, or atomic energy.

It is what you are asked for when new employees need to be broken in at your shop or office, when the woman next door asks how you make that wonderful meringue, when your garden club wants pointers on growing chrysanthemums, when your children ask why the moon shines only at night or where babies come from.

It is ninety-nine percent of the work of our schools, ninety percent of the work of our armed forces in peacetime, and a much greater percent of the work of all industry than is commonly realized.

Few speaking assignments can be easier under one set of circumstances. Few can be harder under another.

It may take a qualified building contractor only two minutes to tell a crew of master carpenters how to frame out a building. But he may never be able to explain to the satisfaction of a white-collar client why it took them so long or cost so much.

The important difference again is your relation as a speaker to your audience.

When the terms of a differential equation can be so arranged that it takes on the form,

$$f(x)\,dx + F(y)\,dy = O,$$

the process is called "separation of the variables" and the solution is obtained by direct integration.

To an audience already acquainted with differential and integral calculus, this is perfectly clear. To any other, it is *mumbo jumbo*.

If you are a surgeon explaining a new surgical technique to other surgeons, you will doubtless start with the physiological conditions to which that technique has been applied, the special instruments needed, and the types of anesthesia recommended. Thenceforth you will describe the steps to follow, merely mentioning the more common ones, and elaborating upon the more unusual ones. Your conclusion may cover postoperative care of the patient, statistics of recovery and mortality, and a final summary of the special precautions to be taken.

Perhaps, in such a case, you can make what you say more clear with good diagrams and fuller explanations of details. But your main problems of organizing what you have to say are taken care of by the lecturing routine of your field.

When you try to tell a lay group about surgery, however, you face an entirely different problem. You can no longer take knowledge of technical terms, familiarity with routines, or even interest, for granted.

The more enthusiastic you are about your subject, the harder it will be for you to realize that your listeners may find it dull. The better you yourself understand what you are talking about, the harder it is for you to grasp what your listeners may not understand about it.

The first question to ask yourself is: Why should the audience consider this matter at all? Yes, it means a lot to me. But what can it mean to them?

If you are a surgeon, you must talk of hospitals not as places where you operate, but as places where most people go only when they are seriously ill.

If you are a builder, you must talk of houses, not as job sites for your crews, but as homes in which people dwell.

If you are a professional athlete, you must talk of baseball not as a means of earning a living, but as a sport which most people enjoy as amateurs, spectators, or fans.

You must set aside, temporarily, your insider's point of view. You must make every possible effort to see your subject matter from your audience's outside point of view.

This applies not only to the preliminary question of arousing interest, but to the very heart of the explanation itself.

Perhaps the greatest single mistake of speakers on technical subjects is to use *technical jargon* without explaining it.

We have all had experience of fakes and showoffs who do this deliberately to "impress" their listeners. Whenever such quackery does not just confuse or annoy an audience, it leaves them suspicious that the speaker is really trying to camouflage his ignorance. The general public is less easily taken in than it used to be by *learned double-talk* with nothing behind it.

But it is easy for you to commit a similar error quite innocently. In so unpretentious a matter as explaining how to bake a particular kind of cake, you may unthinkingly say: "Then fold in the whites of two eggs." Neither you nor any other experienced cook may be aware that any technical term has been used. But the listener who "folds" only letters and newspapers may have a very grotesque picture in his mind of what you mean by "folding in egg whites."

This is not to say that you must never use any such expressions. That would be unnecessarily awkward if not impossible. But do try to use technical terms sparingly.

Unless there is some real point in doing otherwise, call a common cold a "cold" rather than an "acute upper respiratory infection." Or call common table salt just that, not "sodium chloride."

If technical terms are unavoidable or serve a real purpose, explain them simply as you go along. Preferably, describe the action or object *before* you use the term itself.

If you are telling your audience how weather is predicted, you may conveniently speak of "precipitation" once you have mentioned that it means "either rain, sleet, hail, or snow." But then remember that your listeners do not have before them a written copy of what you are saying. They cannot check back if something has slipped their minds, as they could if they were reading your speech. So remind them of technical definitions whenever they are likely to need such help.

It is also a good idea to anticipate in your introduction *common mistaken attitudes* toward your subject. Are you talking about "wonder drugs"? Some people have been so over-impressed by them as to think ordinary health precautions have become unnecessary.

Is your subject golf? Many think of it as "an old man's game"—one in which "you just keep chopping at a ball until you hit it, and then spend the rest of the day walking around looking for it."

Have you been asked for an explanation of the popularity of psychiatry? Some still regard it as an expensive, time-consuming indulgence. You will do well, therefore, to clear away such popular misconceptions as soon as possible.

A more basic need is somehow to connect matter unfamiliar to your listeners with something familiar to them. A common example is the kind of explanation the astronomer gives of astronomical sizes and distances in a popular lecture. He may compare the sun to a handball, two inches in diameter, and then say that, on the same scale, the earth would be no larger than a grain of sand, nineteen inches away, while the star, Alpha Centauri, would be a similar ball a thousand miles away.

A similar example is Dr. Albert Einstein's *popular* explanation of relativity theory. He does not use differential equations, as when addressing other scientists. He refers, rather, to what we experience when riding in elevators or trains; and then he goes on from there by other simple analogies.

Pumpkins, peas, miles, elevators riding up and down, trains passing each other on parallel tracks, these are things our minds can grasp more easily than "light years" or "relatively accelerated coordinate systems."

Even commonplace facts and figures need special treatment when the listener does not have them spread out before him as when reading a book. Charts and diagrams are helpful if you can have them prepared large enough for the audience to see.

But there are times when you cannot have such visual aids on hand for the audience to look at while you are speaking. Then you must make up for the lack of them by the way you present your figures.

The simplest device is to *round off* numbers of many digits. **Do not say:**

"Three million, one hundred and twenty-eight thousand, four hundred and thirty seven; or seventy-nine, point, six, one, eight percent." **Say, rather:**

"Well over three million, or very nearly eighty percent."

Better still, express your statistics in a form which strikes the imagination of the listener and drives home to him what they mean *in concrete terms*.

Speaking at a luncheon meeting of the American Society of Newspaper Editors in Washington, D.C. (1953), President Eisenhower reported military expenses as follows:

"The cost of one modern heavy bomber is this: A modern brick school in more than thirty cities.

"It is: Two electric power plants each serving a town of 60,000 population.

"It is: Two fine, fully equipped hospitals.

"It is: Some fifty miles of concrete pavement.

"We have to pay for a single fighter plane with a half million bushels of wheat.

"We pay for a single destroyer with new homes that could have housed more than eight thousand people."

Figures like these do not put an audience to sleep; seven-digit columns often do. Make your statistics meaningful.

You can do much the same sort of thing with other kinds of ideas. Even when they are not obscure to begin with, you will make the points you wish to emphasize more vivid to your listeners, and easier to remember, if you can point them up with some striking *example, analogy,* or *anecdote*.

When Mr. Charles E. Wilson, as president of General Motors, spoke to the Dallas, Texas, Chapter of the Society for the Advancement of Management (October 10, 1951), he began:

The title I have chosen for my talk, as most of you know, is "The Camel's Nose is Under the Tent." The expression comes from an old Arabian fable, and to an Arab it spells trouble and disaster. The fable of The Arab and His Camel goes something like this:

One cold night, as an Arab sat in his tent, a camel gently thrust his nose under the flap and looked in.

"Master," he said, "let me put my nose in your tent, for it is cold and stormy out here."

"By all means, and welcome," said the Arab, and turned over and went to sleep. A little later he awoke and found that the camel had not only put his nose in the tent but his head and neck as well.

The camel, who had been turning his head from side to side, said, "I will take but little more room if I place my forelegs within the tent. It is difficult standing without."

"You may also plant your forelegs within," said the Arab, moving a little to make room, for the tent was small.

Finally the camel said: "May I not stand wholly within? I keep the tent open by standing as I do."

"Yes, yes," said the Arab. "Come wholly inside. Perhaps it will be better for both of us." So the camel crowded in.

The Arab with difficulty in the crowded quarters

again went to sleep. The next time he woke up he was outside in the cold and the camel had the tent to himself.

Independent of how he got there, the important point is that the camel of government control now has his nose under the tent of free competitive industry and is crowding in. We will all have to watch him or he will take over the tent . . .

The comic picture here given of a clumsy quadruped nosing his drowsy master out of his own quarters is, of course, only a starting point. It does not "prove" anything. It remains to be justified in terms of something which is not a fable. But it does inject new life into the statement of a point of view to which many listeners had long since stopped paying much attention.

Note that this last example of expository technique is also a narrative. We may distinguish different types of speech in terms of the speaker's main intent. But there is no hard and fast difference between the several kinds of speech composition themselves.

Just as narration may serve the purposes of exposition, therefore, both may also serve the purposes of argumentation. And since much of what has already been discussed will consequently carry over, we now proceed to that topic with an emphasis upon the more typical problems of composition which it alone raises.

Argumentation

Argumentation is speaking to persuade. Its practical purpose is to win support for points of view or proposals for action.

For the salesman the outcome may mean the booking of a big order. For a club member, it may mean the soundness of his organization's policy. For a political party it may mean the winning of an election. At the level of international statesmanship even the grim issue of war or peace may be at stake.

In such cases the chips are down. Our convictions, our very hopes and fears are often involved. What then makes argumentation so important also makes it difficult.

To begin with, there are certain **basic ethical questions** as to means and ends.

It would be pointless to ignore the fact that there *are* well established ways of "pulling the wool over people's eyes." The very word **sophistry**—which means deliberately deceptive argumentation—goes back to certain rhetoricians of ancient Greece who, over two thousand years ago, professed to teach how to speak so as "to make black appear white, or the worse the better cause."

Admittedly, the sophists and their followers have been doing a brisk trade ever since. Deliberate quacks, frauds, and demagogues do sometimes have their day.

On the professed theory that "there's a new sucker born every minute," Barnum amassed a fortune. After Adolf Hitler published his belief that the speaker should tell such colossal lies that the small-minded public is overwhelmed by them (*Mein Kampf*), he gained enough popular support to be able, in a moment of manufactured crisis, to seize control of the German government. And such examples can be multiplied many times over.

Now what about such methods of persuasion?

In one set of circumstances, the answer is obvious. A speaker who is peddling Hokum's snake bite remedy will have to talk fast or the yokels will have a chance to think. One who seeks to gain notoriety by "stealing headlines" does not let common decency stand in his way. One who is inciting a mob to riot against the processes of justice will have to work on his listeners' most vicious prejudices and depraved passions.

But how about the speaker who sincerely believes that he is defending all that is sound and good against the attacks of folly and evil?

It is an elementary social fact that many shades of different opinion are sincerely held by different people. Even when standing side by side, looking at the same things, we may see them with different eyes. Depending on our different past experiences or constitutional make-ups, we view the same scene with different sensitivities, different habits of perception.

"This is a wonderfully large doughnut!" says the optimist.

"It has such a terribly big hole in the center!" objects the pessimist.

"We have achieved the highest standard of living in the world!" the administration boasts.

"It is not half of what it could, or should be!" the opposition complains.

There is such a thing as genuine disagreement in the face of identical evidence. In view of the importance of the ends for which we argue, then, are not all devices of persuasion equally legitimate? So long as we really believe in what we are speaking for, are we not within our rights to use cajolery or trickery to win others over to our side?

One attitude is to regard all arguments as *ammunition in a war of ideas*. The front line soldier has no choice. He must use rifle, bayonet, and sheath knife as he can. Otherwise, he will get chalked up as a casualty himself.

According to this view, the world of opinion and policy making is a jungle. You fight with words and ideas as does a beast with tooth and nail. Otherwise your beliefs will become extinct. And then what good is it to have been fair and reasonable?

A book on the art of speaking is, of course, not a place to preach virtue. Yet, *the techniques which a speaker uses in argumentation so obviously depend on his ethical principles that they cannot be discussed realistically as though they existed in a moral vacuum.*

If yours is *the jungle view of human nature,* you will study how best to exploit the ignorance, stupidity and emotional immaturity of your listeners. You will devise "trick cases" and "loaded definitions." You will distort evidence or fabricate your own from rumor and gossip. You will practice the theory of "the big lie repeated loudly enough and often enough until people lose their power to doubt it."

Whenever possible, you will confuse the attempts of others to think critically by intimidation and emotional appeals to prejudice. And to do all this more easily, you will "shift the ground of consideration" from real problems to "false issues" of your own making.

There is, however, another view of man and society. Its articles of faith have been given political expression in such documents as the Declaration of Independence and the Constitution of the United States. And what it means for argumentation was perhaps most simply put by Abraham Lincoln when he said:

"You may fool all the people some of the time; you can even fool some of the people all the time; but you can't fool all of the people all the time."

Although this statement has often been made fun of by garbling, the more you think about it, the more rock-bottom good sense you are likely to find in it. Yes, sophistry does work more than many of us would like to admit. Barnum did not overestimate the rate at which his market was growing.

But perhaps most people "catch on" sooner than the cynics realize. There is little repeat-business in the wooden nutmeg trade. Even in the political field, slick operators eventually have to move along. For there are few people so knowing as the "sucker" who eventually realizes that the aces were really in another deck all the time.

However futile it may at times seem to face up to the issues squarely, perhaps it pays in the long run.

An on-the-level salesman may lose a big order to a tricky competitor. But if he has a good product and has represented it honestly, who is more likely to get the repeat business over the years?

Corporal Hitler may have had a meteoric rise. But the big truths eventually won out over his "big lies," and his name lives only in infamy.

You may lose many of your arguments when you feel you should have won them. But if you have kept your listeners' respect, your credit will still be good with them for the future.

This long-run view of argumentation does not mean, however, that you can ignore the *legitimate* biases and special interests of your listeners. On the contrary, careful audience analysis is still most important to this kind of speaking.

In trying to put your case on a sound logical basis you should not forget that *logic* is, in a sense, relative. It is mainly a way of being consistent with yourself. If you start from different *premises*—basic assumptions—you will arrive at different conclusions by the very same logical steps.

The famous educator and philosopher John

Dewey used to tell his students the story of a mental patient who was quite rational except for one thing. He was convinced that he was dead.

On one occasion a number of psychiatrists were experimenting with this patient to see if there was not some way of reasoning him out of his absurd notion.

One of the doctors finally took the patient's hand, pricked the skin on the back of it with a surgical instrument, wiped off the blood with a piece of cotton, and showing him the bright, red-stained swab, demanded: "Can you look at that and still insist that you believe you are dead?"

With the evidence literally thrust under his nose, the patient was deeply disturbed. His brows knitted in a frown, he bit his lips, and there was obviously a deep struggle going on within him. It looked for a moment as though he had been reasoned out of his delusion. But suddenly his face cleared and he answered:

"Why that only proves dead men bleed!"

Granted his assumption, of course, the patient was perfectly logical. His reasoning went like this:

"I am dead.
I am bleeding.
Therefore a dead man is bleeding."

When we are too naive about reasoning, our evidence often has the effect of helping others to such un-intended conclusions.

The structure of your argument should, indeed, be a logical one. That is the basis on which you should try to arrange your notes as recommended at the beginning of this chapter. But you cannot expect to work solely from your own personal premises.

The chances are that you will never, in a life-time, persuade a real opponent that his premises are wrong. *Conversion* is a remarkable thing—because it so rarely happens.

The most you can realistically attempt in any one speech is to incline in your favor the attitudes of those listeners whose minds are not yet fully made up. If you are both effective and fortunate, you may then also persuade some other listeners that your conclusion is more acceptable to them than they had realized. But you are not likely to achieve either of these results unless you start from those aspects of your audience's genuine interest and conviction which are most closely related to yours.

Suppose, as a parent of children in a community where there are no playgrounds, you feel that something should be done to provide such recreational facilities. Your original concern in the matter may be simply that of a parent for the well-being of his own children.

But let us suppose further that, by means discussed in the next two chapters of this book, you have an opportunity to present a case for such a playground before the following audiences:

A group of other neighborhood parents.
A meeting of a local tax-payers association.
A meeting of a local businessmen's association.
An open hearing of your City Council.

In each of these groups there may be several individuals who will sympathize with your desire as a good parent to see your dear ones have as happy a childhood as possible. But that will not be their main concern. And that will not be what they are there for.

To build a playground takes time, trouble, and money. It will mean work and expense for many people as long as it operates. You need more than a few nods of sympathy.

Your problem in each case is to show how what you happen to be urging is also really good for them. Is it?

The first group will doubtless be easiest to persuade. As parents themselves, some may already feel as strongly as you do the need for such a project. They may merely be waiting for someone like you to take the initiative in speaking up for it.

Still others in the same group may have given their children's welfare less thought. They need to have it called to their attention how dangerous it is for children to play in the street, how many have been injured in this way, and how well other communities have been provided with safe playgrounds.

Here your main obstacle is mere *inertia*. As a speaker you need only to awaken dormant interests.

The composition of the second audience may overlap the first. But the taxpayers will also include people who have no children, or whose children are grown up. Why should they bother about playgrounds? They may wish their neighbors and all young folks well. But they will also be paying the bill. Would they get anything out of it for their money besides the satisfaction of doing good deeds?

Perhaps the old fashioned taxpayer's association was a narrow-minded conspiracy to beat down everything that might raise the tax rate. But the modern one is an alert civic group which seeks mainly to assure that tax payments are good investments. If you can appeal to them on that basis, you may well find them with you as a matter of enlightened self-interest.

How about your playground as a community asset? Can you show that neighborhoods without such facilities tend to run down? Can you show that real estate values tend to go up in neighborhoods with such facilities?

Next comes the businessmen's association. Some of its members are subject to the same appeals as parents and taxpayers. Again there is partial overlapping. But perhaps some do not even live in the community. And they all have a lot on their minds during business hours besides philanthropy. Is there anything in this project to appeal to them specifically as businessmen?

When a community runs down due to inadequate facilities, is that not as bad for local business as it is for property owners? When the community level improves, is that not as good for local business interests as for any other?

Is there not, moreover, an established relationship between lack of playgrounds and juvenile delinquency? When children do not have wholesome places to work off their energy, are they not more likely to form gangs who pilfer merchants' stocks and destroy property?

If you can show that support of such a project as yours is also a good, double-barreled business investment, you will have more than a personal "sob-story" to offer. You will be putting your proposition on a sound business basis.

Before the City Council, finally, you may offer all these arguments. But then you should also emphasize whatever endorsements you have been able to get from other groups.

Honest politicians will not respond to mere pressure when they believe proposals are not in the public interest. But on the other hand, in their busy routines they can give little attention to worthy causes about which no one cares.

You may be perfectly realistic about this without assuming a corrupt attitude toward public life. Political officials do not get reelected by ignoring the legitimate wishes of the voters. They may lead, but they have to glance back over their shoulders to see where their followers are actually going. Your representative may recognize the soundness of the rest of your arguments. But the support of responsible groups is what lets him know that he can afford to act accordingly.

Summarizing, then, your over-all case may look something like this:

A. *Existing playgrounds are inadequate.*
B. *The proposed new one would be good for the community's children.*
C. *It would be good for local taxpayers.*
D. *It would be good for local businessmen.*
E. *It has responsible popular support.*

This is the kind of arrangement of main points which might well come from an early organization of your notes as suggested at the beginning of this chapter.

The first contention would probably be a necessary part of any talk you might give. The others might also at least be mentioned on most speaking occasions. But the amount of time you would spend on each of the last four would most certainly depend on your analysis of your listeners' main concern in each case.

How, next, will you back up these contentions?

Argument *A* may be common knowledge, or it may not. Can you get or make a survey of how many children of different ages there actually are in your community? Can you get comparative figures for other communities? Can you also get the figures on the number of acres of playground, swings, handball courts, etc., in the other communities?

The Art of Speaking Made Simple

The more exactly you prepare such data, the less likely is your proposition to be confused with the vague proposals of fuzzy minded "crack-pots."

Argument *B* is not wholly a factual matter in the same sense. It involves some less tangible considerations which you will have to present in more personal terms:

"After all, one is a child only once. We do not want ours to look back over the years upon bleak memories of street corners and side alleys. . . ."

But perhaps you can also get records of accidents to children playing on your streets, or of cases of juvenile delinquency traced to unwholesome gathering places. These will help to make it clear that you are talking real human values and not sentimental slush.

For arguments *C* and *D,* you may well have to look into the estimated costs of acquiring, equipping, and maintaining a playground. No sound business group is likely to sign a blank check even for the worthiest cause. So you had better calculate what the estimated total cost would come to, per hundred dollars of assessed evaluation on local property. If the resulting figure is higher than you had realized, you may then have to compare it with estimated costs of vandalism, of other delinquency, of injury due to accidents, etc.

For contention *E,* finally, the best evidence is signed petitions or officially prepared copies of resolutions passed at the taxpayers' and businessmen's meetings. Supporting newspaper editorials, if you can get them, are first rate.

Wherever possible, give your **evidence** in specific numerical form. Reliable **statistics** on a wide range of questions like those of populations, national income, employment, exports, imports, economic productivity, etc., can readily be looked up in such convenient sources as *The World Almanac.*

Other issues, of course, do not admit of such treatment. Is euthanasia (mercy killing) in accord with our major moral and religious traditions? This is the sort of question on which we are much more likely to be guided by **authoritative opinion.** Looking up such topics in sources like the New York *Times Index* or the *Readers' Guide to Periodical Literature,* you can find articles by people whose specialized study or official connection gives their judgment more weight with an audience than your own personal say-so.

Be careful, though, that you do not cite "authorities" outside the field of their real competence. Prominent people voice views on all sorts of questions. But it is no more appropriate to quote a famous ballet dancer on the merits of a technological advance in thermodynamics than it is to quote a chemist on the relative difficulty of performing a pas de deux.

In summary, then: It is one thing to think out a case in plausible general terms. But it is quite another to back it up with *evidence.*

Without good organization on your part, your listeners may not even get the point of the data you present to them. But without concrete indications of the grounds on which you maintain your position, they may fail to see any reasons for it.

Your preparation should anticipate both of these needs. Then most of your remaining problems will arise from factors in the larger setting of argumentation to be considered in the two following chapters on business meetings and discussion techniques.

COMPOSITION AS FEELING FOR FORM

We have thus far considered speech composition here only in connection with the organization of specific parts, or specific kinds, of speeches.

But the question of how to organize a speech is but a special instance of the more general problem: how to put first things first, last things last, and everything in between in its proper place. The more we have cultivated our sense of form, direction, structure, or purpose, in other areas, the more easily can we apply it in what we say.

The error to avoid is the idea that speaking is something apart from whatever else you do. The aim is to carry over to your speaking any skill or insight you have already gained in other activities. For, certain basic principles of other arts also apply to the oral articulation of ideas.

As you look at *paintings* or *photographs* you particularly like, ask yourself concerning each:

Is it easy to overlook? Or does it at once catch the eye?

After the first general glance, is your eye drawn by the composition to some sharper focus of attention?

Are there elements in the pictures which keep distracting your attention from the central point of interest? Or do all secondary objects lead back to the main focus?

Does any part of it seem to have no connection with the rest of the picture? Or does all of it obviously belong within the same frame?

If you prefer *music,* consider some of your favorite pieces. Listen to them again, asking yourself concerning each:

Does it take a while really to arouse your interest? Or does it catch your ear with the very first notes?

Do the first measures so arrest your attention that you tend to hum them over rather than listen to the rest of the composition? Or do they rather lead your attention to what follows?

Is the same melodic theme repeated monotonously. Or is it given interesting new variations as the composition progresses?

If there are several melodic themes, do they tend to clash with each other? Or are they so inter-related as to contribute to a common, musically interesting effect?

Is the composition tiresomely padded out? Or does it conclude gracefully before your attention is fatigued?

At the finale are you sometimes uncertain as to whether it has actually reached its end? Or does it finish off with an unmistakable final cadence?

You can ask similar questions for *sculpture,* *poetry, novels, short stories, movies, plays, radio programs, television programs*—anything that requires design or any kind of artistic contrivance.

Note particularly that most of the questions asked above are in pairs.

If your answer is "yes" to the first in each pair, the work you are considering does not have *good structure* for you. For you it is in some respect awkward, confused, jumbled, incoherent, ill-organized, or otherwise badly composed.

If your answer is "yes" to the second question in each pair, the work you are considering is *well composed* so far as you are concerned. You find it clear, consistent, unified, focussed, purposeful, harmonious, well-organized.

Note, next, that each of the art forms considered above has certain elements in common with the art of speaking. All the above questions could be rephrased to apply to public address.

The first eye-catching quality of a painting or the first ear-catching quality of a musical composition corresponds to the interest-arousing phase of the introduction to a speech.

Elements in each which distract attention correspond to a speaker's rambling off on matters which have no bearing on his main theme though they may be interesting in themselves. And so on down the line. Review all the above questions and state the parallels for yourself.

Finally, renew such questions for yourself whenever you are considering any performance which is planned, designed, or in any other way artistic. The more you cultivate your sense of form and order in all matters of art, the more readily will you be able to distinguish between good and bad structure in speech.

CHAPTER V

PARLIAMENTARY PROCEDURE

In our country there are thousands upon thousands of organizations—social, fraternal, political, religious, welfare, business, labor, and civic—which hold business meetings regularly. Almost all of us belong to at least one of these organizations. And when attending their meetings we need to be able to stand up and say what we think about what goes on.

How do *you* make out on such occasions? When matters which concern you are being discussed, do you sometimes hesitate to speak until it is too late?

When you rise to the occasion, are you sometimes cut short with the ruling that you are out of order?

When you have your say without interruption, do you sometimes find that the discussion goes on as though you had not spoken at all?

If any of these things happen, what do you do about it?

All too often, many of us grumble that the organization is being "run by a clique." In protest, we attend meetings less regularly. In the end we may drift away altogether from affairs in which we would like to play an active role.

But the so-called *clique* often consists of overburdened members carrying on to the best of their ability. They may want to consider the views of those who drop out. But they have no direct way of knowing what these views are. They may even wish to be relieved of some of the responsibilities of office and committee membership. But they get re-elected and re-appointed because no one else seems to show ability for such jobs.

So the grumbling makes them feel misunderstood. "Why don't the grumblers speak up at the right time and in the right place?" they ask.

Some meeting groups, it is true, are run in such a way as to discourage participation by the full membership. They *have* been "taken over" by a minority.

But again it is our fault that we let this happen. When the general membership knows its rights and speaks up for them, no such thing can occur.

Are you seriously concerned with the aims of the organizations to which you belong? Then doing your bit includes having your say and speaking your mind.

What does that require?

Careful organization of ideas, clear use of language, effective devices of explanation, good vocal resonance, distinct articulation—all of these help. All are taken up elsewhere in this book.

But you also need to know some basic things about the special speech situation at a business meeting. You need an understanding of the rules of parliamentary procedure, according to which business meetings are conducted.

BASIC DEFINITIONS

Rules of Order

Rules of Order are those laws of procedure by which discussion at meetings is regulated. Collectively they are called **Parliamentary Law** because of their origin in rules worked out over the centuries in the English Parliament.

In this country, the Houses of Congress and of the various State Legislatures each have their own rules of order, modified to suit local purposes. No two sets are exactly alike, and all are too complicated for ordinary business meetings.

Many handbooks have been written to adapt the rules of governmental legislative bodies to the needs of ordinary business meetings. The best known is *Robert's Rules of Order,* first published in 1876. But practically all these manuals retain so many complications of government legislative procedure that the average reader becomes lost in details for which he has no practical need.

The simplified account of parliamentary procedure in this Chapter concentrates attention upon the more basic principles which you will have occasion to apply as a member of the groups to which you belong.

The Chair

The Chair is the office of the person who presides over a meeting as distinguished from the personality of the individual who occupies that office. Although the traditional title of one who presides has been "Chairman," many groups now use the title "Chairperson" or, when the office is held by a woman, "Chairwoman." The Associated Press Stylebook and Libel Manual does not favor coined words like *chairperson,* but the usage is now a matter of choice or preference.

SPECIAL RULES

a. The Chair should preserve order in the meeting and regulate its procedure by applying the rules of order impartially to all members.

b. While occupying the Chair, the Chairman should refrain from speaking for or against controversial motions. If he or she feels an urgent need to speak on a controversial question, he or she should vacate the Chair and speak on the same basis as any other member.

c. The Chair should not vote unless a secret ballot is being conducted, or unless a tie has resulted by other means of voting.

d. Under *formal procedure* (See the next chapter), the Chairman should avoid use of the pronouns, "I" and "me," but should use such expressions as:

"The Chair recognizes the member in the second row."

"The speakers will please refrain from cross-conversation and address all questions to the Chair."

e. Under formal procedure, members should address the presiding officer as "Mr., Ms., or Mrs. Chairperson," or "The Chair."

Not:

"Mr. Jones, I think your decision is all wrong."

But:

"Mr. Chairman, I move to appeal from the decision of the Chair" (See explanation of *Motion I-4,* below).

EXPLANATION

More is involved here than a mere fussiness over words. The distinction between the office of the Chair and the personality of the Chairman is based on the fact, expressed in rule a, that the Chairman is expected to apply parliamentary law impartially at a meeting.

Like everyone else, the Chairman has his own personal views, interests, friendships, and possibly antagonisms. But he is not supposed to allow these to influence his official actions.

Like everyone else, the Chairman also has the individuality of his own character. A warm, friendly disposition is of course an asset; and patience is almost an essential. But he is supposed to apply these desirable personal traits to all members alike.

Rule b, which prohibits him from joining in debate, is to help protect an erring Chairman from himself. The remaining rules are to help protect a good Chairman from others.

When you are Chairman, it may seem artificial to say to your best friend: "The Chair calls the speaker to order." But the formula also says in effect: "It isn't really me who is calling you down like this, Jim old pal, but just the responsibility of the Chair which you yourself helped vote me into."

When the same formula likewise requires a wrought-up member to address you as "Mr. Chairman," it again avoids needless personal unpleasantness.

Notwithstanding such practices, many a Chair of a mixed meeting has still gone home to "catch blazes" from wife or husband for having ruled against spouse in favor of "that busybody who lives down the street." It is just such hazards of the office which the rules attempt to keep to a minimum.

Moreover, an impersonal attitude toward the Chair helps keep a proper tone in discussion at times when it might otherwise be difficult to do so. A good chairman keeps things moving by his energy and obvious fairness. But sometimes a weak personality presides over the best of organizations. Then the established tradition of respect for the Chair can give it needed authority which the chairman cannot command for himself.

These explanations illustrate an important general point: No matter how artificial certain rules of order may appear, they are never mere formalities. They usually embody the practical wisdom of generations of deliberators who have tried to give sense and system to their ways of talking things over.

Practice Exercise No. 26

A session of a Court is a special form of meeting in which the presiding officer is the Judge. In view of what has been said above, consider the following:

What "rules" is the Judge required to apply equally to all parties to a trial?

Is the Judge supposed to prejudice the outcome of a trial in any way?

Why does the Judge customarily say: "The Court rules . . ." rather than "I rule . . ."?

Why does the Judge customarily speak to those in Court as "The Witness," "The Attorney for the Defense," etc., rather than by their names?

Why do others customarily address the Judge as "Your Honor" rather than by his name?

If you do not think highly of the personal ability or character of the Judge, may you speak to him disrespectfully in his official capacity in Court?

Does the personal ability or character of the Judge have anything to do with a citation for Contempt of Court?

SUGGESTION

In answering the above questions you will find parallels between the court and other meeting situations. Because the judge is expected to be impartial, all parties must respect his official role as the presiding officer. Contempt of Court has nothing to do with any individual's personal qualities. It is an act of disrespect for the Court as an institution of justice.

The same considerations apply to respect for the chairmanship of a meeting. It is, in effect, respect for the worth and dignity of the meeting organization itself.

Rising to be Recognized

No one other than the Chair may normally address the meeting unless called upon or recognized by the Chair.

If you wish to speak, therefore, you must first **rise to be recognized.** Formally, this means standing. In small, informal meetings it is usually enough to raise your hand.

Ordinarily you may not interrupt a speaker to do this. The most basic principle of parliamentary procedure is that *only one speaker can be properly heard at a time.* (Certain privileged or emergency exceptions to this rule will be explained later in connection with *Column 2* of the *Table of Motions,* below).

Other things being equal, the Chair will generally recognize that member who rises first.

EXAMPLE

Member A (rising first): "Mr. Chairman . . .
Chairman: "The Chair recognizes Mr. A."

Or, if he does not know A's name:

"The Chair recognizes the member in the second row."

At times, however, the Chair will have to depart from this general rule and use his own judgment where other factors apply.

Practice Exercise No. 27

If you were the Chair, whom would you recognize in each of the following cases:

1. A member who has already spoken twice on the same question. A member who has not yet spoken on the question.

2. A member known to agree with the views just expressed by the preceding speaker. A member known to disagree with those views.

3. A young member who is often quick to his feet. A senior member who rises seldom and with physical difficulty.

SUGGESTIONS

In each of these cases you would do best to recognize the second choice because:

1. Whenever possible, members who have not yet had a chance to speak should be recognized in preference to those who have.

2. Fair practice requires each side to be heard in turn.

3. Considerations of common courtesy apply. Getting recognition should never become an athletic contest with the reward to the nimblest.

Having the Floor

Once you have been recognized by the Chair you are said **to have the floor.** This means that no other member may interrupt you except for certain privileged or emergency purposes (See explanation of *Column 2* of the *Table of Motions,* below).

Subject to any standing time-limits which your organization may have set on individual speeches, you may then continue speaking so long as you remain **in order.** This means that what you say must be: *proper* and *relevant.*

The question of the **propriety** of your speech is no different at a meeting than in any other social situation. The general rule is that you may not use language offensive to your listeners.

This obviously implies a flexible standard. Words which would outrage a meeting of Sunday School Superintendents may sound tame at a gathering of seafarers.

The thing to remember is that the most sensitive member of any audience is entitled to have his reasonable sensibilities respected. Sound policy for you as a speaker is: In case of doubt, cut it out.

Beyond that, make sure not to impugn the character, motives, or personal affiliations of a fellow-member. The only exception to this is discussion on an actual impeachment or censure measure. Then character judgment becomes relevant. And then you should have such proof of your statements as would stand up in Court.

Presumably, you would not want the floor of your organization used to assassinate your reputation. The parliamentary precept on this point is a simple application of the Golden Rule.

The **relevance** of whatever else you say depends upon a number of things such as the *Order of Business* and *Precedence of Motions* discussed further on in this chapter.

The general principle is: One question at a time, and each in its proper turn.

If the Chair has asked for additions or corrections to the minutes, don't bring up a committee report unless it is in connection with the way the minutes have been written (See *Reading and Approval of the Minutes,* below). If the building of a new clubhouse is being discussed, you will be out of order in speaking of a membership drive, unless you do so in connection with the building project. And no matter what is going on, you may not tell about your fishing trip except on the unlikely chance that it has a reasonable bearing on the business at hand.

But if *the floor is clear* of other business, and if the agenda otherwise permits (See *The Order of Business,* below), you may introduce a new item of business. You do so in the form of a motion.

Making and Seconding Motions

This is the general procedure for making and seconding motions:

Member A (Rising to be recognized): "Mr. Chairman."

Chairman: "The Chair recognizes Mr. A."

Member A (After brief explanation of his purpose): "I move that such and such be done."

Chairman (If it is in order): "It has been moved that such and such be done. Is there a second?"

Member B: "I second the motion."

Chairman: "It has been moved and seconded that such and such be done. Is there any discussion?"

SPECIAL RULES

a. When a motion has been *properly* made and seconded, the Chair must refer it to the assembly for discussion.

b. No other discussion is then in order except in connection with motions which properly precede the one thus introduced (See *The Precedence of Motions,* below).

EXPLANATION

The formality of requiring a specific motion is for the purpose of focusing discussion. It serves to establish what is being talked about.

Even with this requirement in force, and even in the best-regulated meetings, discussion may wander far afield. Some speakers manage to twist almost any topic to their own pet themes. Others get so concerned with side issues as to forget the main point.

When this happens, an alert Chair will remind the assembly what the question before them is. If the Chair fails to do so, any member may ask him to (See *Motion I-1*, below).

Sometimes an embarrassed assembly has to wait while the Secretary searches his transcript to find out what the motion before them really is. The practical need for the above formalities then becomes strikingly clear.

Seconding is simply co-sponsoring a motion. It assures that at least one other person is interested in a question before it is considered. But it is not always required (See the explanation of *Column 3* of the *Table of Motions,* below).

THE ORDER OF BUSINESS

The question of whether what you say is in order (See *Having the Floor*, above) is partly determined by the order of business of the meeting.

An organization's **order of business** is the basic schedule which its constitution (See *Constitutions,* in the next chapter) requires its meetings to follow. This schedule consists of a number of consecutive **items** covering regularly anticipated business.

An **agenda** is the order of business with specific sub-items entered under the main headings.

The general rule is that you may not speak on any item at a time when a different item is being considered. To do so is literally *out of order.*

Following are the main items on a typical order of business, with examples of how they are introduced and of what discussion they allow.

1. The Call to Order

EXAMPLE

Chairman (Rapping with gavel): "The meeting will please come to order."

EXPLANATION

Until the meeting is thus officially *called to order,* nothing that is said, even though it may be addressed to everyone in the meeting room, has official status for consideration. The records of the meeting begin with this call.

2. The Minutes

The Secretary of an organization has the duty of noting all important transactions which take place at a meeting, and writing them down in an official permanent record called **The Minutes.** His **reading of the minutes** of the previous meeting is usually the first business of a meeting after it is called to order.

EXAMPLE

Chairman: "Will the Secretary please read the minutes of the last meeting."

Secretary: "The regular monthly meeting of the X Organization was called to order by the President, Mr. John Doe, Wednesday, August 8, at 8:15 P.M. in Y Hall . . . etc."

After the reading of the minutes, they must be *approved by the membership.*

EXAMPLE

Chairman: "Are there any additions or corrections to the minutes?"

Member A: "Mr. Chairman (Pause for recognition), I want to state right here and now that I think this group made a very bad mistake when it passed the second motion the Secretary just read us about . . ."

Chairman: "Sorry, Mr. A., but you are out of order. This is not the time to debate that again. Unless you have some question as to how the minutes have been recorded, the Chair must ask you to be seated."

Member B: "Mr. Chairman (Pause), didn't you include Mrs. D. in your appointments to the Program Committee at the last meeting? I don't believe I heard her name mentioned on the list as it was read to us in the minutes."

Secretary: "No, Mr. Chairman, I don't have Mrs. D.'s name down."

Chairman: "Mrs. D. was included in the appointments, Mr. Secretary. Will you please add her name to the list. Are there any other additions or corrections? (Pause for reply) If not, the minutes will stand as read."

EXPLANATION

Only questions of the completeness or correctness of the record may be raised when the minutes are to be approved.

If there is any serious debate about the correctness of the minutes, they cannot be approved so informally. The procedure then is:

Chairman: "If there is no further discussion concerning the minutes, the Chair will now entertain a motion that they be approved as corrected."

Member E: "I so move, Mr. Chairman."

Member F: "I second the motion."

Chairman: "It has been moved and seconded that the minutes be approved as corrected. All in favor . . . etc."

3. Reports

Reports by Officers and Committees are usually heard in the following order.

Officers: President, Vice President, Secretary, Treasurer.

Committees: Standing Committees, Special Committees.

EXAMPLE

Chairman: "The Treasurer will now please make his report."

Treasurer: "As of the last report of the Treasurer, our cash balance was . . . Receipts since then were as follows . . . Disbursements since then were as follows . . . The cash balance is now . . ."

Chairman: "Are there any questions concerning the Treasurer's report?"

Member A: "Mr. Chairman (Pause for recognition), now that the question has come up again, I'd like to ask this organization why it appropriated so much money for so-called welfare purposes. We need our funds for . . ."

Chairman: "Sorry, Mr. A., but the Chair must rule you out of order. That question does *not* come up at this time. We are not now reconsidering our past appropriations. We are merely hearing the Treasurer's report of his custody of our funds. Are there any other questions?"

Member B: "Mr. Chairman (Pause), I should like to ask if the balance given by the Treasurer includes an estimate of membership fees due but not collected."

Chairman: "Will the Treasurer please answer that question."

Treasurer: "In accordance with the By-laws, Mr. Chairman, our accounts are kept on a cash basis. No fees are recorded until actually collected."

Chairman: "Thank you, Mr. Treasurer. Are there any other questions? (Pause) If not, the Treasurer's report will be referred to the Auditing Committee as usual."

Committee reports sometimes include recommendations for action (See explanation of *Motion S-5,* below). A common error of some chairmen is then to ask for a vote to *accept the report,* without meaning to have these recommendations thereby put into effect. This practice is subject to mis-interpretation.

A report is *accepted* by *being heard.* Any vote taken should be on the question of whether to put its recommendations into effect. The only exception to this is a vote on a motion to thank the committee members for their work.

EXAMPLE

Chairman: "You have just heard the report of the Financial Committee recommending that membership fees in this organization be increased $2.00 per member per year. Since this would involve a change in the By-laws (See *Constitutions, etc.,* in the next chapter), it may not be considered until after it has been announced as a question at a previous meeting. Do you now wish to move that it be so announced as the first general order of business (See following *Item 4*) for the next regular meeting?"

Member A: "I so move, Mr. Chairman."

Member B: "I second the motion, Mr. Chairman."

Chairman: "It has been moved and seconded . . . etc."

4. General Orders

A general order of business is any motion proposed for consideration at the first opportunity in a given meeting. This means immediately after all reports have been heard.

EXAMPLE

Chairman: "As the first general order of business tonight we have to consider the recommendation of the Financial Committee at the last meeting (See preceding EXAMPLE above) that the membership fees of this organization be increased $2.00 per person per year. Is there any discussion?"

EXPLANATION

Passage of the motion to consider this question at the previous meeting makes it unnecessary to go through the routine of moving and seconding it at the present meeting.

Legislative bodies and some large organizations also include **special orders of business** in their agenda. These differ from **general orders** only in that they set a definite hour for the consideration of the question. This would interrupt any other business, except another special order, before the meeting at the set time.

Most organizations obviously do not have to commit themselves to so inflexible an arrangement. Unless there are exceptional reasons, do not try to fix your order of business by the hands of the clock.

5. Unfinished Business

Sometimes a meeting ends without disposing of a motion before it. This motion then becomes **unfinished business** which the next meeting must take up immediately after general orders.

EXAMPLE

Chairman: "At the time we adjourned last week we were considering the motion to discontinue regular business meetings from June 31 to September 1. Is there any further discussion of that motion now?"

EXPLANATION

At any given meeting, unfinished business comes up in the same automatic manner as general orders. For that reason, the two items are sometimes combined in a single order of business under either heading, or under the joint heading: "General Orders *and* Unfinished Business."

6. New Business

If you have a proposal to bring up for consideration for the first time, wait until **New Business** is called for, before rising to be recognized.

It is a good idea to have the exact wording of what you propose written out in the form of a motion. No matter how well you may be prepared to back up your proposal, stumbling over its wording gives the impression that you do not know what you are talking about.

Moreover, phrasing a motion unclearly because you are doing it on the spur of the moment, gives it a bad start. The discussion that follows often then turns on the question of what you really mean and how better to state your meaning, rather than on the merits of your proposal.

For ordinary purposes, keep the wording of your motions as short and simple as possible. For example:

"Mr. Chairman, I move this Sport Club appropriate thirty dollars to provide a trophy as first prize in its annual fly-casting tournament."

But, if what you propose is unavoidably complicated, or is intended to come to some kind of official attention, you may better word it in full-dress traditional form. For example:

"Mr. Chairman, I move the following resolution:
'Whereas, The City of Blank has constructed no public playgrounds in this community; and
Whereas, The City of Blank has constructed adequate public playgrounds in neighboring communities; and
Whereas, Public playgrounds are an essential public facility for the general welfare of the community; therefore be it
Resolved, That this Civic Organization petition the Mayor and the City Council to take all necessary measures promptly to provide this community with adequate public playgrounds; and be it further
Resolved, That the Executive Committee of this Civic Organization be authorized and instructed to call upon all candidates for City office in the forthcoming elections to determine and report to this assembly their policy with regard to action upon this petition.' "

Discuss your motion informally beforehand with some other member who is likely to be willing to second it. An embarrassing pause in the proceedings of the meeting while waiting for the motion to be seconded can thus be avoided.

If possible let the Chairman know in advance —before the call to order—that you intend to ask for the floor for that purpose. He may be able to expedite other items of business to provide more time to consider your motion.

Some organizations require that members desiring to make motions under New Business, file them in writing with the Secretary beforehand. In such cases they may be included in the agenda accompanying reminder-notices of the meeting.

For further details concerning this item of business, see *Main Motions* (below).

7. Adjournment

Once a business meeting has been called to order, it remains in session, except for *recess*, until it is *adjourned*.

A recess is a temporary interruption of a meeting. This may be for such purposes as refreshment or conference among groups of members. At a set time, the *same meeting* reconvenes.

Adjournment is the formal end of a meeting. On the basis of motions explained later in this Chapter (See *Motions P-1* and *P-2*, below), it is formally announced by the Chair:

"The meeting is now adjourned."

Nothing said after adjournment can become part of the official proceedings of a meeting, even though addressed to everyone in the room. Should a group be called back to order after being adjourned, what then takes place is, strictly speaking, a new meeting and it should be so recorded in the minutes.

Practice Exercise No. 28

Under which item of the order of business would it be most proper to consider each of the following:

a. A question as to how many members are behind in dues payments.
b. A motion to hold a special social affair.
c. A question as to what events the Program Committee has thus far scheduled for the coming season.
d. Further discussion of a question under consideration when the previous meeting adjourned?
e. The President's impression of his visit to the organization's national headquarters?
f. A correction to the official title recorded for the guest speaker at the previous meeting?
g. A proposal to launch a membership campaign?
h. Current recommendations by the Ways and Means Committee?
i. Support of a motion specifically assigned for consideration at the present meeting?

EXPLANATION OF THE TABLE OF MOTIONS

Most of the remaining technicalities of parliamentary procedure are summarized on the accompanying **Table of Motions**. Glance at the Table briefly for a general impression of its format and contents. Then proceed to the following explanations of the entries in its nine columns.

Column 1—Precedence

The precedence of motions is a set of rules of order whereby discussion of certain motions may claim the right of way over discussion of certain other motions. Thus, precedence is another aspect of parliamentary law which determines what speaking is *in order* at any given time.

In general, any motion is said to *precede,* or *have higher precedence* over another, if the rules permit it to be introduced at a time when the other motion is already being discussed.

Conversely, any motion is said to *be preceded* by, or *have lower precedence* than another, if the rules do not permit it to be introduced when the other motion is on the floor.

The twenty-six most important types of motions—those likely to come up in the meetings of most organizations—are tabulated in *Column 1* of the accompanying *Table of Motions.* (pp. 88, 89).

Of these, the first twenty-two are listed in the order of their *relative precedence.* Speaking on any of these motions is *in order* when any motion *below* it is on the floor. Speaking on any of these motions is *out of order* when any motion *above* it is on the floor.

The four motions in the last group at the bottom of *Column 1* have special orders of precedence (explained in the notes of *Column 8,* and also in the later, separate explanations of each of these motions, page-referenced in *Column 9*).

Column 2—Authority to Interrupt

Nothing is more basic in parliamentary procedure than the practice of allowing only one member to speak at a time. Hence the requirement that you rise and be recognized by the Chair before you may have the floor.

Sometimes, however, you may have legitimate reason to interrupt a speaker. You may have an urgent *Point of Personal Privilege* to raise (See explanation of *Motion P-4*); or a serious parliamentary objection to make to the way the meeting is being run (See explanation of *Motion I-1*).

In such emergency cases you have a right to speak up without waiting for another speaker to finish. Where such interruptions are allowed is indicated in *Column 2* by the entry, *Int.* (May Interrupt).

For all other motions, of course, you must wait your turn.

Column 3—Need for a Second

Although it is general practice to have a motion seconded before it is further considered (See *Making and Seconding Motions*, above), there are also cases where such a requirement would not be sensible.

For example, you may question the Chair's decision as to a voice vote and may want to have a more accurate count (See explanation of *Motion I-4*). Or you may wish to ask for pertinent information in order properly to follow what is being said on the floor (See explanation of *Motion I-5*).

In such cases parliamentary law does not require that you be seconded. This is indicated by the omission of the entry, *Sec.* (Second required) in *Column 3*.

Column 4—Debatability

Most parliamentary law is concerned with having debate proceed in an orderly manner. But there are times when it can, or must, operate so as to close off debate.

There are cases where you may reasonably object to the consideration of motions made and seconded (See explanation of *Motion I-7*); or, when it is reasonable for you to move to close debate on a question (See explanation of *Motion S-2*).

If either of these motions of yours were to be themselves debatable, their purpose would automatically be defeated. The question to whose consideration or continued discussion you ob-

jected would, in effect, continue to be considered or discussed in the debate over your motion.

Parliamentary rules therefore provide that only those motions may be debated for which debate is appropriate. And these are indicated in *Column 4* by the entry, *Deb.* (Debatable).

Column 5—Amendability

Likewise, some motions may properly be amended, whereas others may not. Those motions which may be *amended* are indicated in *Column 5* by the entry, *Amd.* (Amendable).

For a general discussion of amendments, see the explanation of *Motion S-6*.

Column 6—Required Votes

Since usual democratic practice is majority rule, the usual requirement for the passage of a motion is a simple majority vote. This is indicated in *Column 6* by the entry, *Maj.* (Majority) for motions which require no more than a *majority* vote to carry.

But suppose a simple majority vote could prevent consideration of any motion you made (See explanation of *Motion I-7*), or could stop debate on any motion in which you were interested (See explanation of *Motion S-2*). It would then be possible for a bare majority-of-one, in your organization, to prevent your ever getting a chance to speak on the floor for your proposals.

To avoid situations like that, certain motions must have a two-thirds vote to pass. They are indicated in *Column 6* by the entry, ⅔, after them.

Column 7—Renewability

Suppose there were no parliamentary restriction against moving and seconding a motion again after it had been defeated. A single pair of persistent members could then obstruct the entire procedure of a meeting by repeatedly proposing the same unpopular measure each time it was voted down. To avoid such a parliamentary snarl, there is a general rule that no motion may be renewed immediately after it has been disposed of.

	1 Motions in Order of Precedence (Groups P, I, S, & M only)	2 Authority to Interrupt	3 Need for a Second	4 Debatability	5 Amendability	6 Required Votes	7 Renewability
	PRIVILEGED MOTIONS						
	P-1 To fix Time and/or Place of Next Meeting. (8)	—	Sec.	(8)	Amd.	Maj.	(8)
	P-2 To Adjourn. (8)	—	Sec.	(8)	—	Maj.	Ren.
	P-3 To Recess. (8)	—	Sec.	(8)	(8)	Maj.	Ren.
	P-4 Questions of Privilege.	Int.	—	(8)	(8)	(8)	Ren.
	P-5 To Call for the Orders of the Day.	Int.	—	—	—	(8)	Ren.
	INCIDENTAL MOTIONS						
	I-1 Points of Parliamentary Order.	Int.	—	(8)	—	(8)	—
	I-2 Points of Parliamentary Inquiry.	Int.	—	—	—	(8)	—
	I-3 To Appeal from the Decision of the Chair.	Int.	Sec.	(8)	—	Maj.	—
	I-4 To Call for a Count of the Vote. (8)	Int.	—	—	—	(8)	—
	I-5 Points of Information. (8)	Int.	—	—	—	(8)	—
	I-6 To Suspend the Rules. (8)	—	Sec.	—	—	2/3	(8)
	I-7 To Object to Consideration. (8)	Int.	—	—	—	2/3	(8)
	I-8 To Consider as a Whole or by Parts. (8)	Int.	Sec.	—	Amd.	Maj.	—
	I-9 Request for Leave to Withdraw a Motion.	—	(8)	—	—	(8)	Ren.
	SUBSIDIARY MOTIONS						
	S-1 To Lay on the Table. (8)	—	Sec.	—	—	Maj.	Ren.
	S-2 To Close Debate. (8)	—	Sec.	—	—	2/3	Ren.
	S-3 To Limit (or Extend) Debate.	—	Sec.	—	(8)	2/3	Ren.
	S-4 To Postpone to a Definite Time. (8)	—	Sec.	Deb.	Amd.	Maj.	Ren.
	S-5 To Refer. (8)	—	Sec.	Deb.	Amd.	Maj.	Ren.
	S-6 To Amend. (8)	—	Sec.	Deb.	(8)	Maj.	Ren.
	S-7 To Postpone Indefinitely. (8)	—	Sec.	Deb.	—	Maj.	—
	MAIN MOTIONS						
	M All Main Motions.	—	Sec.	Deb.	Amd.	Maj.	(8)
	REVIEW MOTIONS						
	R-1 To Reconsider. (8)	(8)	Sec.	(8)	—	Maj.	—
	R-2 To Repeal. (8)	—	Sec.	Deb.	Amd.	(8)	(8)
	R-3 To Take from the Table. (8)	—	Sec.	—	—	Maj.	Ren.
	R-4 To Renew. (8)	(8)	(8)	(8)	(8)	(8)	(8)

Left margin labels: HIGHEST PRECEDENCE / LOWEST PRECEDENCE / SPECIAL PRECEDENCE

Int.—"May interrupt." Sec.—"Needing a second." Deb.—"Debatable."
Amd.—"Amendable." Maj.—"Majority." Ren.—"Renewable."

MOTIONS

8 Special Notes (Explanations of entry (8) in other Columns)	9 Page References

P-1   (1) Privileged only when no time and/or place have yet been set. (4) Debatable only if no other question is pending. (7) Renewable only to change time and/or place.   94

P-2   (1, 4) Privileged and undebatable only when made for immediate adjournment.   86

P-3   (1) Privileged only when made for immediate recess. (4) Debatable only when floor is clear. (5) Amendable only as to length of recess.   94

P-4   (4, 5, 6) Usually decided by Chair. Only a resulting motion is debatable, amendable, or needs majority vote.   95

P-5   (6) The Chair normally complies, but a ⅔ vote is needed to postpone a special order.   95

I-1   (4, 6) Debatable and in need of majority vote only if appealed from the decision of the Chair by I-4.   96

I-2   (6) Answered by Chair with help of others if needed.   96

I-3   (4) Debatable only when point is not one of decorum or order of business, or when pending question is debatable.   97

I-4   (1) Also known as: "Call for a Division of the Assembly." (6) No vote is needed since Chair must comply.   97

I-5   (1) Must be addressed to the Chair and must be a genuine request for information.   98

I-6   (1) Applies only to certain rules (See reference in Column 9). (7) May be renewed only by unanimous consent.   98

I-7   (1) Should be limited to grounds of relevance or propriety. (7) Renewable only by opposition to consider.   99

I-8   (1) Also known as: "To Consider *in Toto* or *Seriatim*."   99

I-9   (3, 6) Granted by Chair if there is no objection. Otherwise needs a second and requires a majority vote.   100

S-1   (1) The quickest means of clearing the floor for special purposes.   92

S-2   (1) Also known as: "To Call for the Previous Question."   92

S-3   (5) Amendable only as to time limit proposed. Otherwise identical with S-2.   92

S-4   (1) The preferred motion for postponing consideration without ulterior strategic purposes.   92

S-5   (1) Wording should fully specify to whom referred, which committee, how appointed, etc.   91

S-6   (1) See Column 5 for which motions this one is applicable to. (5) Amendments may themselves be only once amended.   90

S-7   (1) Applies only to Motions M and P-4. See reference, Column 9, for strategic implications of this motion.   93

M   (7) Once defeated, may not be renewed until second session following.   100

R-1   (1) An emergency motion to be made only at same meeting or at meeting following one at which original motion passed. (2) May interrupt only for entry, not for consideration. Hence dual precedence. (4) Is debatable only if original motion was.   101

R-2   (1) Also known as: "To Rescind." Not in order when R-1 is. (6) Needs ⅔ vote unless notice is given at previous meeting. (7) May not be renewed until next meeting.   102

R-3   (1) Reverses action of S-1.   102

R-4   (1) Applicability shown in Column 7. (2, 3, 4, 5, 6, 7) Has same status in all Columns as original motion.   103

It is reasonable, however, to allow many kinds of motions to be made again after conditions have changed.

For example, a group which at 10 P.M. votes down a motion to limit debate or to adjourn, may want to reconsider such motions at 11 P.M.

This possibility is recognized in parliamentary law by a provision for *renewability* in certain cases. All such motions are indicated in *Column 7* by the entry, *Ren.* (Renewable).

Column 8—Special Notes

Certain motions in all the *Columns, 1 through 7,* may carry the entry, *(8)*. This refers you to *Column 8* where special explanations are given.

Column 9—Page References

The last column *(9)* of the *Table* refers to the pages where additional explanations of items may be found.

Use of the Table of Motions

If you have some previous acquaintance with parliamentary law, you can use the *Table of Motions* in this book as a convenient quick reference to decide questions of parliamentary procedure. Take the book with you to meetings for that purpose.

All you need to remember are these few simple abbreviations:

> **Int.** for "May interrupt"
> **Sec.** for "Needing a second"
> **Deb.** for "Debatable"
> **Amd.** for "Amendable"
> **Maj.** for "Majority"
> **Ren.** for "Renewable"

As you read the explanations of the various kinds of motions in the rest of this chapter, keep turning back to the *Table* to review the important points. This will help fix in your mind the relation of each type of motion to the others.

THE CLASSES OF MOTIONS

Motions are usually divided, as in the preceding *Table,* into five general classes: *Privileged, Incidental, Subsidiary, Main* and *Review.* (See general explanation under "Incidental" motions, below.)

Of these, Main Motions are the most basic, and Privileged Motions have the highest precedence. But since the practical applications of Subsidiary Motions require the least prior understanding of the others, we shall begin our more detailed study with them.

SUBSIDIARY MOTIONS

Subsidiary Motions are those which apply to other motions. Having no independent purpose of their own, they serve to help dispose of other motions. And we shall consider them here in groups according to the several ways in which they do this.

For convenient reference, the number of each motion is given as listed in the *Table of Motions.* Thus the following motion, *To Amend,* is identified as *S-6.*

S-6 To Amend

A motion **To Amend** is subsidiary in that it proposes changes in other motions. It may do this for the words, sentences, or paragraphs of an original motion by:

1. Striking out,
2. Inserting,
3. Striking out and substituting.

EXAMPLES

1. "Mr. Chairman (Pause for recognition), I move to amend the motion 'that we be willing to meet earlier hereafter' by striking out the words 'be willing to.'"

COMMENT: This improves the sense of the motion. The words, "be willing to" are unnecessary and can be misconstrued.

2. "Mr. Chairman (Pause), I move to amend the motion 'that we meet earlier hereafter' by inserting the words 'one half hour' between the words 'meet' and 'earlier.'"

COMMENT: This makes the motion more specific.

3. "Mr. Chairman (Pause), I move to amend the motion 'that we meet one half hour earlier hereafter' by striking out the word 'hereafter' and substituting for it the words 'whenever daylight saving time is in effect.'"

COMMENT: This changes a detail of the motion, but in the spirit of the original intent and in a manner more likely to get approval.

SPECIAL RULES

a. The motion to amend may be applied only to those other motions indicated in *Column 5* of the *Table of Motions*.

b. It takes its relative precedence from the motion to which it is applied.

c. It may itself be amended only once.

d. It should relate to the motion amended and not have the effect of making a different motion.

EXPLANATION

Sometimes you may be in favor of most of the provisions of a motion, but object to certain details. Or, you may favor the general intent of a motion, but question whether that intent is correctly expressed by its wording.

If there were nothing you could do about this you might find yourself obliged to vote against motions with whose purpose, or with most of whose provisions, you agreed.

The motion *To Amend* is a parliamentary means of finding out whether the original proposal can be brought more into line with your way of thinking. So do not hesitate to use the device of amendment whenever you believe it will serve to clarify debate.

Members supporting the original motion may appreciate your help because they find your amendment better expresses what they had in mind. Or, even if they do not wholly agree with it, they may be willing to accept it to gain the additional backing of members who think as you do.

The motion To Amend is sometimes called an *Appendage Motion*. This means that it takes its *relative precedence* from the original motion to which it applies.

The precedence order, *S-6*, shown for it on the *Table of Motions* (above), holds when it is applied to a *Main Motion* (see below). But the motion at the very top of the precedence list is also one which can be amended. A motion to amend motion *P-1*, with regard to the proposed time or place of next meeting (see below), will therefore precede any other motion which can be made.

Special Rule c, limiting amendments to one further amendment, is to avoid excessive com-plication. When you get to the stage of putting patches on patches, it is a good idea to start over with a fresh article.

The purpose of requiring an amendment to relate solely to the original motion is to prevent it being used to change the original subject of discussion.

EXAMPLE

Member A: "Mr. Chairman (Pause for recognition), I move to amend the motion 'that we meet one half hour earlier' so as to read 'that we place a time limit on long speeches in order not to have to get here so early.' "

Chairman (Laughing): "We all understand how you feel about that, Mr. A. But your motion is not a proper amendment and the Chair cannot accept it for consideration."

COMMENT: Member A is, of course, only joking. But what he says is technically out of order because, in the form of a motion to amend, he is making a different proposal. In effect it is an argument against the original one. But the same thing is often attempted seriously.

S-5 To Refer

A motion **To Refer** is subsidiary in that it proposes to turn consideration of another motion over to a committee for study and recommendation.

EXAMPLE

"Mr. Chairman (Pause for recognition), we have been debating for the last half hour whether this organization should sponsor these social events. But no one present can now give us enough facts about costs, available halls, and questions like that. I therefore move that we refer the question to our Program Committee for study, and ask that it report its findings and recommendations at our next meeting."

SPECIAL RULE

This motion should specify the committee to which the original motion is to be referred, and what that committee is to be instructed to do with it.

EXPLANATION

The entire membership of an organization cannot possibly work out all the details of all its business. If it tried to do so, it would never catch up with unfinished business.

Most organizations therefore have *committees* to do the preparatory work.

When you sense a situation such as the one described above, do not hesitate to use this motion. It may save much time and pointless discussion.

The motion To Refer is sometimes used *strategically* (See next chapter) with the purpose of removing an original motion from discussion never to be taken up again. This is known as "burying it in committee."

You can avoid such "burial" of a motion in which you are interested if you insist that any motion To Refer state when the committee is to report back.

Lastly, bear in mind that no motion can ever be referred to any sub-group for *decision*.

A motion can be passed only by the regular procedure of voting at a meeting. A committee can serve only to help the membership do this by reporting its *factual findings* and *recommendations*.

Motions Regulating Debate

Two types of motions are *subsidiary* in that they relate to the debating of other motions.

S-3 To Limit (or Extend) Debate

EXAMPLES

1. "Mr. Chairman (Pause for recognition), I move that we limit debate on the question before us to one more speech of at most five minutes for each side."

2. "Mr. Chairman (Pause), I move that we extend debate on the present question one half hour."

S-2 To Close Debate

EXAMPLES

1. "Mr. Chairman (Pause for recognition), I move to close debate."

2. "Mr. Chairman (Pause), I move the previous question." (This is simply old-style parliamentary jargon for the same motion.)

SPECIAL RULES

a. Both motions require a two-thirds vote to carry.

b. Both motions also have the same status in all other *Columns* of the *Table of Motions* except that S-3 may be amended as to the proposed time to which debate is to be limited or extended.

EXPLANATION

If it were not possible to limit or close debate, a minority could prevent any motion from being passed by **filibustering**—talking on and on to prevent a vote from being taken. This has often happened in the United States Senate where the present rule is difficult to apply.

On the other hand, if it were too easy to limit or close debate, a small majority could always shut off opposition to their motions by moving to close debate on them at once. Hence the requirement of a two-thirds vote. This makes it impossible for a majority of less than two-thirds to silence the minority, or for a minority of less than one-third to filibuster.

Most often, however, these motions serve a more simple, routine purpose. When both sides to a debate begin to repeat themselves, or when the whole discussion begins to "go around in circles," you can use them to get on to other business.

Motions Postponing Consideration

The remaining three motions of this general class are *subsidiary* in that they relate to ways of postponing consideration of other motions.

S-1 To Lay on the Table

It was an old Parliamentary custom in England, when consideration of a motion was stopped, to lay its written draft upon the table before the Chairman. Hence, *to table a motion, or to lay a motion on the table* has come to mean to discontinue consideration of it.

EXAMPLE

"Mr. Chairman (Pause for recognition), I move that the motion before us be laid on the table."

SPECIAL RULE

This motion may not be debated or amended.

S-4 To Postpone to a Definite Time

EXAMPLE

"Mr. Chairman (Pause for recognition), the hour is getting late and there is an urgent matter of new business which I should like to bring before this meeting. I therefore move that consideration of the motion now before us be postponed to the next meeting."

SPECIAL RULES

a. This motion may be debated or amended.

b. It creates a *general order* (See *Order of Business, Item 4,* above) if in the form of the above example.

c. It creates a *special order* (See same reference) if a definite hour is specified, in which case a $\frac{2}{3}$ vote is needed to carry.

S-7 To Postpone Consideration Indefinitely

EXAMPLE

"Mr. Chairman (Pause for recognition), I move to postpone consideration of this question indefinitely."

SPECIAL RULES

a. This motion applies only to *Main Motions* and to *Questions of Privilege* (See below).

b. It may be debated.

EXPLANATION

Since all three of these motions have the effect of postponing consideration of an original motion, there is a question of which you should attempt to use in any given case where you would like to put off debate on a question.

For an answer, consider first the main facts about each of these motions with regard to their status in *Columns 1, 4,* and *5* of the *Table of Motions.*

S-1	S-4	S-7
To Table	To Postpone to a Definite Time	To Postpone Indefinitely
High Precedence	Medium Precedence	Low Precedence
Undebatable	Debatable	Debatable
Unamendable	Amendable	Unamendable

Which of these subsidiary motions can most readily be used in an emergency to clear the floor for other business?

Obviously the first, *S-1, To Table.* It has the highest precedence. And no time can be lost on it for either debate or amendment.

The very efficiency of this motion, however, also makes it a dangerous parliamentary instrument. An inconsiderate majority can misuse it to shut out consideration of minority proposals.

Which of the above motions would be fairest to use under normal circumstances?

Obviously the second, *S-4, To Postpone to a Definite Time.* It provides for a specific time to reconsider the original motion. And it admits of both debate and amendment, thus assuring that a generally acceptable time for reconsideration may be set.

The normal purposes of any member who wants to have an original motion considered at a later time, are therefore well enough served by the first two motions above.

Why, then, the other motion, *S-7, To Postpone Indefinitely*?

This is a *strategic motion* (See next chapter) in that it is never used for what it seems to be for, but always for an ulterior end. The key fact is that it is debatable just as the original motion is. By moving it, therefore, the opposition to the original motion has something to gain and nothing to lose.

If the motion *To Postpone Consideration Indefinitely* passes, the opposition has achieved its purpose of preventing the original motion from passing. And it does this, without a commitment for reconsideration, as in the passing of *S-4.*

Even if this strategic motion does not pass, moreover, the opposition is still no worse off than it was before. And, the motion being debatable, it may even have gained some advantage.

First, the opposition will have gained debate time to speak against the original motion without being subject to time limits to which debate on that original motion may later be subject.

Secondly, the opposition will have had an opportunity to learn its strength and weakness by the positions which other members take, and by the count of the vote on the subsidiary question of postponement.

Thirdly, the opposition will have delayed final action on the original question for a period of time which may be long enough to enable them to gather more strength.

Lastly, the opposition will have been able to do all this without the risk of a vote on the original motion which remains to be debated and voted upon after the subsidiary motion is disposed of.

Never be fooled by the motion *To Postpone Consideration Indefinitely*. It is simply a *delaying tactic*.

This does not mean, however, that it is always obstructive. It can also serve to further good democratic procedure.

It has found a place in parliamentary law because well organized minorities sometimes try to rush unpopular measures through at meetings where they chance to have a temporary majority. In such cases, the delaying feature of this motion may be used to postpone action until the normal balance of the voting membership is restored.

SUMMARY

You will find the *Motion S-1, To Table,* the most efficient in clearing the floor quickly for special purposes. But you must beware of its possible misuse as a means of keeping minority proposals from being considered.

You will find *Motion S-4, To Postpone to a Definite Time,* the fairest way of putting off debate under normal circumstances, and the least subject to abuse for strategic purposes.

You should be on guard against *Motion S-7, To Postpone Consideration Indefinitely,* as a parliamentary delaying tactic. But do not hesitate to use it yourself if you find a temporary majority trying to take parliamentary advantage of the absence of fellow members with whom you agree on the usual majority policy of your organization.

PRIVILEGED MOTIONS

Privileged Motions are those which deal with the basic arrangements for a meeting and the comfort and personal rights of the members attending.

The fact that privileged motions have the highest **precedence** (See explanation of *Column 1,* above) does not necessarily mean that they concern the most important items of business. On the contrary, they may relate to minor matters such as the opening of a window for ventilation (See *Motion P-4,* below) or mere details of routine such as the formal ending of a meeting when its real business is finished (See *Motion P-2,* below).

Yet, the reason they are given right of way over more important questions will be clearly seen in each of the following cases.

P-1 To Fix the Time and/or Place of Next Meeting

EXAMPLE

"Mr. Chairman (Pause for recognition), I move that when we adjourn we do so to meet next at this same place at 8:30 P.M. tomorrow evening."

SPECIAL RULES

a. Privileged only when no time and/or place have yet been set for the next meeting.

b. Debatable only if no other question is pending.

c. Renewable only to change the time and/or place.

EXPLANATION

This motion has the highest precedence because it is a necessary preliminary to the motion to adjourn. Since no official action may be taken after adjournment, an organization could theoretically abolish itself by adjourning without a set time and place to meet again.

Most organizations, of course, have regular meeting times and places. They therefore do not normally need this motion at all.

P-2 To Adjourn

P-3 To Recess

Explanations of these terms, and an example of the motion, *To Adjourn,* have been given under *Item 7* of *The Order of Business.*

SPECIAL RULES

a. Have privileged status only when they provide for *immediate* adjournment or recess.

b. When privileged, they may not be debated.

c. They may not interrupt a speaker or a vote.

EXPLANATION

The high precedence of these motions is based on the common-sense idea that members cannot usefully be kept at a meeting when they feel that they must, or would rather, go elsewhere.

The last special rule keeps the motions from being used to deprive a speaker of the floor, or to avoid the tally of a vote.

P-4 Questions of Privilege

An **Ordinary Question of Privilege** is one which relates to the comfort or convenience of the members at a meeting. It requires a formal motion only when challenged.

EXAMPLES

1. *Member A:* "Mr. Chairman (Interrupting if necessary, and not waiting to be recognized), I rise to a question of privilege."

Chairman: "What is your question?"

Member A: "Will the Chair please ask the speakers in the front of the room to speak up more clearly so that we can hear them here in the back of the room?"

Chairman: "By all means. The Chair asks all speakers to comply with the member's request. And will the last speaker please repeat what he just said for the benefit of those in the back of the room."

2. *Member B:* "Mr. Chairman (Interrupting if necessary), I rise to a question of privilege."

Chairman: "State your question."

Member B: "Will the Chair please ask all candidates for election to leave the room while we discuss their qualifications?"

Member C: "Mr. Chairman (Also interrupting), as a point of privilege, I object to our being asked to leave the room while our candidacies are being discussed."

Member B: "In that case, Mr. Chairman, I should like to make my original question of privilege a formal motion."

Chairman: "It has been moved as a point of privilege that all candidates for election be asked to leave the room while their qualifications are being discussed. Is there any discussion on the privileged question? Etc."

A **Question** becomes one of **Personal Privilege** when it involves the reputation or standing of a member.

EXAMPLE

"Mr. Chairman (Interrupting if necessary), I rise to a point of personal privilege . . . The speaker has just misquoted me in a way that reflects upon my personal reputation as a loyal member of this organization. I ask that he correct that impression immediately, or else that I be given the privilege of taking the floor at once to make clear the facts of the matter in so far as my personal reputation is concerned."

SPECIAL RULES

a. May interrupt a speaker if necessary.

b. No vote is required unless a motion is involved.

EXPLANATION

The high precedence given Questions of Privilege is a matter of common sense in all routine applications. Members should not hesitate to raise them for reasons of their comfort and convenience in following the course of business.

The high precedence given Questions of Personal Privilege reflects the importance properly attached in democratic procedure to an individual's personal dignity and security from slander. It is best for any organization, however, to try to avoid the need of raising these questions (See *Propriety* under *Having the Floor,* above).

P-5 To Call for the Orders of the Day

The general plan of a meeting's *Order of Business* has been discussed in detail above. But sometimes a Chairman does not follow this order or he allows others to depart from it on the floor.

EXAMPLES

1. *Member A:* "Mr. Chairman (Interrupting if necessary, and not waiting to be recognized), I call for the orders of the day."

Chairman: "In what particular, Mr. A?"

Member A: "The Chair has just asked for reports from committees. But we have not yet heard the Treasurer's Report."

Chairman: "Thank you Mr. A. That was an oversight. The Treasurer will please make his report."

2. *Member B:* "Mr. Chairman (Interrupting, etc.), I call for the orders of the day."

Chairman: "In what way, Mr. B?"

Member B: "The speaker is introducing new business. But at our last meeting there was a general order of business voted for consideration today."

Chairman: "Is that the case, Mr. Secretary?"

Secretary: "Yes, Mr. Chairman, it is."

Chairman: "The Chair will then have to ask the speaker to yield the floor. Will the Secretary please read the general order of business . . . etc."

SPECIAL RULES

a. Needs no recognition or second.

b. May interrupt a speaker, if necessary.

EXPLANATION

If the Chairman does not use his authority to keep discussion to the proper order of business, this motion is your means of getting him to do so.

"INCIDENTAL" MOTIONS

The traditional distinction between *Privileged, Incidental, and Subsidiary* motions may be summarized as follows:

Privileged Motions are a special group of motions concerning matters of such urgency at the moment that they require a special priority for consideration.

Subsidiary Motions are those which are applied to other motions for the purpose of disposing of them.

Incidental Motions are those relating to questions which arise out of the consideration of other motions.

This division is clear enough so far as Privileged and Subsidiary motions are concerned.

But the so-called "Incidental" motions are much more similar to those in the other two groups than their formal definition would suggest.

For example, *Leave to Withdraw a Motion* (See *Motion I-9,* below) is practically a *Question of Privilege,* and the latter is always classed as *Privileged* (See *Motion P-4,* below). Yet, *Leave to Withdraw a Motion* is also just as much a way of disposing of another motion as any motion usually classed as *Subsidiary.* And in many similar instances there are really no hard and fast lines of division between these so-called "classes of motions."

You will therefore find it simpler to think of "Incidental" motions either as more privileged subsidiary motions or as more subsidiary privileged motions.

I-1 Points of Parliamentary Order

Sometimes the question of correctness of procedure depends, not on the *Order of Business* (See *Motion P-5,* above), but on some other parliamentary rule.

EXAMPLE

Member: "Mr. Chairman (Interrupting if necessary, and not waiting to be recognized), I rise to a point of order."

Chairman: "Please state your point of order."

Member: "The alleged amendment which the speaker has just offered is not a true amendment to the main question. In effect, it is a proposal of an entirely different measure than the one we are now considering."

Chairman: "Quite so, Mr. A. The Chair must ask the speaker to re-word his motion in the form of a proper amendment or else yield the floor" (See *Motion S-6, To Amend,* above).

SPECIAL RULES

a. May interrupt a speaker and needs no recognition or second.

b. Is decided by the Chair and is not debated unless the Chair's decision is appealed (See *Motion I-3,* below).

EXPLANATION

Like a *Call for the Orders of the Day* (See *Motion P-5,* above), this motion makes it possible for you to help keep the Chair alert to correct parliamentary procedure.

You should be careful, though, not to abuse it. Unless the point is of practical consequence, you will only antagonize others by calling constant attention to minor technical "slips."

I-2 Points of Parliamentary Inquiry

A point of correctness of parliamentary procedure may be put in question form.

EXAMPLE

Member: "Mr. Chairman (Interrupting if necessary, and not waiting to be recognized), I rise to a point of parliamentary inquiry."

Chairman: "Please state your question."

Member: "Is the present speaker in order in offering an amendment to my motion at this time?"

Chairman: "Yes, sir, he is. A motion to amend takes precedence over the main motion. The speaker is therefore quite in order and may continue."

SPECIAL RULES

a. May interrupt a speaker, but should not do so for trivial reasons.

b. If the Chairman cannot answer the question he may refer it to the assembly, but a debate is not in order.

EXPLANATION

You should know enough about parliamentary law not to have to raise frequent questions of parliamentary procedure. You are entitled, however, to have your reasonable questions answered officially by the Chair.

You may also use the form of a parliamentary question even when you know the answer. It is a tactful way of calling for the Orders of the Day (See *Motion P-5,* above), or of raising *Points of Parliamentary Order* (See *Motion I-1,* above), without embarrassing the Chairman.

I-3 To Appeal from the Decision of the Chair

EXAMPLES

1. *Question Debatable:*

Member A: "Mr. Chairman (Interrupting if necessary, and not waiting to be recognized), I appeal from the decision of the Chair."

Member B: "I second the motion."

Chairman: "The decision of the Chair has been appealed. Is there any discussion?"

(Discussion)

Chairman: "If there is no more discussion, the question is: 'Shall the decision of the Chair be sustained?' All in favor . . . etc."

2. *Question Not Debatable:*

Member C: "Mr. Chairman (Interrupting if necessary, etc.), I appeal from the decision of the Chair."

Member D: "I second the motion."

Chairman: "The decision of the Chair has been appealed. The question is: 'Shall the decision of the Chair be sustained.' All in favor . . . etc."

SPECIAL RULES

a. Appeals from decisions of the Chair must be made promptly after the decision has been made, and may interrupt a speaker if necessary.

b. They require a second and are debatable unless the question is one of decorum or order of business, or unless the pending question is undebatable.

c. The question is always put to vote as one of sustaining the decision of the Chair, as in the above examples.

EXPLANATION

The ruling of the Chair on points of order is normally accepted. But it does not have to be.

If you believe the Chair in error on an *important* point, you may appeal the decision by means of this motion. Here again, you should not do so for trivial or merely technical reasons. Keep your parliamentary powder dry, for the time when it is really needed.

I-4 To Call for a Count of the Vote

In the older handbooks, the motion for a count of the vote is termed a **Call for a Division of the Assembly.**

EXAMPLE

Chairman: "All those in favor of the motion will please say 'Aye' (*Eye*)."

Response: Chorus of "Aye"s.

Chairman: "All those opposed to the motion will please say 'No.'"

Response: Chorus of "no"s.

Chairman: "The 'Aye's have it. The motion is carried."

Member A: "Mr. Chairman (Interrupting if necessary, and not waiting to be recognized), I call for a count of the vote."

Chairman: "The member calls for a count of the vote. All those in favor of the motion will please stand. Will the Secretary also please count those standing so that we may check our results . . . etc."

SPECIAL RULES

   a. May interrupt a speaker if necessary.

   b. Needs no recognition or second.

EXPLANATION

The usual practice is for a voice vote as illustrated above. Because some people answer louder than others, however, it is often hard for you to tell which side has carried by a voice vote, especially when the vote is close.

If in doubt, the Chair may ask for a show of hands, or a standing vote. But you are also entitled to a careful count if you question the Chair's decision, and you can ask for it by means of this motion.

I-5 Points of Information

EXAMPLE

Member A: (Speaking in possession of the floor).

Member B: "Mr. Chairman (Interrupting if necessary, and without waiting to be recognized), I rise to a point of information."

Chairman: "Does the speaker mind?"

Member A: "Not at all, Mr. Chairman."

Chairman: "You may state your question, Mr. B."

Member B: "Is the speaker taking the figures he has been quoting from our last year's Financial Statement?"

Member A: "No, Mr. Chairman, I am sorry if I failed to mention that these figures are from the Treasurer's current records."

Member B: "Thank you, Mr. Chairman. That was what some of us were wondering about since we could not find them on the last Financial Statement."

Member C: "While such questions are in order, Mr. Chairman, I'd like to ask one. Do you realize, Mr. A., that those figures you have been quoting are misleading because of the unusual expenses we have had this year?"

Chairman: "Sorry, Mr. C. That is not a proper point of information. The Chair will be glad to recognize you next if you wish to raise such an issue. But Mr. A. has the floor now and may proceed."

   NOTE: Member C was also out of order in addressing his question directly to Member A. All questions and answers should be addressed to the Chair. Cross-conversation is not allowed in formal parliamentary discussion.

SPECIAL RULES

   a. Should be limited to genuine inquiries.

   b. You need not first be recognized to rise to a point of information, but the speaker may decide whether he will yield the floor to hear your question.

   c. Both questions and answers must be addressed to the Chair.

EXPLANATION

The high precedence given to a request for information is to help you follow what the speaker is saying. Member B is *in order* in the above example because he is making a genuine inquiry.

Member C is *out of order* because he is obviously trying to use this high-precedence motion to get speaking time for which he should properly wait his turn.

If someone rises to a point of information while you have the floor, you must decide whether you will agree to hear his question. When your time is limited and you have important points still to make, you may be reluctant to do so, since both question and answer will be clocked against you in limited debate.

The question to be asked, however, may be troubling other members as well. Answering it may help your case more than saying what you had planned to say. You will do well, therefore, to yield to members from whom you can anticipate intelligent questions.

I-6 To Suspend the Rules

Many of the preceding motions provide means of keeping the procedure of a meeting regular. This motion and the following one, however, provide emergency means of avoiding usual procedure.

The fact that there is a general class of motions, To Suspend the Rules, does not mean that all rules can be suspended by any organization. Each society's constitution or by-laws (See next chapter) specifies which rules, if any, can be suspended at its meetings.

It is commonly possible to suspend rules which relate to:

   a. The order of business.

   b. Limitations on debate.

c. Exclusions of non-members from attendance of discussion.

It is generally *not* possible to suspend more basic rules which relate to:

a. The rights of members.
b. Voting requirements.
c. Rules of parliamentary procedure not specifically excepted.

EXAMPLES

1. *Permissible:*

Member A: "Mr. Chairman (Pause for recognition), in view of the importance and complexity of the motion on the floor, I move to suspend the rules in order to extend debate on it beyond the limits imposed by our By-laws."

Member B: "I second the motion."

Chairman: "It has been moved and seconded . . . etc."

2. *Not permissible:*

Member C: "Mr. Chairman (Pause for recognition), the motion which was just barely defeated required a two-thirds vote to pass. In view of the importance of the action, I move to suspend the rules in order to make a simple majority vote enough to pass it."

Chairman: "Sorry, Mr. C., but the Chair cannot entertain such a motion. A rule of voting is not one which can be suspended."

SPECIAL RULES

a. Is limited to specified rules.
b. May not be debated or amended.
c. Requires a two-thirds vote to carry.

EXPLANATION

This motion is more limited than is generally realized. It is strictly a special-purpose measure for setting aside minor regulations when there are good grounds for doing so. It is *not* a way of getting around really basic parliamentary principles.

The rules governing it assure that no time will be lost on it, and that it will not pass without substantial majority support.

I-7 To Object to Consideration

EXAMPLE

Member: "Mr. Chairman (Interrupting if necessary, and not pausing for recognition), I object to consideration of this motion."

Chairman: "Objection has been made to consideration. Do you wish to consider the original motion to which objection has been made? All those in favor of considering the original motion please say 'Aye' . . . etc."

SPECIAL RULES

a. Should be made when the original motion is first presented.
b. Should be based upon a presumption of bad taste or irrelevance in the original motion.
c. Requires no second, and cannot be debated or amended.
d. Is put to vote by the Chair in the form illustrated above, and a two-thirds vote in the negative excludes the challenged motion from further consideration.
e. May be renewed only by the negative.

EXPLANATION

Most parliamentary law is designed to give all members and all points of view a fair chance to be heard. Sometimes, however, a minority may take advantage of this fact to impose upon a meeting motions out-of-line with its purpose.

For example, a pair of members of a social or business club may repeatedly introduce resolutions for "world peace" or "clean living." You may have no objection to these in themselves, but may well feel that they are out of place at that meeting.

You can give such offending members a gentle hint by first moving To Table their motions (See *Motion S-1,* above). If they persist, it is your right to object directly to the consideration of their proposals by means of this motion.

The rules assure that no time will be lost in applying it, and that a small majority will not misuse it to prevent consideration of proper minority motions.

I-8 To Consider as a Whole or by Parts

In the older manuals of Parliamentary Law this motion is usually given the Latin phrasing: Consideration *in toto* (as a whole) or *seriatim* (in a series, and so by parts).

It is customary to consider any motion as a whole unless a motion is passed to consider it by parts.

EXAMPLE

"Mr. Chairman (Pause for recognition), discussion of the motion before us is becoming so complicated, I move to consider it paragraph by paragraph."

SPECIAL RULE

If this motion is passed, separate votes are taken on the separate parts into which the original motion is then divided.

EXPLANATION

By moving to consider a complicated motion by parts, you may obtain *two advantages:* You can speak for or against each part separately in debate. And you can register your support or opposition on each part separately when the vote is taken.

Thus you can help to keep separate issues from being confused, and can better express just where you stand on each part of the original question. Give its possible use careful thought whenever debate becomes too involved.

Where necessary this motion may be applied to break down an original motion, sentence by sentence or phrase by phrase.

I-9 Request for Leave to Withdraw a Motion

EXAMPLES

1. *Situation with no objections:*

Member A (Original Mover): "Mr. Chairman (Pause for recognition), in view of what has just been said by the last speaker, I should like to withdraw my motion."

Chairman: "The member requests leave to withdraw his motion which we are now considering. Are there any objections? (Pause for response.) If not, that leave is granted and the floor is now open for other business."

2. *Situation with objections:*

Chairman: "The member requests leave to withdraw his motion. Are there any objections?"

Member B: "I object, Mr. Chairman."

Chairman: "In that case the Chair will have to ask if anyone is willing to move that Mr. A. be granted permission to withdraw his motion."

Member C: "I so move, Mr. Chairman."

Member D: "I second the motion."

Chairman: "It has been moved and seconded that the member be granted leave to withdraw his motion. All in favor . . . etc."

SPECIAL RULES

a. Only the mover may request leave to withdraw a motion.

b. The Chair can grant the request only if there are no objections.

c. When there are objections, a formal motion to grant it must be made, seconded, and voted upon without debate.

EXPLANATION

No one but you can reasonably be allowed to withdraw a motion which you have made. In the absence of objection, it can be regarded as your personal right to do so.

Since other members have accepted consideration of your motion, however, the rules give them the right to object to your trying to take it back from them.

MAIN MOTIONS

Original Main Motions supply the grist for the parliamentary mill because they introduce those basic proposals of action for which the organization exists.

The other classes of motions considered above—Privileged, Incidental, and Subsidiary—serve merely to help an organization to function so that it can deal with these basic motions more efficiently.

Typically, an Original Main Motion is the kind you may most properly make as a point of *New Business.* In connection with that *Item, 6,* of the Order of Business, we have already given as examples: the proposal at a meeting of a Sports Club to purchase a contest trophy; and a proposal at a meeting of a Civic Association to petition City officials for the construction of a playground (above).

Review those examples for formal wording and for recommendations as to what preparations you should make before trying to introduce such motions.

Motions to introduce main points of new business, however, are not the only ones included in this general class. There are also **Incidental Main Motions.**

Consider, for example, the question of when and where the next meeting of an organization will be held. We have already seen that, if this question has not been decided, a motion concerning it is classified as Privileged and has the highest precedence (See *Motion P-1,* above).

Yet, if a time and place have already been set for the next meeting, a motion to propose a different time or place is not so privileged. It then has no more priority for consideration than an ordinary Original Main Motion.

Moreover, even when such a motion is privileged, once it has been introduced it becomes a main motion in the sense that subsidiary and incidental motions may be applied to its discussion. If the floor had been clear at the time when it was introduced, it would be treated like any Original Main Motion so far as parliamentary routine is concerned.

The same is true of a motion *To Adjourn* if it is not for *immediate* adjournment; or of a *Question of Privilege* once it has been put as a motion before the meeting.

All such motions are therefore classed as **Incidental Main Motions**—"Incidental," to distinguish them from "Original" main motions introducing essentially new business; and "Main" because incidental and subsidiary motions may be applied to them.

SPECIAL RULE

Main motions are last in order of precedence.

EXPLANATION

The low precedence of main motions means that none can be made while any other motion, including another main motion, is being discussed.

This may at first seem unsound, since the most important business considered at a meeting must be introduced by means of main motions. Why put first things last in order of priority?

Subsidiary, incidental, and privileged motions take precedence over a main motion,

however, only because they enable a meeting better to consider the more basic proposals which are contained in a main motion.

Beyond that, the purpose of the rule of precedence is simply to assure that no more than one main motion be discussed at a time.

REVIEW MOTIONS

Review Motions are those which direct attention back to a motion previously considered. You may therefore quite correctly think of them as a special class of *Incidental Main Motions.*

The form which they take, and their precedence order, depends upon the manner in which previous discussion of the original motion was ended.

R-1 To Reconsider

If previous discussion ended in the *passing* of the original motion, that motion may be reviewed, under certain conditions, by means of the motion *To Reconsider.*

EXAMPLE

"Mr. Chairman (Interrupting a speaker, if necessary), having just learned from a late arrival that the Fire Department has declared X Hall unsafe for occupancy, I move to reconsider our vote earlier this evening to hold our next meeting there."

SPECIAL RULES

a. May be moved only by a member who voted for passage of the original motion, and only during the same meeting, or the meeting immediately following the one at which the original motion was passed.

b. May interrupt a speaker on any other motion.

c. Once seconded, it automatically stops all action carrying out the motion to be reconsidered.

d. Discussion must await clearance of the floor, but precedes any other main motion not actually under discussion.

e. May not be renewed.

EXPLANATION

The motion, *To Reconsider,* is primarily an emergency measure. Its main purpose is to stop action on a previous motion when new information puts that action in a different light. Rule *b* therefore, gives it the same high precedence for entry as a Question of Privilege (*Motion P-4* above), and rule *d* assures that its discussion will follow at the earliest reasonable opportunity.

Like other devices for quick action, however, this motion can be *abused.* Rules *a* and *c* which limit its use to supporters of the original motion and forbid its renewal if defeated, are intended to prevent a defeated side from using it to block action on a motion.

But sometimes a scheming minority will have some of its members vote with an anticipated majority just in order to make them eligible, later, to delay action by moving To Reconsider.

Likewise, a scheming majority will sometimes automatically move To Reconsider a motion which they have just passed themselves. Their purpose, then, is to vote down the motion To Reconsider at once so that rule *c* makes it impossible for real opposition to the original motion to stop action on it later.

For comment on all such parliamentary maneuvers see the section on *Parliamentary Strategy* in the next chapter.

R-2 To Repeal

After the meeting following the one at which it is passed, an original motion can no longer be reached by the motion To Reconsider. If you then wish to review the action approved by a previous vote, you must do so through the motion **To Repeal,** sometimes called **To Rescind.**

Under either name, this is a motion to undo whatever was done by the original motion. And so it is reasonable only when the previous action is one which *can* be undone.

EXAMPLES

1. *Member A:* "Mr. Chairman (Pause for recognition), I move to repeal the motion we passed two years ago increasing membership fees by two dollars per year."

Member B: "I second the motion."

Chairman: "It has been moved and seconded, etc."

2. *Member C:* "Mr. Chairman (Pause for recognition), in view of the recent conviction of the Trustees of the Z Foundation for misuse of funds, I move to repeal the motion we passed last year making a donation to the Foundation."

Chairman: "Many of us regret that action as much as you do, Mr. C. But in accordance with our instructions, the Treasurer mailed out our check to the Foundation the next day and it has long since been cleared through the bank. So I do not see how the Chair can entertain a motion such as you offer now."

SPECIAL RULES

a. Has the same precedence status for entry as any other main motion.

b. Requires a two-thirds vote to pass unless notice of consideration has been given at the previous meeting, in which case only a simple majority vote is required.

EXPLANATION

The preceding motion, *R-1, To Reconsider,* makes any action subject to quick review within a reasonable period of time. But if past actions could always be so easily reviewed, it would be theoretically possible for a conspiring minority to reverse your organization's entire past policy at a single meeting in which they chanced to have a temporary majority.

Once the period of the motion, To Reconsider, has expired, therefore, the review of past actions is made more difficult. The rules governing Repeal Motions give them the lowest possible precedence rank to insure that your organization's considered policy will not be too easily reversed.

R-3 To Take from the Table

A motion which has been removed from consideration by being *tabled* may be renewed by means of a motion *To Take from the Table.*

EXAMPLE

"Mr. Chairman (Pause for recognition), in order to clear the floor for the guest speaker whom we just heard, we tabled the motion then on the floor. I now move to take that motion from the table."

SPECIAL RULES

a. Is in order only when no other motion is before the meeting.

b. Is undebatable.

EXPLANATION

This motion simply undoes the action of *Motion S-1, To Table*. It is your means of having a meeting take up again a matter in which you are interested.

It is undebatable, of course, for the same parliamentary reasons that the motion *To Table* is (See detailed explanation of *Motion S-1* above).

R-4 To Renew

Strictly speaking, there is no such thing as a separate motion "to renew consideration." But when a motion is made again, after having been previously moved and defeated, the new motion is said **To Renew** the original one.

The conditions under which each type of motion may or may not be renewed are indicated on the *Table of Motions* and discussed in the explanation of *Column 7, Renewability* (above).

EXAMPLES

1. *Member A:* "Mr. Chairman (Pause for recognition), I should like to move once more as I did earlier this evening, that . . ."

Chairman: "Sorry, Mr. A., but that motion was defeated when you first introduced it. We may therefore not take it up again until the meeting after next when the Chair will be glad to have you re-introduce it if you then wish to."

(NOTE: See *Table*, Line *M*. Columns 7 and 8.)

2. *Member B:* "Mr. Chairman (Pause for recognition), I again move to reconsider the motion we have passed to appropriate . . ."

Chairman: "Sorry, Mr. B., but you are out of order. Since a motion to reconsider cannot be made a second time after it is once defeated, the Chair can entertain no such motion."

(NOTE: See *Table*, Line *R-1*, Columns 7 and 8.)

3. *Member C:* "Mr. Chairman (Pause for recognition), a full hour has gone by since my motion to close debate on this question was defeated. I therefore again move to close debate."

Member D: "I second the motion."

Chairman: "It has been moved and seconded to close debate. All in favor . . . etc."

(NOTE: See *Table*, Line *S-2*, Column 7.)

The application of parliamentary procedure to organized discussion is taken up in the first section of the following chapter.

CHAPTER VI

DISCUSSION TECHNIQUES

PARLIAMENTARY DISCUSSION

Formal and Informal Procedure

Perhaps the most commonly misunderstood aspect of parliamentary practice is the difference between **formal** and **informal** procedure.

When strictly following the formalities described in the preceding chapter of this book you may at times have felt stiff and unnatural. Taking your cue from such experiences, you may have departed from such formality at other times only to find yourself called to order.

What, then, is the best policy to follow in this matter?

As a general rule, you will do best to keep to formal procedure when the members at the meetings you attend are: Large in number; not well acquainted with each other; concerned with major issues; sharply divided in opinion.

Any one of these factors alone may decide the question. There is a limit to how casual a large assembly can be without becoming too disorganized to accomplish anything. And even two people tend to be more formal in their attitude when they are comparative strangers, when they are engaged in serious dealings, or when they are not seeing eye-to-eye.

Conversely, parliamentary procedure may become more informal when the members at your meeting are: Few in number; well acquainted; dealing with routine matters; in agreement as to views.

Most of these factors are of course relative. We could say that a meeting has few participants when less than some arbitrary number like *fifteen* are present. But the questions of how well acquainted or in agreement with each other people really are, is a matter of nice judgment.

In doubtful cases it is always best to err, if you must, on the side of formality. You can soften the strictly correct formulas of speech with a smile and a casual tone of voice. The ludicrous impression of over-formality, after all, is as much a matter of how you speak as of what you say.

Then, if the general tone of response seems to justify it, you can shift to more informal wording later.

As the Chair, you should be particularly sensitive to this problem and give the speakers cues on how to proceed.

Whenever informality seems possible, you can speed matters up by cutting corners a bit. But when objections arise you must be prompt to return to strict procedure.

EXAMPLE

Member A: "Mr. Chairman (Pause for recognition), in view of the information that has been brought out in the discussion, I move to amend the main motion by striking out the word 'Wednesday' and substituting for it the word 'Thursday'."

Chairman: "Perhaps that change will be acceptable to Mr. B., who made the motion. If so, we won't need to take time for discussion and vote on the motion to amend."

Member B: "Yes, Mr. Chairman, that would be perfectly all right with me."

Member C: "Mr. Chairman (Pause, etc.), I wonder if Mr. B. would also be willing to have his motion read 'next September' instead of 'next August'."

Member B: "No, Mr. Chairman, I most definitely would not agree to any such change!"

Chairman: "In that case, Mr. C., the Chair must ask if you want to put what you have in mind in the form of a motion to amend."

COMMENT: In this example the Chairman was able to save time by treating A's formal action informally. But on seeing that C's informal suggestion could not be handled in the same way, he correctly put the discussion back on a formal footing.

The main error to avoid is that of confusing informality with **irregularity.** When your meeting is conducted informally, you should do substantially the same things as under formal procedure, only in a more relaxed and streamlined manner. Never use informality as an excuse for avoiding the substance of the rules of parliamentary procedure.

EXAMPLES

1. At a regular business meeting:

Chairman: "Support for this appropriation measure seems to be so strong that I don't believe we need bother taking a vote on it. The Secretary can record it as passed."

COMMENT: This Chairman is not just being informal. He is being highly irregular. Unless there has been a proper majority vote, any dissenting member has the right to charge that there has been a misappropriation of funds.

2. At the quarterly meeting of the 450 members of the Suburban Civic Association:

Chairman: "Will the Secretary please read the minutes of the last meeting."

Secretary: "Nothing much happened at the last meeting. I don't think we need take the time to read the minutes. I have a copy of them here on my desk if anybody wants to look them over on the way out."

COMMENT: Here the Secretary is being much too informal for the occasion. He cannot reasonably expect that many people to read a document of any length while walking past it on their way home at a late hour. Moreover, it is a long time between quarterly meetings, and those who attend them may need reminders of what took place at the last one.

3. At a luncheon meeting of the four like-minded members of the Trophy Committee of a Fishing Club:

Committeeman A: "Mr. Chairman, I rise to a point of parliamentary inquiry."

COMMENT: This is, of course, absurdly over-formal. The committeeman, we may hope, is joking over the cocktails.

Parliamentary Strategy

In the explanation of different kinds of motions in the preceding chapter, attention was called to the **strategic possibilities** of several.

In certain cases such tactics are strictly **irreg-**ular. For example: attempts to change the intent or substance of a motion by *Amendment* (See explanation of *Motion S-6,* above), or attempts to interrupt a speaker and gain debate time by improper *Points of Information* (See explanation of *Motion I-5,* above).

An alert Chairman should prevent such abuses. Or you can influence him to do so by the use of *Points of Parliamentary Order* and *Appeals from the Decision of the Chair* (See explanation of *Motions I-1* and *I-3* above).

But other strategic moves are perfectly **regular.**

Perhaps the most unblushing example of this is use of the motion, *To Reconsider,* so as actually to prevent the possibility of reconsideration (See explanation of *Motion R-1,* above).

Its purpose, as we have seen, is to enable a parliamentary group quickly to stop action, for emergency reasons, on a motion previously passed. And to prevent one possible kind of abuse, the motion, *To Reconsider,* is classified as un-renewable.

But we have also seen that a majority may take advantage of this un-renewability feature. They may themselves immediately move and vote down the motion, *To Reconsider,* thus making it technically impossible for others to reconsider the same action later.

Moreover, by the motions, *To Refer* or *To Table,* a bare majority can sidestep consideration of a proposal at will (See explanations of *S-5* and *S-1,* above).

By the motions, *To Limit Debate, To Close Debate,* or *To Object to Consideration,* a two thirds majority can confine discussion of any question as they wish, even to the extent of preventing it altogether (See explanations of *S-3, S-2,* and *I-7,* above).

The motion, *To Postpone Consideration Indefinitely,* we have also seen, is always a tactical move to delay action on a main proposal (See explanation of *S-7,* above).

Each of these motions, including the last, has a perfectly legitimate purpose. It is a useful part of the whole plan of parliamentary procedure.

Yet, the very effectiveness of such motions for their intended use makes them subject to misuse. And there is no formal parliamentary means of distinguishing between their intended and unintended application. So the question is: What should be *your* policy regarding them?

One thing should be perfectly clear in any case. You should fully understand the possibilities of such tactics if only to be prepared to *counter* them when used against you in parliamentary discussion.

Do not hesitate to challenge *Amendments* which tend to change the substance of motions in which you are interested.

Do not allow improper *Points of Information* to interrupt your speaking or be clocked against your allotted debate time.

When a motion is made *To Refer* a proposal in which you are interested, see to it that, through discussion and *Amendment,* it is referred to a committee which will really work on it and report back its recommendations in due time.

When a motion you are interested in is *Tabled,* do not lose sight of it. Use the motion, *To Take from the Table,* to bring the question up again at an appropriate time.

Do not hesitate, moreover, to use any of these motions yourself for their legitimate purposes. As we have seen, there are often reasonable grounds for moving *To Table, To Close Debate, To Object to Consideration,* or *To Postpone Indefinitely.*

But what about the purely **obstructive** use of such motions?

A book of this sort is not the place for exhortations to virtue. Still, it can be reported as a fairly clear lesson of practical experience that parliamentary skulduggery tends to defeat itself in the end. In our imperfect world, tactics of this kind sometimes enjoy a limited success. But in the long run, they satisfy those whom they serve no more than those whom they frustrate.

When you are working with a comfortable majority, it may seem an easy matter to steamroller a measure through by arbitrarily closing off debate. But there are several questions which you should ask yourself.

What happens to your respect for those who join you in such an action? How, then, must it affect their respect for you? And what kind of a basis is that for working together in the future?

What kind of precedent does it set for your organization as a way of handling its business? This time it may have worked out to your advantage. But how about the next time? And the next, and the next?

What is the effect of such an action on the minority of the moment who are over-ridden? Do you want them as loyal, interested members of your group for other projects? Is this kind of treatment calculated to make them such?

Reasonable answers to the above questions would suggest this practical conclusion: A measure must be very, very important indeed to be worth winning by questionable parliamentary means.

You are advised to study tactical devices with great care. But you will do so most profitably if you go at it in the spirit of the law-abiding citizen who takes up jujitsu as a manly art of self defense, "just in case."

It is worth mastering the technicalities of the rules of order explained in the preceding chapter. Then you will know how to speak up at the right time and in the right way. You will have the assurance that goes with knowledge. You will be spared the embarrassment of being found out of order. And you will be able to block irregularities of others, disadvantageous to the motions you are interested in.

Do not, however, make the opposite mistake of becoming a "stickler" for technical trifles—a parliamentary show-off who parades his knowledge of the rule book.

Many so-called "irregularities" are as harmless as they are innocent. They are the fumblings of people who have not yet learned the parliamentary ropes. If you are Chair when such individuals blunder on the floor, you will accomplish little by lecturing them. Often all that is needed is a tactful suggestion:

"Perhaps, Mrs. Smith, you would want to put what you are saying in the form of a motion to . . ."

Or:

"I wonder, Mr. Jones, if the Chair may not call upon you to explain the point you are making later on, when we come to the question you have in mind under Unfinished Business."

Thoughtfulness like this may be appreciated even though it *is* educational.

Or, if you are not the Chairman, consider the possibilities of a *Point of Parliamentary Inquiry* before you raise a *Point of Parliamentary Order*. Better still, do not raise either, unless the irregularity is really serious or appears to be made with bad intent.

Even the best parliamentarians make occasional slips. And you may have more than one occasion to be grateful for similar thoughtfulness on the part of others.

Organizing a Parliamentary Group

Much of the instruction given the speaker advises him how to find the right things to say to a given audience. But in certain practical situations your problem may be the very different one of finding the right audience for a given speaking purpose.

Here are three typical *examples* of purposeful speakers whose difficulty is getting the kind of hearing which will make their speaking effective.

Mrs. K. and *Mr. L.* are neighbors in a new housing development. Over the back fence they exchange gripes about the Town's delay in putting lights in the streets, extending school-bus service to the new community, and other such matters. Mrs. K.'s letter to the Mayor has gone unanswered; Mr. L.'s visit to Town Hall got him a "run around."

Mrs. M. and *Mrs. N.* often meet at the playground of the large apartment house where they both live. They agree that the equipment in the playground is inadequate and that a needed service is supervision of the children while the mothers attend classes. They have told the apartment-house manager that they would be glad to share the costs in both cases. But the manager's abrupt answer was he did not want to "get into anything like that."

Mr. P. and *Mr. Q.* run small neighborhood businesses. At lunch, in a nearby restaurant, they compare notes and find that an increasing number of their old customers are doing their buying at the shopping mall. Neither has been able to do much by himself to recover the lost trade.

The chances are that none of these people will get very far merely by organizing their ideas better and expressing them more forcefully. So long as their audience is confined to individuals they can buttonhole, their words will be without effect.

What they all need is the kind of audience to whom they can bring their facts and figures with some hope of getting action. Their first speaking job is **the formation of an appropriate parliamentary group** to back them up.

If you find yourself in such a situation, this is the way to go about it.

First sound out others who face the same problems, with a view to forming an **Organizing Committee** with a **Temporary Chair.**

Mrs. K. and *Mr. L.*, for example, might spend a few evenings calling on their immediate neighbors, *Mrs. M.* and *Mrs. N.* might begin with the other mothers who use the playground. *Mr. P.* and *Mr. Q.* can call on other business places at lunch time or during the slack hours of the day.

Be ready, if you can, to make a fairly specific suggestion—the formation of a Civic Association, a Playground Project Group, a local Better Business Bureau. But avoid giving the impression that you have everything worked out and just want the other fellow's backing.

He may have better ideas than yours, or he may not. In either event, he is more likely to respond if you give him reason to believe that he has a part to play.

Do not make the mistake of "pressuring" obviously reluctant individuals. If you keep their goodwill they may tag along later. But if you are too insistent at the outset, you may antagonize them forever. The popularity ratings of the know-it-all and the busy-body are low. So be careful not to be officious or hustling.

The best technique is to ask the right questions. "Do you feel that the Town has been giving us service in this community as efficiently as it has been billing us for taxes? Have you ever had any experience with a Civic Association? How do you suppose one would work out for us here?"

In the answers to such questions you may find broader experience than your own with such matters, and better ideas as to how to deal with them.

Remember also, an Organizing Committee has work to do. Never load it up with indifferent, half-hearted, or obviously incompetent people. Invite into it only the best talent you can get.

This is especially important in the case of the **Chairmanship.** You may be of the stuff of which leaders are made. So do not hesitate to accept the responsibility if you are willing to carry the ball, and if the others obviously show that they expect you to.

On the other hand, if it is results you want rather than doubtful glory, be ready to support for that job the man who seems most to command the confidence of the others. He may not be the one you know best. He may not even be one of the founding members. But if he has what it takes to put the plan over, you will serve your cause best by supporting him.

Once an Organizing Committee is thus formed, it should plan an **Organizing Meeting.**

This means, first of all, arranging an appropriate time and place—details, which are not as simple as they may seem.

No **time** is ever really convenient for everyone. The chief mistakes to avoid are conflicts with peoples' working hours, periods of religious observance, or already scheduled events likely to interest the same potential audience.

Beginning too early discourages those who like leisurely dinners. Beginning too late discourages others addicted to regular bedtime.

Try to canvass a typical sample of the people you would like to reach. Find out their commitments and preferences. Then settle on the least inconvenient time for the greatest number.

The possibilities of a **place** to meet may be even more limited.

If there is no alternative to the local school auditorium, the matter is settled. If you are fortunate enough to have a choice, pick a hall which will be large enough to seat all comfortably, but not so large that a good turn-out will look like poor attendance.

For non-partisan and non-sectarian groups, you should avoid meeting places with a partisan or sectarian atmosphere. And do not sign up for anything like the back-room of a bar if you hope to bring out people who are diffident about such surroundings.

These arrangements are only the beginning of your job. The Committee should also prepare a brief, pointed announcement of the Organizing Meeting.

This should cover not only such details as the time and place, but the purpose of your Committee in calling the meeting, and what you hope to accomplish by it.

The announcement should also be an *invitation* not merely to come and listen, but to present ideas as well. "We want to hear from YOU!" is a good approach whether the individual wishes to speak or not. Just so long as he feels welcome to put in his own word, he is more willing to hear what others have to say.

But do not assume there is any magical drawing power in the best-written open invitation. We all have many demands upon our time. Even when we are interested, we misplace a sheet of paper and the event slips our mind while we are thinking about something else.

An Organizing Committee that takes its job seriously should spend a lot of time in **personal follow-up** of mimeographed or printed notices. A word or two at the front door or on the phone with enough people can make all the difference between a good or poor start.

Here again, the makeup of the Organizing Committee will be an important factor. A "wind-bag," who holds people back from what they are doing while he gossips about anything and everything on the pretext of your Committee's business, can be fatal to your plans. Those whom he calls on may be left grimly determined never to have anything to do with the organization he represents.

Come quickly to the point in such interviews. Leave promptly after you have given a friendly personal touch to the written invitation. That will encourage people to come and bring others along with them.

The Committee's preparations, moreover, should include careful planning of **The Organizing Meeting** itself.

Your purpose will be little served by a big

turn-out if you fumble the program. Each member of the Committee should know exactly what he is to do, and when, without any need for last-minute consultations.

By all means, start promptly. A wait of more than fifteen minutes before starting a meeting makes an audience restless. "If these fellows can't even start on time," they begin to think, "what good can come of the whole thing?"

Bear in mind also that a meeting such as this has no regular parliamentary authority as yet. The Committee members extended the invitation. But they have no more to say about its outcome than those who appear by invitation.

The proper thing is for an agreed-upon member of the Organizing Committee to stand up before the audience, call the meeting to order, and nominate an agreed-upon person to serve as **Temporary Chair.** This motion should be seconded promptly by another agreed-upon Committee member, whereupon the first one can put the question to a vote.

Normally, the election of a Temporary Chairman for a not-yet organized group will go through automatically. And he can then proceed to the election of a **Temporary Secretary** to record the minutes.

Next the Temporary Chairman should explain the general purpose of the meeting and sum up the thinking of the Organizing Committee as to what it might accomplish. Or, he can call upon some other agreed-upon member of the Committee to do this.

If the responsibility falls to you, be careful to take account of the possible interests and apprehensions of your listeners. What most of them want to know is why they should take part in this sort of affair at all. Address yourself to that question first.

Anything vague like: "Some of us just sort of thought it might be a nice idea if we were to get some kind of group organized around here . . ." will very likely draw the reaction: "Why bother?"

On the other hand, do not try to deliver a complete pre-packaged program. Avoid the attitude that all the others need to do is to have the good sense to come along and back it up.

Most people like to be addressed as though they might have a few good ideas of their own. And the chances are that many of them do.

If it is to be a Civic Association, go into the issues of civic welfare which have stirred up your Committee. Describe, too, the experience some of you may have had elsewhere in organized dealing with such problems.

So far as you go, be as concrete and as emphatic as you wish. But do not give the impression that you or your Committee believe this to be the last word on the subject.

The test of your Meeting will be the reaction you get *from* the audience. Let them understand that you honestly want to find out what they know and think about the situation. And keep your own speaking brief enough to leave them time to have their say.

Once the discussion is started, the Chairman will do well to recognize as many different speakers as will volunteer from the audience. He can remind the long-talkers and the repeaters, in a friendly way, of the number of others who have not yet been heard from.

Members of the Committee should stand by, ready to speak up in case of a lull. But as much as possible they should let others make the points.

Finally, be careful that the discussion does not fade out as a general gripe-fest. You are there for a more important purpose than just blowing off steam.

As soon as it is clear that a need for organization is widely felt, and as soon as all present have had a reasonable chance to have their say, an agreed-upon member of the Committee should introduce a motion that a permanent organization be formed.

EXAMPLE

"Mr. Chairman (Pause for recognition), in view of what has been said here tonight, I wish to offer the following motion:

"Whereas we residents of Airy Acres believe that our community interests would be better served by a permanent civic association; therefore, be it

"Resolved, that the Chair appoint a committee of five to draw up a proposed constitution for such an association; and be it further

"Resolved, that we meet again at the same hour four weeks from today to consider the recommendations of that committee for such a constitution."

The original Organizing Committee should, of course, be prepared promptly to second this motion and speak in explanation and support of its previously agreed-upon text. But they should be careful not to give the impression of trying to force something through by pre-arranged plan.

The purpose of the advance preparation of the motion is to make sure that discussion will not dissipate into mere talk. If you depend on inspiration, you may lose your chance to get action started at the opportune moment. But that does not mean you are committed to a conspiracy.

The audience may want to load the Whereas clause with a list of grievances, make the committee larger or smaller, and meet again sooner or later. This may, or may not, be wise. But it can be done by amendment and consideration by parts (See *Motions S-6* and *I-8* of the *Table of Motions*). And it is the right of the assembly to do so if they think best.

Do not make the mistake of holding out for mere details of your plan. That would risk arousing distrust for the entire project. If this organization is to accomplish anything, its members will have to compromise their differences in a spirit of give-and-take. Start practicing this nice social art yourself from the beginning.

For a committee such as is proposed by the above motion, a gathering will normally draw on the experience and interest already shown by the Organizing Committee. But the members of this initial group will also do well to try to bring others into responsible jobs as soon as possible. Once you give the impression of trying to hold on to the ball, others may decide to let you run with it—all by yourself!

The temporary chairman should therefore call for volunteers and try to appoint members of the audience who have shown intelligent interest in their contributions to the discussion. But he should also know, by previous agreement, in what order to call upon the members of the Organizing Committee as they are needed.

Use the interval between the first and second organizing meetings for **further promotion and canvassing.**

You will never get out all the people you want the first time. Some who came may be too half-hearted about the project to return. So let the announcement of the second meeting be your calling card for a second round of personal interviews.

Prospects who were obviously annoyed by a first contact may not warrant a second try. But reporting the results of the first meeting is a good point of entry for any sort of follow-up. And try not to have any likely prospects for your group feel they were deliberately overlooked.

If all goes well, the **Second Organizing Meeting** will end the work of the Organizing Committee.

The Temporary Chair should preside over the opening of this meeting, calling first for the **Minutes** from the Secretary, and next for the proposed **Constitution** from the Constitutional Committee.

Procedure may be as at any meeting of an established organization. The main motion before the assembly is the proposal to approve the Constitution. It may be amended, considered by parts, and otherwise treated as described in the preceding chapter.

If the constitution is referred back to the Constitutional Committee, a third organizing meeting will be necessary to continue discussion in the same way.

Once a motion to adopt the constitution is passed by a majority vote, however, qualifications for membership will have been determined.

All those eligible and willing to join should then do so by signing the approved draft of the constitution and paying whatever dues are required by it.

This may be done during a recess. When the meeting is called back to order, the Temporary Chair should call upon the Secretary to read the list of members. These are the people now eligible to vote for the permanent officers provided for by the constitution.

The Temporary Chair's last responsibility is

to conduct the election of the President, as provided for in the Constitution. Once elected, the President takes over as chairman, conducts the election of the other officers, and a new organization is on its way to do its part of the world's work.

Practice Exercise No. 29

In the preceding text, three examples are given of pairs of individuals who face the need of forming an appropriate parliamentary meeting group. Consider in detail how you would apply each step of the recommended procedure to their organization problems.

Whom should they sound out to form an organizing committee? And how should they go about contacting these people?

What would be a good text for their announcement of an organizing meeting? What likely time and place should it propose? And how should they follow it up by personal interviews?

What would be the text of a good resolution to introduce at each organizing meeting?

With what arguments would you support such a text? And what details of such a text should you stand ready to have modified by amendment?

Consider, also, how you might form a parliamentary group by similar steps to better serve some of your own speaking purposes.

Constitutions, Bylaws, and Rules

The basic regulations which govern the procedure of any meeting are those contained in the organization's constitution, bylaws, charter, or standing rules. If you are to take an active part in the formation of a parliamentary group, you will need to know what they should contain.

Even if all the organizations to which you belong were going concerns when you joined them, however, you still need to get acquainted with such basic documents. Officers or older members may refer to their provisions as reasons why you can or cannot make particular proposals. So you should have more than a general awareness of what they are about.

We are all familiar with the Constitution of the United States as the basic law of the land. The **Constitution** of any organization is a similar sort of document.

Some older societies with a complicated structure have only a few articles in their Constitutions with such headings as:

I. Name of the organization.
II. Purposes of the organization.
III. Requirements for membership.
IV. Officers and their election.
V. Provisions for meetings.
VI. Method of amending the constitution.

In such cases, other basic regulations are contained in a separate document known as **Bylaws**. For example:

I. Duties of officers.
II. Standing Committees and their duties.
III. Methods of Admitting members.
IV. Custody of funds.
V. Definition of a Quorum.
(The number of members who must be present to hold a meeting and cast valid votes.)
VI. Parliamentary authority.
(The standard work on parliamentary law to be followed at meetings.)
VII. Method of amending the bylaws.

More commonly, however, all the provisions belonging to either of these are now combined in one known as either the **Constitution** or **Bylaws**. The first name is of Latin origin; the second of Anglo-Saxon origin. There is just about the same difference between the two words as between "residence" and "home." Although they mean the same thing, however, you should, in each case, use whichever term appears in the document itself.

Standing Rules usually cover such additional matters as:

I. Set hours and places of meeting.
II. The order of business.
III. Limitations on debate.
IV. Limitations on attendance or speaking by non-members.

These are usually the only "rules" which may be suspended by the motion, *To Suspend the Rules* (See *Motion I-6,* above).

If your organization is a local Chapter of a larger body, it may have a **Charter** instead of either a Constitution or Bylaws.

This is a similar document, issued by the parent organization, and authorizing your group to operate locally under the name and Constitution of the parent organization. Its provisions will therefore be much the same except that they will also state in what ways the local group is responsible to the larger one.

Whatever the basic documents which govern your organization, they should state in black and white just what your rights and responsibilities are as a member. And they should do the same for all the officers and major committees.

Study them carefully. You may well be able to quote them to good effect later.

Practice Exercise No. 30

If you do not have copies of the Constitution, Bylaws, Charter, or Standing Rules of any organization to which you belong, get a copy from the Secretary. Then check the text carefully with such questions as these in mind:

What is the stated "purpose" of the organization? Is that the purpose for which you joined it? Are most of its meetings conducted in the spirit of such a purpose? Have most of the motions it has recently passed tended to carry out that purpose? Do some recent actions of the organization have a contrary effect? Can you think of any proposals that would better carry out the stated purpose?

What are the stated "duties" of the officers? Are your officers, in fact, fulfilling those duties? Are they in some cases, perhaps, overstepping their authority? How about yourself, if you are an officer?

What *standing committees* are provided for, and what are their *duties*? Are they functioning as they should? Or have some tended to become *paper committees* while others *took over*? Is this a better set-up? If not, what might you say at meetings to correct the situation? Or, what amendment might you propose to clarify it?

What is defined as a *Quorum* to conduct business at your meetings? Are that many members always actually present? If not, what should be done about it? Should you support a drive for better attendance? Should those who do not attend be stricken from the membership roll? Or should the quorum requirement be cut by amendment?

What handbook is used as *parliamentary authority*? Is it being followed? Does your Chairman need to be reminded of its provisions?

Are there any stipulated *limits on debate*? Are these observed by you and your fellow-members at meetings? If not, would it be better to do so, or to amend the limitations?

Which rules, if any, may be *suspended* by a motion to do so? Are any others ever sidestepped at your meetings? Have you always realized and made use of allowed suspensions yourself?

On the model of the texts examined above, try drafting proposed constitutions or bylaws for one of the proposed new organizations in the preceding part of this chapter.

Do the same for a parliamentary group which you would like to organize.

PROGRAM FORMS OF DISCUSSION

Most purposeful speaking in organized groups is carried on in the parliamentary manner already described. But sometimes, even in the course of regular business meetings, we may hold discussions as special **program events.**

No immediate practical decisions may result from platform debates, symposia, and forums. But they can serve the ends of popular education.

Platform Debates

As a matter of general interest to the membership, your Program Committee might schedule a **platform debate** on a current topic.

In that case the question is called a **proposition,** and you should word it in a way that admits of a simple *yes* or *no* answer.

A mere topic, such as "Our National Farm Policy," would not do because it invites explanation rather than argument.

"Resolved, that the present administration's sound farm policy be enacted into law," is an improvement. Yet this wording illustrates the different error of **loading the question.** Whether the administration's farm policy is indeed *sound,* is what the debate should be about. So never put any such prejudicial terms in the proposition itself. Strike out "sound," and the above wording is good.

Speakers who support the proposition are called the **Affirmative.** Those who oppose it are called the **Negative.**

There may be no more than one speaker on each side. Two is usually the best number for general interest value. You are quite sure to have planned badly if you schedule more than three. And of course there should always be the same number on both sides.

The customary form of debate, called **Oxford style,** is divided into two general parts—presentation and refutation.

In the **Presentation phase** each speaker is

given an equal amount of time to present his constructive case.

The Chairman for the occasion introduces the debaters to the audience in the order: first affirmative, first negative, second affirmative, and so on. The idea is that the affirmative begins and that the sides alternate thereafter throughout the presentation.

You should, of course, relate what you say in such a speech to what the other speakers are saying. But you are supposed to concentrate on the more positive aspects of your own case.

As an affirmative speaker, you should emphasize your positive reasons for supporting the proposition. As a negative speaker you should emphasize equally positive reasons for opposing it.

A much repeated saying which you may have heard is that "the burden of proof is always on the affirmative." On this theory, a smug negative will sometimes assume that it has nothing to do but wait for the affirmative to put up an argument, and then criticize it.

This makes some sense in a court of law where our legal tradition presumes a man to be innocent until proven otherwise. The proposition before the court is that the accused is guilty. The (negative) defense technically has no obligation except to show how the (affirmative) prosecution is in error.

But elsewhere the circumstances can be quite different. A popular proposal may easily be carried, unless an aggressive negative builds up a very strong opposition to it. That could be the case, for instance, with regard to the above proposition to enact an administration's farm policy into law.

Thus, in practical situations, the burden of proof may fall to either side. For platform purposes, therefore, it is sensible to think of both sides as having an equal obligation to give convincing positive arguments.

A *program difficulty* which sometimes arises is that the different speakers on each side do not have enough opportunity to confer with each other beforehand. As a result, they may duplicate each other's material. Or, at the other extreme, they may present such different lines of argument that there is little tie-up between them.

In the latter case, such serious inconsistencies may arise that the other side spends too much of its speaking time asking where their opponents really stand. So make every possible effort to get each set of speakers together well before the event.

Usually there is an intermission of at least five minutes after the presentation speeches in an Oxford style debate. Then the second phase, called the **Refutation,** begins.

This time the Chairman introduces the negative first, and the others alternately by sides, so that the affirmative has the final speech as well as the opening one. The theory is that the affirmative should have both the first opportunity to present its proposal and the last opportunity to pick up the remaining pieces of it after all has been said.

A generally accepted rule is that you should not try to develop essentially new constructive arguments in refutation speeches. You should concentrate, rather, on rebuttal and rejoinder.

Rebuttal is your criticism of the arguments made by your opponents in presentation.

Rejoinder is your renewed explanation and defense of your own previous arguments after rebuttal by your opponents.

The general plan of a constructive argumentative speech has already been discussed in chapter four. But something should be added here on **refutation technique.**

While preparing your own presentation you will have become fairly well acquainted with the more common arguments for the other side. It is a good idea to jot these down on separate cards as you go along, with notes as to how you would answer them if you had to.

Then, as the opposition speakers present their case, you can pick out already prepared notes on many of their points. And you can use these for most of your refutation speech which you would otherwise have to pull together on the spur of the moment.

Be careful, however, not to let yourself be distracted by obvious errors which they make on minor points. Concentrate, rather, on possible major fallacies.

Check first to see whether your opponents' arguments are **consistent** with each other. Do they all fit together logically? Or do some contentions contradict others?

Check next to see whether your opponents' arguments are **adequate** in their over-all structure. Even if you were to agree with all they contend, would you then be compelled to join their side? Or, could you accept what they say so far as they go, and still reasonably maintain your own conclusion?

Nothing is so devastating to an opponent's platform position as a rebuttal in which you can accept his premises but show that they serve your purposes.

This was the embarrassing position of one speaker against the proposition that teachers belonging to subversive organizations be dismissed. He made a major issue of figures to show that there are actually fewer such teachers in our schools than there are bankers in our prisons who have been convicted of embezzlement.

His opponent accepted the statistics, but pointed out that, if there were fewer embezzling bankers than there were subversive teachers, the same line of reasoning would lead to the conclusion that we should retain embezzlers in banking jobs merely because there would then be so few of them. Since that was obviously ridiculous, the admittedly striking statistics were shown to be beside the point.

This kind of refutation penetrates to the underlying errors in the other fellow's thinking. Attend to it first. You can always put the commas and decimal points in the right places later.

The usual time-table for an **Oxford-style debate** runs as follows:

Affirmative Speakers	Phase	Negative Speakers	Minutes
	Presentation		
First			10
		First	10
Second			10
		Second	10
	Intermission		
			5 or 10
	Refutation		
		First	5
First			5
		Second	5
Second			5
		Total	65 or 70

With a single speaker on each side there may be only one presentation speech of about fifteen minutes, and only one refutation speech of about eight minutes for each side. In either case, with the time needed for opening remarks and introductions, the event takes at least an hour and a quarter without any audience participation.

The chief shortcoming of platform debates from the audience point of view is failure on the part of the speakers to get down to brass tacks on basic issues. Both affirmative and negative usually attempt to include every major point. Thus, in their concern for comprehensiveness, they tend to distribute their time almost equally over all possible issues, leaving themselves relatively little time to discuss specific points of difference.

The problem is particularly acute in radio and television debates, which are seldom good examples of the form. Because of the expense factor, so little time is allotted that a real meeting of minds is difficult at best. But, to make matters worse, no sooner do speakers begin to come to grips with an underlying problem than a nervous chairman, working for the network, hastily changes the subject for fear some listener may switch his dial.

Whenever speaking on a traditional Oxford-style program, therefore, avoid harping on points which are not seriously challenged. Concentrate your attention on the main issues of actual contention on that particular occasion. And fill in the details of the over-all argument only to put these points in perspective.

One formal solution to this disadvantage of Oxford style debating is the alternative **Oregon style,** cross-examination debate.

Here the first affirmative and negative speakers each make a single presentation speech of from ten to fifteen minutes in length.

Next, the first affirmative is cross-examined by the second negative, usually for a period of ten minutes.

Then the first negative speaker is cross-examined in turn by the second affirmative speaker.

After an intermission, each of the second speakers sums up for his side, negative first. Thus the **Oregon Style Time Table** runs:

Affirmative Speakers	Phase	Negative Speakers	Minutes
	Presentation		
First			10 to 15
		First	10 to 15
	Cross-Examination		
		Second	10
Second			10
	Intermission		
			5 to 10
	Rebuttal and Summation		
		Second	10
Second			10
		Total	65 to 80

It is understood, of course, that speakers being cross-examined should not be deliberately uncommunicative or evasive. They are supposed to answer only the questions asked them and not try to change the subject to make additional speeches of their own.

One advantage of the Oregon style debate is that a good cross-examiner can direct attention more sharply to basic points of difference.

Another advantage is that a good cross-examiner can heighten audience interest. He may at first ask a series of seemingly casual questions which get equally casual answers. This leaves all but the sharpest listeners puzzled. Then, suddenly, he uses everything he has brought out from his *witness* to penetrate, with a final question, to the very heart of the other side's argument just where it is weakest. There can be something approaching drama in this.

The technique, however, is extremely difficult to handle on the platform. The inexpert cross-examiner too often just lectures his respondent, and then says: "Don't you admit that?" To which the answer is invariably: "No!" Or he asks obvious questions to which the respondent replies by repeating what he has already said in presentation.

"Do you mean to say that you believe this administration's farm policy is a sound one?"

"I most certainly do! And I thought I explained why!"

This can become a bore even to the most tolerant audience. So do not attempt the form unless you have cross-examiners with proven ability to handle **questioning technique.**

It takes a lot of practice to develop the art, but a few simple *rules* will help. In addition to avoiding the above-mentioned errors:

Break down the line of reasoning in the back of your mind into several separate steps.

Try to phrase a separate question for each step in such a form as to admit a short, direct answer.

Put that question first which is farthest from the conclusion you intend to reach, and which most certainly will have to be answered as you wish.

Then work backwards through the sequence of questions until you have enough answers to use your respondent's admissions to establish your own conclusions.

For *example,* the refutation point mentioned further above was actually made in cross-question form somewhat like this.

"I understand, Mr. X., that you do not yourself approve of subversive teachers. Isn't that so?"

"Of course it is."

"But you contend there are so few of them, there is no need to dismiss them."

"That is correct."

"And you report as an example of the integrity of the profession in general that all your own children's teachers are staunchly loyal citizens."

"I'd vouch for them any time."

"Now I also gather from what you said that you also disapprove of embezzlers."

"Naturally."

"And you pointed out that annually there are an alarming number of cases of embezzlement in banks?"

"Yes, I did."

"But let us suppose, Mr. X., that there were only a few such cases. Suppose even that there were just one. In that event, would you approve of keeping this one embezzler working in the bank to which you entrusted *your* funds?"

"I should say not!"

"Ah, Mr. X., you are a hard man indeed! Just one poor solitary little embezzler, and you would have your bank fire him! How much, I am tempted to ask, could this one poor fellow embezzle by himself that he should be fired for it? But you need not answer that. Instead I am going to ask you a different question: Which, would you say, is the greater trust—the trust which you put in your bankers for the care of your funds, or the trust you put in your children's teachers for the training of their minds?"

"You know the answer to that one as well as I do."

"Well now, Mr. X., perhaps we have both been fortunate in having the typical sort of American bankers who handle our funds honestly, and the typical sort of American teachers who develop our children's minds loyally. And perhaps there are even fewer disloyal teachers than there are dishonest bankers. But you admit that even one embezzling banker should be fired. And you admit that the trust you put in your children's teachers is greater than the trust which you put in your banker. So what is the point of telling this audience that subversive teachers should not be fired merely because there are so few of them?"

"The difference is just this: We don't usually convict a banker of embezzlement on the basis of gossip and slander. But in some of our schools . . ."

"Pardon me, Mr. X., but that is a different matter! It is a question of legal method on which it will be my turn to agree with you later. But on the present question of principle I must point out to this audience what you have just, in effect, admitted: If a teacher is proven to be subversive by the proper legal American methods which we would normally apply to a banker, he should be dismissed even if he were the only one in the entire nation!"

Note that, in his last answer, the above speaker tried to change the subject. This is called **shifting the ground of consideration**. It is a natural tactic when a speaker is caught in a tight spot. You always need to be on your guard against it in all forms of discussion. So observe how the above cross-examiner handles it here.

Symposia

If your membership finds debates too formal, you may wish to try scheduling a **Symposium**. This is a more informal kind of platform discussion in which a number of speakers—usually three to five—state their attitudes on a common question.

Propositions such as are necessary for debating will not do then because they allow for only two approaches—affirmative or negative.

The **question** must be posed in an **open form** which allows any kind of approach. For example:

"What should our national farm policy be?"

"How can we best deal with the problem of juvenile delinquency?"

"If I were President . . ."

"What's right with American agriculture?"

From the above list it is clear that subjects may be serious or light. One of the main advantages of a symposium, as a program item, is its broad adaptability to almost any sort of theme.

In a platform symposium, you may also feel free to express the most personal aspects of your way of thinking. Clear reasoning and sound substance are of course as desirable here as anywhere. But you need not limit yourself to weighing evidence as much as in a debate. The main purpose is to stimulate thinking by refracting the common theme through the prisms of the different personalities of the speakers.

Approach the occasion as an opportunity to get audience reactions to some of your more novel ideas. Take a cue from the literal Greek meaning of the word, **symposium**, "a drinking together." That hardly places you under an obligation to be grimly sober.

Forums

A **forum** is a discussion event in which the audience takes part. It may follow a single guest speaker, a debate in any form, or a symposium; or, it may be a special event in itself.

From a program point of view, you will generally find it wise never to schedule platform speaking without a *forum period*. A verbal exchange of ideas strikes sparks in the minds of listeners. They feel frustrated without the chance to have their own say. Some even regard saying their own bit afterwards as the main reason for coming. So do not let them down.

There is the danger, of course, of having such a period monopolized by cranks and bores. And there is a limit to what the most tactful chairman can do about this if others do not ask for the floor. So don't make the mistake of assuming you must plan only the platform part of the program. You should also have a few prepared questioners in the audience.

One might be assigned, for example, to start off the forum period with a provocative question:

"Mr. X., what would you do in your farm policy about our present stockpiles of hundreds of millions of pounds of butter?"

Or:

"Mrs. Y., after all you have said about what is right with American agriculture, could you now say which policies need improvement?"

Never interrupt good, spontaneous discussion from the unrehearsed audience. But be prepared to supply leads or cues if they are needed. Then you may feel assured that you have done all you possibly can to make the event click.

INFORMAL GROUP DISCUSSION

In some conference situations you may feel confident of your own conclusions, and you may be in a position of authority to command a hearing for them.

Let us say you are a sales manager and believe that your merchandising campaign is falling flat because your men in the field are using the wrong approach to their customers, or are not keeping up with new developments in the market. In that case, you may call them in and try to straighten them out. Your talk will point out their faults, show them what they could do if they went about it in the right way, and encourage them to try to do better with a fresh start.

But often, in a small discussion group, no one has such authority. If you are a member of the Program or Welfare Committee of a Social Club or Civic Association, you are in no position to take the others to task on the basis of your ideas of what should be done.

Sometimes, too, you may have more questions than answers in your own mind. All present may be looking for possible solutions to common problems. Then it is important for you to realize that group meetings need not be a backdrop for contention. Discussion can also be a method of inquiry and discovery.

It may indeed be well to remember this even when you believe you know the answers, and even when you have the authority to call the tune.

Discussion as Group Thinking

Yes, perhaps you, as Sales Manager, are the most experienced member of your staff. In your time you have seen many salespeople come and go. When you were out in the field yourself, you booked record orders. Perhaps that is how you got to be Sales Manager. And that proves you know how your product can be sold.

But wait a minute! When you take *all* the responsibility for thinking things out, the entire sales program is going to be limited by your ability, as a single individual, to foresee everything. That is a lot to expect, even of a genius.

Nobody really knows all the answers. Times change. And there is more than one way to do the same job. A tried-and-proven method for Jim may not work for Mary at all.

And what about **motivation?**

When the ideas themselves are all yours, you have to charge others with the enthusiasm which goes with your creative planning. That will be hard if you are the sole powerhouse for all you hope to get done.

Suppose, however, you take a different approach to the conference situation. Suppose you put the lagging sales record up to your group, not as a matter of reproach, but as a mutual problem. Suppose, instead of "bawling them out," you take them into your confidence. Very briefly:

"Well, now let's have a look at the scoreboard. As you see, *we* haven't been doing as well as *we* had hoped to. What do *you think* is the trouble? And what are *your ideas* as to what *we* can do about it?"

This is the only approach you can take when membership in your group is purely voluntary. And it may also be used to advantage in other cases. The results of recent research suggest that you can get the most out of a discussion by regarding its members as human resources in dealing with a problem.

Every participant, after all, is a potential source of information and ideas. Even the least informed may possess some useful bit of special knowledge. Even the least acute may have some insight which has escaped the thinking of the others.

Moreover, by cutting them all in on it, you give all members of the group a stake in the outcome. Since they have had a part in making whatever decisions are reached, they feel a more personal responsibility for the results.

They are no longer just following orders like sheep. They are in the business of thinking for themselves. The project is theirs just as much as it is yours. Its defeat would also be their personal defeat. So they are more likely to do everything possible to ensure its success.

Thus, by facing the problem *with* the group, you can tap abilities and energies which you might otherwise have to contend with as opposition in trying to make your solo-thinking prevail.

This sort of group-participation discussion is the **group dynamics theory.** Behind it is a metaphor—a figure of speech which pictures each participant as a bundle of human energies that can generate social forces in different directions.

What the domineering discussion leader attempts, according to this theory, is to counteract those forces which oppose him, and to reinforce those which have the same direction as his. Thus, he must be a *forceful* speaker in a more literal sense than usual. But what the *dynamic leader* does is to draw upon all the energies of the group, to determine in what direction they may be most effectively applied together.

Do not take this figure of speech too literally. The problems of how best to talk things over are much too subtle to be explained by a simple physical analogy. But bearing it in mind may help you to visualize an important truth.

Discussion may be a way of making many minds better than one by enabling them to think things over together.

In any event regardless of the theory by which it is explained, many responsible organizations are giving the approach a serious trial today. Also, colleges are doing similar things with student participation in their campus government.

Traditionally, the military services were a rigid set-up with a chain-of-command from top to bottom. Wrote Tennyson in his *Charge of the Light Brigade:*

> "Theirs not to make reply,
> Theirs not to reason why,
> Theirs but to do and die."

Today the armed forces train men and women officers in the use of such conference techniques, wherever they can be practically applied, to give a broader base to military decision.

Requirements for Cooperative Discussion

Thinking together in any way, however, requires a reasonably like-minded group.

People who are over-enthusiastic about discussion techniques seem to think these are ways of ironing out really basic differences of view. That is an illusion.

As sales manager you may be able to confer to advantage with members of your sales staff. But you can hardly expect to get helpful counsel from a cut-throat competitor by inviting him to your sales conference.

At an anti-crime meeting, you may confidently discuss ways to improve law-enforcement with representatives of civic organizations and public agencies. But you are foolish indeed if you think you can sit down and reach an acceptable deal on such matters with gangsters.

As a loyal citizen of your country you may honorably confer with others who wish to amend its constitution by constitutional means. But it would be a phenomenal conference where you could come to a satisfactory working agreement with those who would subvert it from the left or from the right.

When some people get to "understand each other better" they find all the more reason to disagree. Techniques of mutual understanding only serve to drive them further apart.

This does not mean that the members of your discussion group must be entirely of one mind. Then conference would be pointless. But all who take part do need to have **common ends in view.**

They may differ, within reason, as to what they think is wrong. Or they may differ, within reason, as to how to go about setting things right. But they must all want to see the sales campaign go over. They must all want to see the forces of law and order prevail. Or they must all want to see that, in the words of Abe Lincoln, "a nation so conceived and so dedicated can long endure."

No mere discussion technique can reconcile the irreconcilable. So first do your best to make sure you have a reasonable basis for sitting down around a conference table.

Beyond that, the important thing is to encourage the right **social attitudes.** An atmosphere of courteous consideration is absolutely necessary. A spirit of positive friendliness is ideal.

The general rule is to avoid any form of expression which would sound a sour note in ordinary conversation.

Some sharpness of tongue, tempered with ironical wit, may be effective in a lively debate against aggressive opponents. But if you are serious about cooperation, and if only those who should be are present, you will have no "opponents" in this set-up.

There is no magic merely in calling a discussion "cooperative." Even when there is a good basis for it in the more basic convictions of the participants, you may still need considerable tact to keep the exchange from becoming a verbal free-for-all.

Even when something is said with which you violently disagree, avoid saying so too emphatically. If the matter is one you feel it is imperative to straighten out, explain your "difficulty" in agreeing with it.

Do not rush in to refute. Instead, explain what "troubles" you when you "try to see the point" of such statements. Not:

"I wish you people would quit talking about having our club social in the Ritzworth Ballroom. Anyone with any sense ought to realize we couldn't afford it!"

Rather:

"It certainly would be wonderful if we could have our reunion at the Ritzworth. But do we have the figures on what it would cost? And have the members been asked if they would be willing to pay that much?"

The best way to appear openminded is really to keep your mind open. It could be that *you* have overlooked a few important points.

Try thinking of your part in discussion as *an exercise in objectivity*. Take your ideas out for an airing. Set them out before the group. Then try to see them yourself as though they belonged to somebody else. It is surprising how they sometimes begin to take on a new look.

Pointers on Agenda

Since informal group discussion has no set parliamentary order of business, there is always the danger that it will wander aimlessly.

One speaker after another may digress on a point in the previous speaker's remarks. Before you know it, you are all far from the subject and getting rapidly nowhere.

After a number of such experiences some people become cynical about group discussion. It is reported that after Lindbergh's first Trans-Atlantic flight, a young woman gushed to a certain corporation executive: "Don't you think it wonderful that he did that *all by himself!*" The terse reply was: "Well frankly, Miss, I'd be much more impressed if he had flown the Atlantic with the help of a committee."

The first step in dealing with this general problem is to set up an **agenda**—a list of the items you hope to cover, in the order you'd like to have them covered. Then you will at least have landmarks by which to plot your progress and tell when you are getting off the course.

The chairman can draw up the agenda in advance and announce it at the outset of the meeting. But this procedure fails to get everyone into the planning.

"We are perfectly free to speak our minds," the others may think, "just so long as we talk only about what you tell us to."

A more tactful start is for you to announce only the subject at the outset, and then ask: "How do you feel we could best go about talking this over?"

If someone suggests pretty much what you had in mind, so much the simpler.

But if impractical suggestions are offered, you can ask appropriate questions to bring out better ones.

If the group obviously prefers to have you take the initiative, by all means be prepared to "propose an agenda for their approval."

There need be no formal voting or show of hands for this or for any other decision. Put the question by asking: "How would that be?" Or: "Is that agreeable?"

Any member of the group should feel free to suggest possible changes. When none does, that is taken to be *tacit approval*.

What **items** should such an agenda include?

A common mistake is to assume there is a universal basic pattern to follow. But the content of the agenda will depend upon the circumstances in each case. Items which would be of key importance in some cases, would be quite pointless in others.

Here are a number of possibilities from which to choose to suit your purposes on different occasions.

Clarification of the Question. A conference on ways to promote sales of Sudsy Soap is not likely to have any real problems of definition. Everybody present knows very well what Sudsy Soap is. They know equally well why they want the public to buy more of it.

But suppose your problem is "How to promote interest in more cultural broadcasting programs." Just what is meant by "more cultural?" Coming to an understanding about

such terms sooner rather than later, may avoid wasting a lot of time speaking at cross-purposes.

This does not imply you must get unanimous consent on a water-tight definition of so elusive an idea as that of "culture."

It is silly to suppose there is a single "correct answer" to such a question. And pretending so results in **quibbling**—needless bickering about the meaning of words—which can break up a discussion before it even gets properly started.

It will serve your purposes simply to know, by a few concrete examples, what each of you has in mind when he uses such terms. Then you will not mistakenly think you differ in opinion only because you are using different words for the same thing. And you will not mistakenly think you agree only because you are using the same word for different things.

That, by the way, is the main point of a subject sometimes made very complicated as a presumed "science" of *Semantics*. If any member of your group springs "semantic analysis" on you, he cannot really mean anything more profound than what has just been said.

Surveying the Facts of the Problem. You have doubtless heard comical examples of discussions which have no point because the facts are the exact opposite of what they are assumed to be—conferences on how to increase production in an industry whose real problem was to dispose of surplus inventories. They remind one of the story of the family discussion on how to marry off the daughter—when she had eloped.

But even when there *is* a sound factual basis for discussion, it helps to have a clear picture of the details of what you are talking about before you get in too deep on false assumptions.

It is announced that "Sales of Sudsy Soap are not up to quota this year." But how you will react to that statement, and what you can intelligently say about it, depends upon the answers to a number of factual questions.

Sales could actually be better than ever. They may not be "up to quota" only because the quota was unreasonably high. Or sales could indeed be falling off, but not nearly so much as in the rest of the industry and in other industries.

So: How large *is* the quota for this year? How

does this quota compare with the quotas for the past ten years? How do all those quotas compare with sales during the past ten years? What have sales been for the entire industry over the same period of time? And what are the corresponding trends in other industries?

Since no really practical discussion can take place without such facts, you should bring them up as soon as possible. This not only promotes clear thinking, but it also helps to sound a good keynote for what is to follow.

Even a review of familiar facts helps to give ballast to a discussion. Your more fuzzy-minded members are then less likely to speak on a vague It-rather-seems-to-me basis. And others are encouraged to offer the more solid sort of contributions of which they are capable.

Diagnosing Possible Causes. Suggesting Possible Solutions. If your idea for improving the sales of Sudsy Soap is to change the product itself, this implies a corresponding belief as to what is causing its sales to lag. In the back of your mind must be the conviction that the public does not like its texture, its odor, its size, its shape, or its lather.

If your idea is to lower the price, in the back of your mind must be the conviction that the public is going for a cheaper competitive brand.

These two related points—possible cause and possible solution—are hard to separate in discussion. Surely there is no need to do so artificially when they come together naturally as in the above examples.

Yet, in preparing for your own participation, and in keeping a box-score of how the discussion is actually getting along, there are several good reasons for noting these two kinds of points separately.

A single effect may have several causes. These causes may admit of different solutions. Not all causes may be equally easy to deal with. Different possible solutions may have different degrees of practicability. And all may be interrelated with each other in complicated ways.

It is therefore sometimes difficult to keep track of interweaving lines of discussion. They may run, for example, something like this:

Speaker A suggests that lowering the price of Sudsy Soap will attract so many more buyers as to make the cut profitable.

Speaker B, from the Production Department, reveals that the price is already down so low that it could only cut further by changing the product.

Speakers C and *D* thereupon suggest changes in the product which might increase its appeal.

While these are being questioned, *Speaker E* mentions the tie-up between product and advertising.

But then *you* may be able to point out that there is also a tie-up between advertising appeal and the previously dropped subject of price:

"We are offering this product in our ads as 'More Suds for Your Money.' The appeal is an economy appeal. Yet people who go for an economy appeal shop around and find they can do better. Perhaps what we need to do is change the advertising angle: 'Here is a soap of distinction. It may cost a little more. But it's worth a lot more to those who insist on the best.' For people who respond to so-called 'snob appeal' the present price may seem a bargain for a quality product."

As chairman, or even as one of the other participants, you are more likely to be able to see the possibility of such remarks if you have sketched your notes on a diagram something like this:

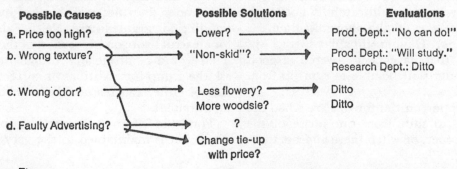

Possible Causes	Possible Solutions	Evaluations
a. Price too high?	Lower?	Prod. Dept.: "No can do!"
b. Wrong texture?	"Non-skid"?	Prod. Dept.: "Will study." Research Dept.: Ditto
c. Wrong odor?	Less flowery? More woodsie?	Ditto Ditto
d. Faulty Advertising?	? Change tie-up with price?	
e. Etc.		

With your own abbreviations and other such short cuts, you can do this for quite a complicated discussion, on a small sheet of note paper. And it will give you a bird's eye view of what is being said when others find themselves getting lost.

Evaluation. It is one thing to suggest an idea in plausible general terms. It is quite another to examine it for what it is really worth. The latter is what is meant by **evaluation.**

Sometimes all a discussion group can do along this line is to see how their suggestions square with information already available to them.

Perhaps your group has been talking about the problem of juvenile delinquency just for the sake of exchanging ideas on the subject. They plan to take no immediate action on the outcome. Reliable statistics and the opinions of authorities in the field may then enable you to agree, for example, that more public playgrounds might help reduce juvenile delinquency.

But, in practical situations, you need to decide further how to go about *checking* what you think *may* be the answers to your problem.

The marketing discussion for Sudsy Soap is not likely to change the corporation's merchandising policy at once. But it may lead to a request that the Production Department estimate the costs of certain changes in the product. And it may lead to a merchandising research study of potential consumer reactions to such changes, or to different advertising appeals.

It is well to recognize, therefore, that evaluation is still another phase of group deliberation. Live discussion will also cut across this distinction at almost every stage. In the above example, for instance, the impossibility of price-cutting is pointed out as soon as the suggestion is made.

But to keep the several threads of discussion clearly in view, you should carefully note such points separately as on the above diagram.

Summarizing. Having thus kept track of major points that have been covered, a good discussion leader will be able to **sum up** from time to time.

The best opportunities for this are when the talk is about to shift from one phase of the agenda to another, or when there appears to be

uncertainty as to just where it has arrived. This helps to clarify the sense of what has been said, in case it was not fully clear to all the group. And it helps those who lose sight of the various trends of the discussion to get their bearings again.

But whether or not partial summaries are given earlier, a good complete summary is always needed at the very end. For then it serves, like the minutes of a regular parliamentary meeting, to confirm what has been agreed upon.

EXAMPLE

"Well, colleagues, we have faced the fact that sales of Sudsy Soap are down ten per cent this year. And we have recognized that our loss of sales compares with a two per cent increase in the rest of the industry and a five per cent average increase in other industries.

We thought our trouble might be that our price was too high. But the Production Department tells us present costs will not allow a price cut. So that was a dead end.

Mrs. C reported customers as saying that our soap was too slippery, and suggested a 'non-skid' texture. Mrs. D reported customers as saying it was too fragrant, and proposed giving it a less flowery odor.

We are asking the Production Department to make a study of costs of both those changes. And we are asking the Consumer Research Department to try to find out how the general public would be likely to accept them.

Lastly, Mr. E suggested that our price trouble might be due to its tie-up with an economy appeal in our advertising. That is another point we are putting to the Consumer Research Department. And I gather you want me to take it up also with the Advertising Department and the Executive Board.

Am I correct in these understandings? If so, are there any important points to be added?"

Note that even in summing up, the discussion leader does not take his/her own understanding for granted here. Neither does he ask for an actual vote on his version of the outcome. That would be artificially formal. But he does ask the group for additions or corrections. And lack of either can reasonably be taken as common consent.

Thus, the informal, cooperative spirit of the discussion is maintained to the very end.

CHAPTER VII

DEVELOPING YOUR VOICE

The voice you now have depends upon many factors:

The *physical make-up* of your voice mechanism, such as the size and shape of your mouth, nasal passages, vocal bands, etc.,

Your *general health,* and the consequent *physical tone* of your muscles,

Your *temperament* and *personality*—your outlook and the way you respond to the happenings of daily life,

The social influence of family, friends, associates, and others you speak with,

The *vocal habits* you formed in early childhood and adolescence.

Developing your voice may involve doing something about any or all of these. Your physical make-up cannot usually be changed, but surgery may be resorted to if some organic structure needs repair. You can keep yourself physically fit. You can adopt a more positive attitude towards life. You can choose what social influences you will allow to influence you. You can retrain your muscular habits.

In other words, you can improve and develop your present voice. Be confident of that.

Do not expect miracles, however. Do not expect to improve overnight. Above all, do not expect that mere wishing will bring improvement.

Many speakers before you have improved their voices. But it has taken *time, patience,* and the *knowledge* of how to go about it.

Voice training takes intelligent practice.

PRINCIPLES OF PRACTICE

Set aside regular practice periods each day. Two short periods will probably suffice, but choose times when you are not likely to be interrupted.

In addition, plan to use spare moments to advantage. Certain simple voice exercises can be done while showering, dressing, walking, driving.

Approach the practice periods willingly and with enthusiasm. No relaxed voice ever resulted from a feeling of constraint. No lively, vital one ever developed from a dull, formalized approach.

Practice one thing at a time. Split a big problem into parts and take up each separately. At the start, work on small, easy projects whose success will give you confidence, spur you on.

Make the transition from practice to performance gradually. Confine your new skills to your practice periods until you feel them well-established. Then try them out in conversation at home, and after that with friends. Put off any public test till the last.

If you must deliver a talk during your early training, avoid trying to judge how you are doing while speaking. Concentrate on what you want to say. Save appraisal of your performance till afterwards.

EAR TRAINING

Begin by training your ear. Cultivate sensitivity to sounds and voices and their characteristics. It will prove an invaluable tool for guiding your progress.

Every sound we hear has four characteristics: **pitch, volume, quality,** and **duration** or **rate.**

Pitch is the highness or lowness of a sound. On the musical scale, C is higher than B and lower than D.

Volume, or intensity, is the loudness of a sound. We speak of a *loud* clap of thunder, a *soft* whisper.

Quality, or timbre, is the identifying character of a sound. It is that characteristic by which we distinguish the sound of a violin from the sound of a trumpet, the vowel EE from the vowel OO, the voice of Jim from the voice of Joe.

Duration is the length of time a sound lasts. In voice-training, the term *rate* is used. Whether one's rate of talking is fast or slow depends on the duration of the individual sounds of which words are made up, the length of the phrases used and the duration of the pauses between phrases.

To train your ear, that is, to cultivate your sensitivity to these four characteristics of sounds and voices:

Develop the habit of alert listening.

Practice Exercise No. 31

a. In a bus or train, close your eyes and listen to the noises about you. Single out in your mind buzzes, hums, rattles, whistles, horns. Which are loudest? Which farthest away? Which is highest in pitch? Which lowest? Which do you find pleasant? Which unpleasant?

b. Compare the use of the voice in different situations: the calls at a ball game; a secretary reading the minutes; conversation at a reception.

c. Notice how a good speaker varies his voice to fit his material: a preacher making announcements, reading from the Bible, delivering his sermon; an announcer handling news, commercials, sports, a symphony concert. Notice how actors use voice for characterization. Notice how voices change with mood, how they reflect personality.

d. Collect a list of pronunciations which differ from yours. On the radio or television, note varying dialects or types of speech. Try to identify what makes the difference: the sounds, the speech melody, the quality of voice.

Increase your listening experiences.

Practice Exercise No. 32

a. Listen to radio programs of the same type as your favorites. Compare styles and techniques.

b. Listen to programs of a different type from your favorites. Attend meetings and programs in your community. Note the various kinds of talking you hear.

Become a more critical listener.

Practice Exercise No. 33

a. Compare speakers you consider good with those you think poor. Try to account for your likes, dislikes.

Do you have difficulty hearing the speaker? Does he bellow? Does he adjust volume?

Is he too fast, too slow? Is his rate fast, but fitting? Is he slow, but impressively so?

Does the speaker sound whining, apologetic, vital; muffled, clear; vigorous, weak; harsh, colorless, pleasant?

Is the speaker's pitch high, too high; low, too low; monotonous, varied; stiff, flexible?

Does the speaker sound sincere, or is the voice used for its own sake? What impression of his personality do you get from his voice? Does the voice fit the occasion, the auditorium, the topic?

b. Ask your friends what speakers they consider good, poor. Compare your list with theirs. Discuss your agreements and disagreements. Listen together to those speakers you disagree about. Try to understand your friends' reactions. Can you arrive at some generalizations about voice and its use?

Combine the above suggestions until you have fixed the habit of alert, varied and discriminating listening.

ANALYZING YOUR VOICE

When you think you have trained your ear to analyze the voices of others, begin analyzing your own in the following ways.

Practice Exercise No. 34

a. Listen critically to your own voice: in conversation, reading aloud in a small and a large room. You will not hear it as others do, for this is physically impossible. But make mental notes as to your pitch, volume, quality, rate.

b. Make a tape of your voice. Record both talking and reading aloud. Include such details as your name, the date, the place. Decide beforehand what topic you will discuss, jot down some of your ideas about it, but don't memorize. For reading, choose material with some dialogue.

You probably will not recognize your voice when you replay the tape. You will say, "Is that me?" disbelievingly. But the sound will probably be fairly close to your voice as others hear you.

If you like what you hear, good. If not, do not be discouraged. Play the record over several times and, as objectively as possible, analyze your voice as you analyzed the voices of others in your ear-training exercises above.

Write down your decisions about your rate, flexibility, pleasantness, vitality, expressiveness, intelligibility.

Ask your family and friends to give their

opinions on your voice. (Do not expect them all to agree.) Compare their reactions with your own. Balancing the several judgments, set goals for your guidance in practice.

When you have done this, study the following sections on *Basic Concepts, The Voice Mechanism,* and *Good Phonation,* and practice all the exercises. Then skim through the remainder of the chapter, selecting for particular study those sections which, according to your voice analysis, will most repay careful practice.

Plan to make recordings at regular intervals so that you can modify your original judgments and determine progress.

BASIC CONCEPTS IN DEVELOPING YOUR VOICE

Begin practice with the following exercises. They embody certain **basic concepts** for developing your voice and expression which you will use throughout all your later practice.

Free the Voice. You used your voice freely enough as a child. But with maturity your vocal habits may have become ruts. You may no longer realize the extraordinary variety the voice is capable of.

Revive the sense of freedom in using your voice. Exercise your imagination. Experiment. Have fun with your voice.

Practice Exercise No. 35

a. Try imitating animals. Moo like a cow, crow like a rooster, quack, caw, meow.

b. Imitate musical sounds. Hear the sound inside you before you voice it.

Imitate a bell. Say *Ding-dong, Ding-dong.* (Concentrate on the *ng;* let the sound die out very slowly.)

Imitate a drum. Say *Boomlay, boomlay, boom.* (Try for a sharp, percussive effect with your lips.)

Imitate a bugle. Say *Blow, bugle. Blow.* (Try for a clear, free tone.)

c. Get your arms, face, voice, your whole body into the exclamations below. Imagine a variety of situations; try to respond as you would in those situations.

Hurray!	Hush!
Come on, let's go!	Hold on there!
So!	See! They're coming!
So what?	Ouch!

d. See in how many ways you can say these simple words. Be hearty, then perfunctory; show dislike, then conceal dislike; act surprised, then casual. Say one thing, but imply something else.

Good morning!	Yes
Hello!	No

Concentrate on Meaning. In reading aloud, always analyze your material beforehand for its meaning. Then try to communicate, to project, that meaning clearly. In talking, too, think what you say, and think hard. Your brain will help control your voice.

Practice Exercise No. 36

In the selections below, concentrate on making the meaning crystal clear. Stress the basic thought, its development, the balance of ideas, the contrasts.

Liberty and Union, now and forever, one and inseparable.

Beauty is truth, truth beauty—that is all
Ye know on earth, and all ye need to know.
The evil that men do lives after them;
The good is oft interred with their bones.

Never before in the history of human conflict have so many owed so much to so few.[1]

Now faith is the substance of things hoped for, the evidence of things not seen.

To strive, to seek, to find, and not to yield

I never could believe that Providence had sent a few men into the world, ready booted and spurred to ride, and millions ready saddled and bridled to be ridden.

That which hath been is that which shall be; and that which hath been done is that which shall be done; and there is no new thing under the sun.

If we spoke as we write we should find no one to listen; if we wrote as we speak we should find no one to read.[2]

Let Emotion Help You. The aroused state of the body which accompanies (or is) emotion will help you to vocalize.

Practice Exercise No. 37

Say the lines below, trying to feel the emotions asked for. As an aid, recall situations in which you have had similar feelings.

Feel the angry scorn of the tribune, Marullus, as he seeks to curb the mob:
You blocks, you stones, you worse than senseless things!

Feel the loneliness of the Ancient Mariner as, gazing at the waste about him, he says:
Alone, alone, all, all alone,
Alone on a wide wide sea.

[1] Winston Churchill.   [2] T. S. Eliot.

Feel the exuberant, physical joy of:
How good is man's life, the mere living!
Feel the terror of Hamlet, on first seeing the ghost of his murdered father:
Angels and ministers of grace defend us!
Feel the lover's affirmation of love eternal:
And I will love thee still, my dear,
Till a' the seas gang dry.

Practice drills on the mechanics of voice. A pianist practices scales, arpeggios, finger exercises. Drills on vocal mechanics will help develop the strength and dexterity with which you control your voice.

The exercises below introduce types of voice drills used throughout this chapter:

Practice Exercise No. 38

a. Say a low-pitched *OO*. Glide smoothly up in pitch about an octave on the *OO*. Glide smoothly down.

b. Prolong an *OO* on any pitch. Prolong *OO* on several other pitches. Do the same for *AH, OH, EE.*

c. Prolong an *OO*, starting softly and gradually increasing the volume. Then let the sound die away. Similarly swell to loud and then die away to soft on *AH, OH, EE.*

d. Say *MU, mu, mu, mu, mu*
    mu, MU, mu, mu, mu, etc.,
separating the syllables and shifting the accent to the third, fourth, and fifth syllables. Repeat the drill, joining the syllables as if you were saying a long word of five syllables: *MUmumumumu, muMUmumumu,* etc. Do these drills first fast and then slow.

THE VOICE MECHANISM

In further developing the voice, it will help to know a few simple facts about its mechanism.

All sound-making devices have at least two elements: a vibrator and a motor. The **vibrator** may be anything that vibrates readily—a taut rubber band for example. The **motor** may be any force that will set it in motion—the finger that plucks the rubber band, thus making it vibrate and produce a sound.

Most musical instruments have a third element: a resonator, which amplifies and enriches the original tone. In a violin the strings are the vibrator, the moving bow is the motor, and the body of the violin and its enclosed cavity form the resonator.

The voice also has **articulators,** which modify the amplified tone into the vowels and consonants of speech.

Thus, the voice mechanism has four parts:

The **vibrator is the vocal bands.** The production of sound by the vibration of the vocal bands is called **phonation.** (The root *phon-* is the same as that in the word *phonograph,* and comes from the Greek for *voice, sound.*)

The **motor** is the exhaled *breath* stream.

The **resonator** is chiefly the system of cavities above the vocal bands: the **throat,** the **mouth,** the **nose.**

The articulators are the **lips, gums, tongue, teeth,** and the **hard** and **soft palates.** Articulation is discussed in *Chapter IX.*

The Vocal Bands and Phonation. The **vocal bands** are situated in the larynx, or voice-box. (What we call the Adam's apple is the top-front edge of the larynx.) They are wedge-shaped folds of muscle, covered with mucous membrane. They project from the inner walls of the larynx, extending along the sides from front to rear.

During breathing, the bands are close together in front, apart in the rear. The triangular opening between them is called the **glottis.**

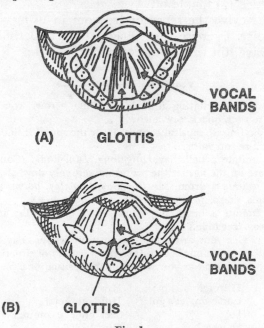

Fig. 1.

The Vocal Bands Seen from Above: A. During Breathing; B. During Phonation

For phonation, that is, the production of voice, the bands are pivoted together, closing the glottis. The exhaled breath stream, building up pressure from below, forces the bands apart and causes them to vibrate.

The vocal bands are tensed or relaxed, lengthened or shortened, separated or closed, and moved upward or downward by the **intrinsic** muscles of the larynx: those pairs of muscles **within** the voice-box. The larynx itself is moved up and down and tilted by its **extrinsic** muscles: those which are attached to adjoining parts of the body, such as the jaw and the breast-bone. These movements are related to pitch, and phonation.

Phonation is essentially an automatic process. Start to speak, and immediately all the activities of phonation are coordinated to produce tone.

This does not imply that phonation may not be faulty. Developing good phonation, that is, the production of a good basic tone, is discussed below.

The Breath. Normally, we breathe in and out with no conscious effort. When the oxygen of the blood-stream is low and the carbon dioxide content high, the chest walls rise and expand, the dome-shaped diaphragm flattens downward. Air pours into the lungs to equalize the lowered pressure in the expanded chest cavity with that of the outside air. Air is pushed out as the diaphragm rises and the chest walls fall.

This automatic process will serve most of us for voice and speech as well as for sustaining life. Many of the breathing muscles, however, are voluntary, i.e., we can control them. For some persons, conscious control of breathing is helpful.

Resonance. Resonance, the re-enforcing and enriching of the original tone, is achieved in several ways:

The sound produced by the vocal bands is reflected from the walls of the throat, mouth, and nose.

The air in the cavities of the mouth, throat, and nose vibrates with and thereby amplifies the tone coming from the vocal bands.

Possibly the head and chest act as sounding-boards.

It will easily be appreciated that the ways in which the chief resonators, the mouth, throat, and nose are used will have an important effect upon the voice. This is particularly so for developing volume and quality.

PHONATION—THE PRODUCTION OF THE BASIC TONE

Good Phonation. When the vocal bands vibrate freely and at maximum efficiency, producing a tone easily and without strain or unnecessary effort, you have good phonation.

Good tone begins smoothly, is clear and not breathy, and can be sustained clearly and easily over a considerable period of time.

Essential conditions for good phonation are:

Good posture, standing or sitting, so that the mechanism is not cramped.

A feeling of aliveness, of alert readiness from the toes up, so that the whole body "supports" the tone.

Concentration on what you are saying, so that the mechanism is properly directed.

Absence of strain or constriction in the throat and neck (the extrinsic muscles of the larynx) so that the vocal bands may vibrate freely and the larynx move easily.

Practice Exercise No. 39

Stand tall, with the feet comfortably apart. Hold the chest high. Don't stiffen the shoulders or over-arch the back. Be sure you are comfortably balanced. Say a long, sustained *AH*.

If your posture feels too stiff, bend forward from the hips, and let the arms and head hang limp. Then slowly uncurl, straightening first the small of the back, the upper back, the neck, before vocalizing. Don't adjust the shoulders at any time.

If you tend to slouch, lift your arms high above your head. Stretch upward, rising on your toes. Feel the tingling in your fingers, your whole body. Then sink back to normal posture and vocalize on *AH, OO, EE.*

Practice Exercise No. 40

Letting breath escape with the voice (half-voice, half-whisper), say: I am now talking with a very breathy voice.

Straining hard, say: I am now talking with a tight, hard, straining voice.

With as easy and relaxed a tone as you can, say: I am now trying to talk with as easy and relaxed a voice as I possibly can.

Hear the difference between the several tones. Feel the difference in your muscles as you say the sentences.

Practice Exercise No. 41

a. Yawn widely, with an open throat. To start a yawn, close the lips and drop the jaw. Softly and lazily, say a prolonged *AH, OH, OO.*

b. Breathe in easily, feeling that you have an open throat. Softly, easily, and on a low pitch, say *one,* holding the tone for a silent count of three. Breathe in, count aloud *one, two,* holding each word for three silent counts. Similarly, count aloud to *three, four.* Very slowly and on a low pitch, say: *who are you; how now; a yellow, mellow moon.*

c. Say *AH, AH, AH,* lightly and quickly, several times over. Try for a clear, sharp tone.

Prolong an *OO* for as long as you can without strain. Keep the tone clear and strong.

d. Before and while phonating, imagine you are drinking very slowly from a glass of water. Concentrate on feeling the water slip down your throat as you vocalize on *OO, AW, AH.* Though this may seem contradictory, it helps counteract a tendency to force the voice.

Practice Exercise No. 42

Read the opening of Gray's *Elegy* in a clear, soft tone:

The curfew tolls the knell of parting day,
   The lowing herd winds slowly o'er the lea,
The plowman homeward plods his weary way,
   And leaves the world to darkness and to me.

Achieving Relaxation. Tonicity is that state of the muscles in which they are ready to act. They are neither too tense nor too relaxed.

Worries, anxieties, or poor health may overtense our muscles and keep us from vocalizing efficiently. In such cases, building up the body or a program of mental hygiene, and possibly that great healer, time, are needed. And physical exercise may well be part of the therapy.

If, while doing the preceding exercises, you found your neck muscles too tense, or if you are too tense generally while talking, the following exercises will help to relax you.

Practice Exercise No. 43

a. Stand at exaggerated "Attention!", your legs, arms, fingers, tense. Hold this stiff posture a moment. Then relax, sag, droop. Feel the difference in the muscles. Repeat, to make yourself more conscious of the difference. Learn to recognize this difference in other situations and while producing tone.

b. Stand at exaggerated "Attention!" for a few moments. Then sink into an easy chair. Lean back, let your arms and head lie limp, close the eyes, think of dozing off. When you feel relaxed, try to recall the earlier feeling of tension. Compare the two muscle sensations. Try to carry the relaxed feeling into voice exercises.

Practice Exercise No. 44

a. Stand tall, erect and tense. Then bend forward at the waist, letting arms and head hang down. Jiggle the fingers, the hands, the arms, the head. Swing them slowly back and forth. Feel the limpness.

b. In front of a mirror, grit the teeth, tense the neck muscles. See the cords tighten, the neck swell. Let the jaw drop, the neck muscles relax. *See* the relaxation.

Put your fingers lightly on your neck. Repeat the above exercise. *Feel* the tension, then the relaxation with your fingers.

c. Let the head fall forward, the jaw sagging open and touching the chest. Slowly roll the head around, avoiding any stiffness or jerkiness of movement. Vocalize on *AH* while letting the head roll around.

Toning Sluggish, Lax Muscles. Debilitating illness or a depressed state of mind will produce sluggish, lax muscles. Physical and mental hygiene and a strengthening of the muscles through toning exercises may all be part of a therapeutic program.

If your muscles lack proper tonicity for good phonation, if your body slouches or droops, if your voice sounds dull and lifeless, the following exercises will prove helpful.

Practice Exercise No. 45

a. Act out physical actions which are accompanied by voice:

Pull on a rope in a tug-of-war. Strain, grunt.

Be your own baseball team. Pitch a fast ball; swing at it; as umpire, fling your arm wide and call, "Strike!"

Call the cows home. Cup your hands to your mouth. Call "Co-boss, co-boss!"

Feed the chickens. Walk about scattering corn, calling, "Here, chick, chick, chick, chick!"

Devise similar exercises of your own.

b. Act out a situation where speech is accompanied by vigorous physical action:

Invite an audience to rise and sing the national anthem. Swing the arms wide.

Say, "No, no, no!" pounding a desk.

Say, "From Heaven above, to Hell beneath," swinging your arm high, low.

Act out: "So I ups to him, and he ups to me."

Be an oratorical District Attorney. Wag your finger at the jury, with "Now, gentlemen." Point to the learned judge with one hand, "As His Honor has told you," and the cowering defendant with the other, "Can you believe what this man has told you?"

Practice Exercise No. 46

a. Practice exclamations and sharp commands: *OH! SHHH!* Halt! Forward march!

b. Let your imagination and feeling help you to achieve tonicity. Imagine and feel yourself:

Othello, intent on death and defiant of his captors, as he draws himself up: "Behold I have a weapon!"

Macbeth, with shuddering suddenness, catching sight of his blood-stained hands: "This is a sorry sight."

Henry V, exhorting his army to battle: "God for Harry, England, and St. George!"

c. Practice the exercises for achieving relaxation (in the preceding section) in reverse, trying to achieve the feeling of muscle tension.

Faulty Phonation. Faulty phonation produces, or is partly responsible for, several unpleasant vocal effects: **Breathiness and glottal shock; huskiness and hoarseness; pinched** or **strident** tone.

Breathiness occurs when unvocalized breath is allowed to escape along with the voice. The glottis, the space between the vocal bands, does not close completely during tone production. Slight breathiness is not objectionable, but the voice lacks strength and may tire quickly.

Glottal shock is the use of a sharp, staccato click to begin a tone. It usually occurs on words beginning with a vowel, such as *and, open*. In glottal shock the closure of the vocal bands is too tense and the bands are blasted or coughed apart by breath pressure.

To Help Correct Breathiness

Practice Exercise No. 47

a. Prolong a whispered *AH*. Gradually add phonation, making the tone less and less breathy, more and more clear. Repeat until you achieve a completely clear, non-breathy tone.

b. Start *AH, OO, EE* with a sharp, glottal shock. (In this exercise one fault is used to help correct another.) Break off the tone immediately. Start the vowels with a sharp, but somewhat slighter shock. Sustain the tone,

keeping it clear. Start the vowels with a sharp, clean-cut attack. Make sure there is neither breathiness nor glottal shock. Sustain the clear tone.

Practice Exercise No. 48

Read the following paired words. Blow out hard on the *h* of the first words of the pairs, and allow the breathiness to carry over into the vowel; start the second word of the pairs with a glottal click:

hall	all	hill	ill	hive	I've
hone	own	hale	ale	whose	ooze
harm	arm	hand	and	hurl	Earl
heave	eve	hem	em	howl	owl

Read the pairs again. But this time say the *h* of the first words very lightly, without much breath, and try to begin phonation as quickly as possible. Begin the second words of the pairs without breathiness or click. This, of course, is the way the words should be said.

Practice Exercise No. 49

Read this paragraph very loudly, and without breathiness. Read it again, and again, each time less loudly, until you are reading it very, very softly and without breathiness.

To Help Correct Glottal Shock

Practice Exercise No. 50

a. While whispering a prolonged *AH,* begin phonation with the softest tone you can. Do not sustain this tone, but repeat the exercise several times, each time trying to make the beginning of the tone easier, gentler, softer.

b. Sustain a whispered *AH* and, as above, begin to phonate with the softest tone you can. Gradually let it swell out till the tone is firm and strong.

c. Begin a tone so softly you can barely hear it yourself. If you are satisfied that you began without a click, gradually increase the volume.

Practice Exercise No. 51

Glottal shock is often associated with the too-frequent breaking off of tone. Say these phrases as if each was one word:

a. onanoldocean   d. onaneveninginApril
b. airisallIown   e. nowIamalone
c. nomanisanisland   f. everyoneIknow
       g. everywhereyougo

Practice linking words together in this way in your talking and reading aloud.

Huskiness is excessive breathiness of tone. It may result from: abuse of the voice, such as yelling or talking for a long time with a strained throat; swelling of the vocal bands during a cold or chronic laryngitis; growths on the vocal bands; certain diseased conditions, some of them very serious. In persistent huskiness a physician, preferably an otolaryngologist, should be consulted.

Hoarseness resembles huskiness except that the tone is harsh, with added raspy noises from the throat. Like huskiness, it may result from abuse or misuse of the voice, or from disease.

To Help Correct Huskiness and Hoarseness

First, visit a physician. If no treatment is required, or *after* medical or surgical care, the next steps are careful practice of relaxation and controlled breathing exercises, easy phonation on soft tones, the gradual development of volume. Yelling, throat-strain, and over-use of the voice must be avoided, and a period of rest for the voice is often suggested.

Huskiness may be due to an improper, usually a too-high **pitch level,** discussed later in this chapter.

Pinched (or *strident*) **tone** results when a person talks as if trying to be heard over noise. He seems to talk only from the throat, as if the breath and the body had no part in speech. The larynx is held so tightly that it up-tilts to an abnormal position. The term *strident* is used when the tone is excessively loud and strained, with the throat walls excessively constricted.

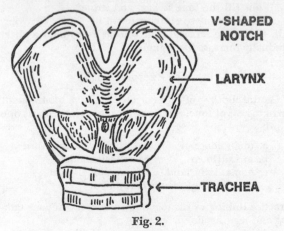

Fig. 2.

Diagram showing the larynx from the front. The V-shaped notch at the top may be felt by lightly touching the fingers to the Adam's apple.

To Help Correct Pinched or Strident Tone

Practice Exercise No. 52

During normal breathing, feel the V-shaped notch at the top of your Adam's apple. Phonate on a moderately low pitch. You should be able to feel this V-notch. If you cannot, if the larynx has up-tilted so that you can feel only its front edge, you must bring the larynx back to its normal position for phonation. With the neck muscles relaxed, feel the notch with your index finger. Phonate on *AH* as softly as possible and with such little effort that you can still feel the V-notch. Your tone should be much less pinched. Repeat on other vowels.

Practice Exercise No. 53

a. Yawn audibly, enjoying your yawn. After the last sound has died away, take an easy breath and begin to phonate on *AH* with the same relaxation.

b. Sigh deeply. Trying to keep the relaxed throat feeling that followed the sigh, phonate on *OH, OO, AH.*

c. Massage the neck muscles during vocalization. Try to get them feeling relaxed.

d. Chant *AH, OW, OY,* on very low pitches. Drop the jaw well down. Feel that you are using a wide, open throat.

e. Practice the selections for developing oral and pharyngeal resonance given later in this chapter.

Practice Exercise No. 54

If you are a chairman, instead of banging the gavel and shouting to get order, rap once, wait for order and then talk quietly.

If you must talk in a noisy room, instead of trying to talk *over* and *louder* than the noise, listen for the approximate pitch of the noise, and talk quietly while trying to pitch your voice *under* the noise.

CONTROLLED BREATHING

Learning to control the usually automatic process of breathing helps to develop a feeling of "support" for the tone. It also helps to reduce strain and tension in the neck and throat during phonation. By concentrating on the chest and diaphragm, one tends to forget the region of the vocal bands and so to relax the neck muscles.

Many methods to control breathing have been taught. Probably there is only one bad method, raising the shoulder blades for inhalation, and dropping them for exhalation.

Effective Methods of Breath Control. Upper

chest breathing. The breast-bone is raised during inhalation, lowered for exhalation.

Lower chest breathing. The lower ribs are moved out and up for inhalation, in and down for exhalation. The abdomen moves only slightly.

Lower chest-abdominal breathing. The lower ribs are moved out and the abdominal wall is relaxed for inhalation. For exhalation, the abdominal wall is pulled in sharply to help the diaphragm in its rise, and the lower ribs are drawn in. (See Figures 3 and 4.)

To learn this method: Lie down, placing the right hand on the abdomen, the left on the left lower ribs. Inhale, forcing the right hand up, the left to the side. Exhale, pulling in and down.

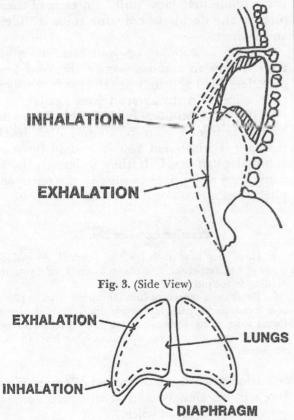

Fig. 3. (Side View)

Fig. 4. (Front View)

Diagrams showing the chest, lungs, diaphragm, and abdominal wall in inhalation and exhalation. For controlled breathing, concentrate on moving the upper chest, the lower chest, or the lower chest and abdominal wall.

Stand up, hold a book against the abdomen with the hands. Breathe as you did while lying down.

Try these several methods of breath control to decide which you prefer.

To Coordinate Controlled Breathing and Phonation

Practice Exercise No. 55

a. Breathe in to the silent count of *one*, out to the silent count of *one-two*. Breathe in to the silent count of *one*. Breathe out to the silent count of *one-two-three*. Increase the count till you are breathing out to the silent count of *ten*.

b. Breathe in to the silent count of *one*. Say *AH*, while silently counting *two*. Breathe in, silently counting *one*. Say *AH*, while silently counting *three*. Continue till you are prolonging *AH* for a count of *ten*. Keep the tone steady.

c. Count aloud in march time: 1, 2, 3, —; 1, 2, 3, —; 1, 2, 3, —; keeping silent for the fourth beat. Do the three groups in one breath.

d. Count loudly in march time, 1, 2, 3, 4; 1, 2, 3, 4; 1, 2, 3, 4; taking a short catch-breath after each count of 4.

Practice Exercise No. 56

a. Say the following sentence slowly, taking a small breath at each (|): Now is the time | for all good men | to come to the aid of the party.

Say the sentence more quickly on one breath with a slight pause at each (|).

b. Breathe in. Letting the breath flow out very smoothly, say the following, taking one breath to each group:

Now fades the glimmering landscape | on the sight, |
    And all the air | a solemn stillness holds, |
Save where the beetle | wheels his droning flight, |
    And drowsy tinklings | lull the distant folds.

c. Breathe in. Force the air out sharply on:

"Forward, | the Light Brigade! |
Charge | for the guns!" | he said.

d. Deciding how you will control your exhaled breath, say:

Speech is silver, silence is golden.

The Owl and the Pussy-cat went to sea
In a beautiful pea-green boat.

I hear America singing, the varied carols I hear.

The earth is the Lord's, and the fullness thereof.

Ready! Set! Go!

PITCH

Changes in pitch are produced by changes in the tension, length and thickness of the vocal bands.

Men's voices are lower in pitch than women's because their vocal bands are somewhat longer.

The vocal bands of the average person allow a pitch range of almost two octaves.

Since the muscular adjustments for changes in pitch take place automatically, training in pitch is accomplished by thinking, by feeling, and by training the ear.

Pitch-training involves:

The selection of the optimum, or best, pitch level for the voice, and

The fuller use of the pitch range through the development of varied pitch levels, intonation, and inflection.

The Habitual Pitch Level. Each of us has a habitual pitch level: the pitch he uses most frequently in conversation, and around which the other pitches he uses cluster.

If this habitual pitch level is too high or too low, variety and flexibility are impaired, the voice sounds strained or affected, or does not seem to fit the personality. The voice mechanism itself may be so harmed that huskiness results.

To Find Your Habitual Pitch Level

METHOD 1. With a pitch pipe or piano at hand, read a passage of unemotional prose in a conversational tone. Listen for the pitches you think you use most often, and find them in the musical scale. (The pitches for women are usually slightly below middle C; for men, around the C an octave lower.)

Try to determine your average pitch from the pitches you use most often, and read the passage several times again to refine your judgment. The average pitch you finally decide on is probably your habitual pitch level.

METHOD 2. If you find the above process difficult, ask a friend to sit at the piano and pick out the several possible pitches lightly as you read. Together, work out your habitual pitch level.

The Optimum Pitch Level. The optimum pitch level is the pitch at which your voice sounds clearest and fullest or strongest.

To Find Your Optimum Pitch Level

METHOD 1. At the piano, determine your pitch range. Hum up as high as you can without strain; hum down as low as you can. Note the limits and determine the mid-point of your range. Your best pitch level is probably about ⅓ below the mid-point.

METHOD 2. If you can sing a scale with ease, hum down to your lowest pitch. Taking this as ONE, count up the scale, a number to each tone. Either *three, four* or *five* should be your best pitch. Say a simple sentence, such as, "This is the house that Jack built," on each of these pitches, and decide where your voice is fullest and clearest.

METHOD 3. Stopping up your ears with your fingers, hum up and down the scale. Your best pitch level will approximate the pitch at which your voice rings strongest in your head.

Using the Optimum Pitch Level. Once you have determined your optimum pitch level, compare it with what you judged to be your habitual pitch level. If they differ, try in as many ways as possible to shift to the optimum pitch level and make it a part of you:

Practice Exercise No. 57

a. Hum your best pitch level to yourself. At various times of the day, check at a piano to make sure you are holding to the pitch.

b. Read short sentences in a monotone on this pitch.

c. Read prose paragraphs out loud in a conversational tone, using your optimum pitch level as a base.

d. Finally, try to use the optimum pitch level in conversation.

Varied Pitch Levels. The use of varied pitch levels in emotional material will help develop variety in your use of voice.

While your best pitch level is the one used for conversation and general reading, a somewhat higher pitch level would be more suitable for excited emotional states, a lower pitch level for depressed or serious states:

Practice Exercise No. 58

a. Use a fairly high pitch level for:

On with the dance! Let joy be unconfined!

The sea! The sea! The open sea!
The blue, the fresh, the ever free!

Sail on, and on, and on!

Hey diddle, diddle, the cat and the fiddle.

My heart leaps up when I behold
A rainbow in the sky.

b. Use a fairly low pitch level for:

Now he belongs to the ages.

The day is cold, and dark, and dreary.

With malice toward none; with charity for all.

The sea is calm tonight,
The tide is full, the moon lies fair
Upon the straits.

Without a grave, unknelled, uncoffined, and un-
known.

c. Read the selections in *a* above with low pitch levels, in *b* with high. What happens to the meaning of the selections?

Practice Exercise No. 59

As you read these selections, notice how your pitch levels change to fit the meaning:

Exult, O shores, and ring O bells!
But I, with mournful tread,
Walk the deck my Captain lies,
Fallen cold and dead.

"A merry Christmas, uncle! God save you!" cried a cheerful voice . . .
"Bah!" said Scrooge. "Humbug!"

There was a sound of revelry by night . . .
And all went merry as a marriage bell;
But hush! hark! a deep sound strikes like a rising
knell!

Intonation. Intonation is the melody pattern of the voice in speech. It resembles the melody of song, except that in singing we usually leap from one tone to the next, whereas in speech we glide up or down toward the next tone. (See *Inflections,* below.)

The most important words, those that carry the meaning, are usually lifted well above the pitch level, less important words not quite so high.

EXAMPLE

MONEY
He gave me the
HE
    gave me the money.
       ME
    gave
He   the money.

The faults of intonation are usually (1) talking almost in a monotone with few and relatively small changes in pitch, and (2) using stereotyped intonation patterns.

Example of Stereotyped Intonation

off-   col-   use   fine   lec-
    ered   lege   of   tion
He   the   the   his   col-   of prints.

To Help Develop Variety of Intonation

Practice Exercise No. 60

a. Change the meaning of the first sentence used above by lifting still other words well above the pitch level:

He GAVE me the money.
He gave me THE money.
HE gave me the *money*.
He *gave* me the MONEY.

b. Try saying the following sentences with different meanings, first lifting one word well above the pitch level, then another:

This is the spot.
Who did you say it was?
I'm very sorry about the whole matter.

Practice Exercise No. 61

Analyze the following sentences for meaning. Decide which words should be emphasized. Say these words louder and longer than the rest, but try especially to lift them above the pitch level:

a. I come to bury Caesar not to praise him.
b. Cowards die many times before their death,
    The valiant never taste of death but once.
c. Our birth is but a sleep and a forgetting.
d. He who knows, and knows he knows,
    He is wise—follow him.
    He who knows, and knows not he knows,
    He is asleep—wake him.
    He who knows not, and knows not he knows not,
    He is a fool—shun him.
    He who knows not, and knows he knows not,
    He is a child—teach him.

(see key to this exercise in answer section at back of book)

Practice Exercise No. 62

Use pitch (and quality and rate) changes on the adjectives below to characterize the rats:

Great rats, small rats, lean rats, brawny rats,
Brown rats, black rats, grey rats, tawny rats,
Grave old plodders, gay young friskers.

Practice Exercise No. 63

Read the selections in the exercises above (1) in a monotone, (2) with only slight pitch changes, (3) with moderate pitch changes, (4) with as wide pitch changes as you can achieve. Check the last readings at the piano to see if you are using a good portion of your range. Do not feel that you must avail yourself of the whole range in every selection, for this would sound artificial.

Inflections. Inflections are the glides in pitch on single words. We are chiefly interested in the inflections on words that end sentences and phrases.

A rising inflection (/) indicates that the thought is incomplete and so connects one idea to the next. It is used in questions which do not begin with question-words. It also implies doubt and uncertainty.

EXAMPLES

We bought apples, / peaches, / bananas, / . . . (incompleteness)

Are you going? / (question without question-word)

Perhaps / (doubt)

A falling inflection (\) indicates that the thought is complete, and so it serves to disconnect ideas. It is used in questions which begin with question-words. It also implies certainty and finality.

EXAMPLES

We bought the apples. \ (completeness)

Where are you going? \ (question with question-word)

Yes! \ (certainty)

A falling-rising inflection (\/) is used at the end of a phrase when the sense is not gramatically complete.

EXAMPLES

As I was saying, \/

One day, \/ as he was driving by, \/

Circumflex inflections (⟨⟩) are associated both with spontaneous emotional reactions (surprise, delight) and with calculated implications and double-meanings (suspicion, irony). They may range from the heaviest sarcasm to the subtlest nuances of feeling.

EXAMPLES

You say you arrived home at 12 ʃ o'clock? (implying, "I don't believe it.")

He's a splendid ⟩ chap. (Far from it.)

Faults associated with inflections are (1) a lack of inflection or (2) over-use of one type. Too many falling inflections make for dullness. Too many rising inflections give an impression of light-headedness.

To Help Develop Variety of Inflection

Practice Exercise No. 64

a. Say *AH* on a low pitch. Glide swiftly up about a half-octave. Glide down. Glide up about an octave. Glide down.

b. Clearly distinguish between rising and falling inflections in the following:

A, / B, / C, / D. \
Are you going? / No! \
I've information vegetable, / animal, / and mineral. \
Bold, / cautious, / true, / and my loving comrade. \

c. Speak as if to a very large audience, slowly, with short phrases, and with long inflections:

a friend of the poor, / of the aged, / of the ill, / of all who are in need. \
He speaks to us as a business man, / as a citizen, / and as a parent. \

d. Say with falling-rising inflections:
That \/ I need hardly tell you, \/
Once before, \/ when he came here, \/
Never, \/ to my knowledge, \/

Practice Exercise No. 65

a. Say the following words with falling, rising, and circumflex inflections. What do the several inflections imply?

Go	Where	See
Please	When	Stop
Oh	I am	Never

b. Imagine a variety of situations, of emotions, in which the above words might be used. Say them, then analyze to see what types of inflections you used.

VOLUME

Volume, the loudness of the voice, is dependent on the strength of the original tone and the degree of reinforcement of that tone by resonance.

A voice has good volume (1) when it can be heard, (2) when it is adjusted readily to varying physical conditions, such as the size of a hall—a voice can be too loud—(3) when changes in volume are used effectively for emphasis, and (4) when the voice, whatever its loudness or softness, is produced efficiently and without strain.

Training in volume involves training the ear to become sensitive to changes in loudness, the development of better habits of phonation, and the better use of the resonators: the mouth, throat and nose. Therefore, review the material and exercises on ear-training and phonation, and study this section in conjunction with that on quality.

To Strengthen a Weak Voice. Your vocal equipment is probably adequate to produce the degree of volume needed in almost any situation. If your voice sounds weak to your friends, the fault may be due to a variety of causes, psychological or physical. Try all the types of exercises below to see which of them best helps to strengthen your voice.

Practice Exercise No. 66

You may be talking absent-mindedly, i.e., with little attention to your listeners. Remember that speech is communication *to* an *audience*, and try to develop a lively sense of communication.

In conversation, look directly at the person you are talking to.

In talking to a group, let your eyes move from person to person.

In reading aloud to your family, try to *share* the information, the experience, with them.

When next you talk to an audience, let your eyes swing from section to section, side to side, forward and back.

Practice Exercise No. 67

You may lack a sense of, or may have forgotten, the varying degrees of energy with which you can produce tone.

Imagine you are conducting a meeting. Say, "The meeting will please come to order," to an audience of (a) 10, (b) 100, (c) 1,000.

Say, "Go all the way down," to a person (a) 10 feet away, (b) 50 feet away, (c) 100 feet away. Avoid straining the throat, or raising the pitch.

Practice Exercise No. 68

You may have fallen into the habit of talking only to the person nearest to you.

In an auditorium, talk to the person half-way back, to the person in the last row. Try to make your voice bounce off the back wall.

Practice Exercise No. 69

You may not be using the resonators sufficiently.

In talking, open the mouth more. Use wide-swinging jaw action for the vowels. Focus the tone forward. Round the lips well on *oh, oo, oh, aw*. Make strong, firm *m, n, ng*, and *l* sounds. (See the section on oral and pharyngeal resonance.)

Practice Exercise No. 70

You may be talking too fast, clipping off sounds or letting them die away.

Prolong vowels with good support from the body, the breath.

Say *all, nine, awning, maim*, prolonging both the vowels and the consonants.

Read a paragraph aloud slowly, concentrating on holding your tone strongly to the ends of the phrases, the sentences.

Practice Exercise No. 71

Call out with an open throat:

Apples, peaches, bananas!

Come and get them!

Ship ahoy! Ship ahoy!

Awake! Awake!
Ring the alarm bell! Murder and treason!

To Develop Responsiveness to the Requirements for Volume

Practice Exercise No. 72

a. Say, with varying volume:
Company, HALT!
Column right, MARCH!
ONE, two, three, four. ONE, two, three, four.
b. Just as in pitch training you changed meaning by lifting words above the pitch level, now emphasize by saying single words much louder than the rest.
HE said she wanted you to go.
He said SHE wanted you to go.
He said she wanted YOU to go.
He said she wanted you to GO.
c. In this selection from Mark Twain, vary the volume to fit the description and the characters:
When (the mate) gave even the simplest order, he dis-

charged it like a blast of lightning, and sent a long, reverberating peal of profanity thundering after it . . . If a landsman should wish the gangplank moved a foot farther forward, he would probably say: "James, or William, one of you push that plank forward, please"; but put the mate in his place, and he would roar out: "Here now, start that gangplank for'ard. Lively, now! *What're* you about! Snatch it! *snatch* it! There! there! Aft again! *aft* again! Don't you hear me? Dash it to dash! are you going to *sleep* over it? . . . WHERE're you going with that barrel! *for'ard* with it, 'fore I make you swallow it, you dash-dash-dash-*dashed* split between a tired mud-turtle and a crippled hearse-horse!"

I wished I could talk like that.

Practice Exercise No. 73

Talk or read in a medium-sized room. As you say the first few words, listen for your voice to be reflected back from the walls. Experiment with larger and smaller degrees of volume to hear the effect of each.

Do the same in a small room, a large room, in an empty auditorium. When next you talk to a large group, let the sound of your first few words tell you how loudly you must talk.

QUALITY

There are many pleasing qualities of voice. We enjoy brilliant sopranos, mellow contraltos, heroic tenors, basso profundos. We use such different words as velvety, flute-like, vibrant, pure, to describe qualities we like.

Quality will be improved if we focus the tone, so that the resonators—the mouth, throat and nose—may operate freely together as a well-balanced unit. It will also be improved if we develop the individual resonances of the mouth, nose and throat.

To Focus the Tone. The tone will be well focused if the throat is open and the voice is "placed" forward in the mouth.

Practice Exercise No. 74

a. Hold a pencil about eighteen inches in front of the mouth. Focusing on the pencil point, prolong *AH, OO, EE.* Try to feel that lines drawn from the lips would all converge on the pencil point.

b. With the tip of the tongue behind the lower teeth, inhale lightly, feeling as if you were going to yawn. Prolong the *AH,* rolling the head around and feeling the openness of the throat. Repeat for *OO, EE.*

c. With tongue-tip behind the lower teeth, say *we* half a dozen times, focusing the tone well forward in the mouth. Similarly, say *be, pea, me.* Move from *we* to *wah,* from *be* to *bah,* etc., still thinking of sending the tone against the gums.

Say *tea, dee, lee.* Move the tongue-tip quickly forward from the *t* and *d*-positions on the upper gum to the rest-position behind the lower teeth. Let the movement help you to "place" the tone forward in the mouth.

d. With open throat and a forward-focused tone, say:

Over the hills and far away.

Where are the snows of yesteryear?

Little Tommy Tucker, sing for your supper.

Build thee more stately mansions, O my soul.

To Develop Nasal Resonance. By nasal resonance is meant the reinforcement of the original tone in the nose cavity.

Practice Exercise No. 75

a. Hum a strong *mmm.* Feel the vibration in your lips, on the bridge of your nose, at the base of your cheek bones. Prolong *n* and *ng* with ringing quality.

b. Chant with strong nasal consonants: *meem, maim, mime, mohm; neen, nain, nine, nohn.* Try to "tie" the vowels onto the nasal resonance, keeping the tone as vibrant for the vowels as for the *m* and *n.*

c. Say with ringing nasal resonance:

Mumbo Jumbo, god of the Congo.

Five miles meandering with a mazy motion.

The moon never beams without bringing me dreams.

The moanings of the homeless sea.

To the noise of the mourning of a mighty nation.

O Wind, if winter comes can spring be far behind

O wind, a-blowing all day long,
O wind, that sings so loud a song.

Faulty Nasal Resonance. 1. Nasality is a dull, smothered quality. It occurs when a lazy soft palate drops during the production of vowels so that too much tone is allowed to reverberate in the nose.

A test for the presence of nasality is to say a sentence without any nasal consonants, such as, "This is the house that Jack built," first in the ordinary way and then holding the nose tight shut. There should be no appreciable difference in the sound of the two sentences. If there is a difference, nasality is present.

To Correct Nasality: work for an active soft palate, one which drops low for the nasal consonants, and is held high against the back wall of the throat for the vowels and the other voiced consonants. Focus the tone forward, round the lips well, move the jaw actively. (See *Articulation*, Chapter IX)

Practice Exercise No. 76

Holding a mirror in front of your wide-open jaw, say: ung-ah-ung-ah-ung-ah. Let the soft palate drop down for the *ung*. Lift it up high for the *ah*.

2. **"Nasal" twang** is a hard, metallic, whining quality, as much due to tight, pharyngeal resonance as to too much nasal resonance. It occurs when with the jaw tight, the mouth opening very small, and the throat tense, the voice is forced through the nose.

To help correct "nasal" twang: in all talking and reading aloud, move the jaw actively, use a wider-open mouth than before, exaggerate lip movements, keep an open relaxed throat, and focus the tone forward.

3. **Denasalization** is the dull, "cold-id-the-dose," quality. It results from a severe cold, enlarged adenoids or other nasal obstructions, or a soft palate held so high and tense that the nasal consonants, *m, n,* and *ng* become *b, d,* and *g,* and the voice lacks resonance.

To help correct denasality (after medical or surgical care, if necessary): practice a free-swinging soft palate, low for the nasal consonants, high, but not too tight and tense, for the vowels and the other consonants. Try for strong, vigorous nasal consonants. Practice carefully the exercises for nasal resonance.

4. **Assimilation nasality** is the substitution of a nasalized vowel for a vowel plus a nasal consonant in such words as *my, time, find.* (Assimilation is the term used for the changing of one sound to another through the influence of a neighboring sound. In this case, the *n* changes the vowel, but itself disappears.)

To Help Correct Assimilation Nasality

Practice Exercise No. 77

In words with nasal consonants, sharply separate the vowels from the nasals. Say *time* as *tie-, tie-, tie-, tie-m.* Keep the vowel free from nasal resonance all four times

you say *tie*, but after the fourth *tie-* quickly press the lips together for a firm, strong *m.* In a similar way, practice all the words with nasals in Exercise No. 75, c.

To Develop Oral Resonance. By oral resonance is meant the reinforcement of the original tone in the mouth cavity.

Practice Exercise No. 78

a. Say *woo, woh, waw,* exaggerating the rounding of the lips. Say each of these syllables rapidly several times with agile lip movement.

b. Say *hoh, poh, boh* strongly with well-rounded lips. Hold the tone a moment, keeping the lips rounded.

c. Open the mouth wide, round the lips, concentrate on projecting the voice through the mouth on:

Oh, what a beautiful day!

Who are you?

How do you do?

So all day long the noise of battle rolled.

Gold! Gold! Gold! Gold!
Bright and yellow, hard and cold.

CAUTION: Guard again trying too hard for oral resonance, for this will merely make you sound affected. You do not want "pear-shaped tones," too mellow and too beautiful.

To Develop Throat Resonance. By throat or pharyngeal resonance is meant the reinforcement of the original tone in the throat cavity.

Practice Exercise No. 79

a. With open throat, wide-swinging jaw, say: *wah, wow, woy; hah, how, hoy.*

b. Yawn. On a low pitch and very slowly, say the syllables above.

c. With low pitch and open throat, say:

And yonder all before us lie
Deserts of vast eternity.

The barge she sat in, like a burnished throne
Burned on the water.

Earth has not anything to show more fair.

d. With very low pitch, and almost as if the voice came from the chest, say:

I am thy father's spirit:
Doom'd for a certain term to walk the night.
And for the day confined to fast in fires
Till the foul crimes done in my days of Nature
Are burnt and purged away.
Now o'er the one-half world
Nature seems dead, and wicked dreams abuse
The curtain'd sleep.

The gaudy, blabbing and remorseful day
Is crept into the bosom of the sea,
And now loud-howling wolves arouse the jades
That drag the tragic melancholy night.

Loud from its rocky caverns, the deep-voiced neigh-
    boring ocean
Speaks, and in accents disconsolate answers the wail
    of the forest.

A faulty pharyngeal resonance is part of stridency. The voice sounds pinched (see under *Faulty Phonation*), the walls of the pharynx are held tight and tense.

To correct this faulty resonance: Review the earlier exercises under pinched voice, and practice vocalizing with relaxed throat and low pitch.

RATE

The normal rate for speaking in public is about 125 words per minute. Radio talking averages about 150 words per minute.

Practice Exercise No. 80

With your normal rate, read the following paragraphs adapted from Samuel Butler's *Erewhon*. Have someone time you to see the place you reach in one minute, the length of time you take to read the whole selection:

When I talked about originality and genius to some gentlemen whom I met at a supper party given by Mr. Thims in my honor, and said that original thought ought to be encouraged, I had to eat my words at once. A man's business, they hold, is to think as his neighbors do, for Heaven help him if he thinks good what they count bad. And really it is hard to see how their theory differs from our own, for the word "Idiot" only means a person who forms his opinions for himself.

The venerable Professor of Worldly Wisdom, a man verging on eighty but still hale, spoke to me very seriously on this subject in consequence of the few words that I had imprudently let fall in defense of genius. He was one of those who carried most weight in the university, and had the reputation of having done more perhaps than any other living man to suppress any kind of originality.

"It is not our business," he said, "to help students to think for themselves. Surely this is the very last thing which one who wishes them well should encourage them to do. Our duty is to ensure that they shall think as we do, or at any rate as we hold it expedient to say we do." In some respects, however, he was thought to hold somewhat radical opinions, for he was President of the Society for the Suppression of Useless Knowledge, and for the Completer Obliteration of the Past.

(There are 93 words in the first paragraph. The 125th word is *imprudently* in the second paragraph; the 150th is *done* in the next sentence. There are 253 words in all.)

A good rate for you may well be somewhat above or below the average rates mentioned. It is the rate that is both comfortable for you, and easy for listeners to understand.

Read the paragraph above for several listeners to get their reactions to your rate.

If you decide, with their help, that your rate is too fast, too slow, or too jerky, go over the paragraph from *Erewhon* once again to see whether the fault lies with the length of the individual sounds, the number of pauses—that is, the way you *phrase* the selection—or the length of your pauses. After making this analysis, study the section below on *Phrasing* and practice the appropriate selections which follow.

Phrasing. We do not talk in single words, but in groups of words. In speech, such a group of related words is called a **phrase**. The phrase is said as if it were one long word.

An article is attached to a noun. We say:

Not, The book	*But*, Thebook
Not, An apple	*But*, Anapple
Not, A road	*But*, Aroad

Adjectives are joined to nouns, adverbs to verbs. We say:

The open book	as Theopenbook
Ride quickly	as Ridequickly

A prepositional phrase is said without a break or pause: totheend; ofthelastchapter. Or two prepositional phrases may be joined: totheendofthelastchapter.

A short sentence may be said as a phrase: Hewentaway.

Where, then, do we break the tone? Where do we pause? Where does one phrase end and another begin? The answer depends upon several factors.

From the point of view of ideas and grammatical relationships, note the following:

We usually pause, of course, at the end of a sentence.

When a sentence is of some length, the subject-portion will be separated from the verb-portion: ThemanIhopedtoseeelected | madeaverypoorshowing.

An interpolated phrase will be set off by pauses: Butsuddenly | asIpeereddown | Isawawhiteformrising.

If we talk in a very large hall, we must shorten our phrases, use more and longer pauses. The prizefight announcer calls: Inthiscorner | inblacktights . . .

A very serious subject, a very dignified occasion, will also cause us to use many short pauses and a generally slow rate.

And we may pause, break a phrase even, for special emphasis: Isawawhiteform | rising.

Finally, personal taste enters into phrasing and rate. One person might read the opening of the *Erewhon* selection above as: WhenItalked | aboutoriginalityandgenius. Another might say this as: WhenItalkedaboutoriginalityandgenius.

Mark the selections below for phrasing before you practice them, and then do the same for the *Erewhon* selection.

Practice Exercise No. 81

a. With long-held vowels, and many and long pauses, say:

Lord God of Hosts, be with us yet,
Lest we forget, lest we forget!

The quality of mercy is not strained;
It droppeth as the gentle rain from heaven
Upon the place beneath.

Tomorrow, and tomorrow and tomorrow,
Creeps in this petty pace from day to day
To the last syllable of recorded time;
And all our yesterdays have lighted fools
The way to dusty death. Out, out, brief candle!
Life's but a walking shadow, a poor player
That struts and frets his hour upon the stage
And then is heard no more. It is a tale
Told by an idiot, full of sound and fury,
Signifying nothing.

b. With a fairly rapid rate—short vowels, and few and short pauses—say:

The year's at the spring
And day's at the morn;
Morning's at seven;
The hillside's dew-pearled;
The lark's on the wing;
The snail's on the thorn:
God's in his heaven—
All's right with the world.

I am the very model of a modern Major-General,
I've information vegetable, animal and mineral,
I know the kings of England, and I quote the fights historical,
From Marathon to Waterloo, in order categorical.

c. Experiment with the selections in exercises 1 and 2 above, keeping the meaning clear, yet varying somewhat the length of vowels, and number and length of pauses.

d. Say, as smoothly as possible:

On either side the river lie
Long fields of barley and of rye.

Far from the madding crowd's ignoble strife,
Their sober wishes never learn'd to stray;
Along the cool sequester'd vale of life
They kept the noiseless tenor of their way.

Earth has not anything to show more fair:
Dull would be he of soul who could pass by
A sight so touching in its majesty:
This City now doth like a garment wear
The beauty of the morning . . .

CHAPTER VIII

PRONUNCIATION

Those of us who wish to improve our speech want to use correct pronunciations. We want to be considered careful, not careless, in our speech habits; we want to avoid being caught in simple mistakes. We seek the assurance and confidence that comes from knowing we are doing something the right way.

In English, however, there is no such thing as a "correct" pronunciation, in the sense that the answer to an arithmetic problem is correct. There is no *one* right way to say a word. English-speaking peoples have no national academy to determine matters of pronunciation.

Therefore, it is better to think of pronunciations as being acceptable or unacceptable, that is, in good usage or not.

ACCEPTABLE AMERICAN PRONUNCIATION

A pronunciation is acceptable in the United States if it meets the following requirements:

1. If it is native, not foreign. In any area with large numbers of immigrants, one must be wary of unconsciously adopting foreign pronunciations.

2. If it is also native, in that it is American, not British. For a person born in the United States to affect a Cockney, Oxford, or BBC accent is downright silly.

3. If it is characteristic of some region of the United States, not some small locality, such as a town. Coastal New England, the middle Atlantic area, the coastal and the mountain South, the West, are examples of such regions.

A corollary, here, is that no one region is superior to others in pronunciation. A New Yorker should not attempt to talk like a Texan, nor a Texan like a citizen of Portland, Maine.

4. If it is used by educated and cultured people. We should take as guides those who know something about the language and treat it with respect. We can get little help from those whose vocabulary is meager and who do not care how they say the words they do know.

5. If it is modern. Pronunciations change, and there isn't much sense in adopting a pronunciation last heard 500 years ago or one we think will be popular twenty-five years hence.

A corollary here is that while one need not use the pronunciations of one's grandmother, one should not criticize *her* for using those she was taught.

From these criteria it is clear that more than one pronunciation of a word may be acceptable, that is, in good usage.

A pronunciation may be unacceptable because it is foreign, provincial, pedantic, affected, or obsolete.

THE DICTIONARY

The best aid in finding and selecting acceptable pronunciations is a good dictionary.

For Americans, probably the most authoritative dictionary is the *Merriam-Webster New International Dictionary,* second edition. This unabridged, library-size volume, with well over 400,000 entries, should be consulted on all fine points of pronunciation.

Convenient dictionaries to keep on the desk for home use are: the *Merriam-Webster Collegiate Dictionary,* based on the unabridged volume mentioned above; and the *American College Dictionary,* published by Random House and Harper and Brothers.

Both are of high quality. Each has well over 100,000 entries. Each, therefore, can well take care of the needs of the average educated person in matters of word meaning and pronunciation. The chief difference between them is probably that the Merriam-Webster (hereafter called WEB) tends to be more conservative than the American College Dictionary (called ACD).

HOW TO USE A DICTIONARY

A dictionary does not legislate about pronunciation. It records present good usage. It points out choices in pronunciation. It indicates regional variations. It suggests levels on which certain usages are appropriate.

A dictionary, therefore, furnishes the necessary information for a sound judgment as to what is acceptable pronunciation in a given situation. It must be used with care and discrimination.

In learning to use a dictionary:

Familiarize yourself with its symbols indicating pronunciation.

These are listed in a *PRONUNCIATION KEY* or *GUIDE TO PRONUNCIATION* at the beginning of the volume. A short form of the key is usually printed at the top or bottom of all the pages of the text.

Both WEB and ACD use diacritical markings to indicate pronunciation. The word is re-spelled and certain marks are placed above or below the re-spellings to give the pronunciations more accurately. Thus, in both dictionaries the symbol ā is used for the vowel of *cape, ale, fate*.

You must realize, in following these markings, that your pronunciation will only be as accurate as your interpretation of them. If you mistake the meaning of the marks, your pronunciation will be mistaken. Dictionaries help to guard against this by printing several key words for each diacritical mark in the full key at the beginning of the volume. Refer to these whenever you are in doubt about any sounds.

Make sure you are looking up the right word, the one you want.

Sometimes words are spelled in the same way but have such different meanings that they are printed as separate entries. *Indict*, in the usual sense of "to charge with an offense," has different pronunciation (in·dīt′ in *WEB*) from *indict*, in the unusual sense of "to proclaim" (in·dĭkt′). As a matter of fact, the latter is a common mispronunciation of the word in its usual meaning.

One word may be used as several different parts of speech with possibly different pronunciations (*perfect* as an adjective and a verb). These may be listed together or separately.

In all dictionaries, check the meaning of the word and its part of speech before you look at its pronunciation.

Examine **all** the pronunciations given for a word. Two, three, or more may be offered. The adjective *alternate* has four acceptable pronunciations.

The first listing is usually the most widespread and therefore the preferred pronunciation.

Note the special comments that may be made about particular pronunciations.

Pronunciations may be called British, local, colloquial, provincial, popular, or poetic. The phrases "older," "formerly," and "less often" are also used.

Finally, if the dictionary offers a choice of pronunciations, you should ask your friends for their vote. In general, you should try to conform to the pronunciations of your region.

A NOTE ON THE PRONUNCIATION LISTS

The remainder of this chapter is devoted largely to pronunciation lists.

These are not intended to be a substitute for a dictionary.

Rather, their purpose is to point out common types of mistakes in pronunciation, to show how these mistakes may be corrected, and to illustrate or emphasize certain principles that will be a help in improving your pronunciation generally.

Practice the lists only in conjunction with, and as illustrations for, the observations which precede them. Take up one list at a time. Read through it, saying aloud both the acceptable and the unacceptable forms. Note particularly those words which you have been mispronouncing. Say the correct pronunciation over several times, trying to fix it in your mind. Say the word in a short sentence. Keep a notebook of such words, and each week try to work three or four into your conversation.

PRONUNCIATION KEY

In the lists that follow, the pronunciations are indicated by a simple system of re-spelling.

Vowels

SYMBOL	KEY WORD	RE-SPELLING
EE	seem	SEEM
AY	say	SAY
Y	buy	BY
OH	no	NOH
OO	ooze	OOZ
AW	taught	TAWT
AH	farm	FAHRM
UR	burn	BURN
OY	toy	TOY
OW	now	NOW
YOO	use	YOOZ
AYR	air	AYR

The remaining vowels are usually indicated by a vowel plus two consonants.

VOWEL	as in WORD	RE-SPELLING
I	ill	ILL
A	bat	BATT
E	end	ENND
O	hot	HOTT (This sound varies from short AH to short AW.)
U	cup	KUPP

The vowel of *push, pull* is usually indicated by U, and a key word is supplied. In the chapter on *Articulation,* the symbol UU is used for this vowel.

The vowels of unaccented syllables are weak, and have only a part of the quality of the original or else are completely blurred or indeterminate in quality. For these, the original spellings are usually retained: alone (a-LOHN), system (SISS-tem), easily (EE-zi-lee), honor (ONN-or), campus (KAMM-pus).

Consonants

These letters have their usual value: **b, d, f, h, k, l, m, n, p, r, s, t, v, w, y** (before vowels, as in *yes*), **z**. The remaining consonants are indicated as follows:

SYMBOL	KEY WORD	RE-SPELLING
G	gay	GAY
J	jay	JAY
TCH	chief	TCHEEF
NG	sing	SING
SH	shoe	SHOO
ZH	measure	MEZH-ur
TH	thin	THINN
~~TH~~	than	~~TH~~ANN

NOTE: *W* is used for words spelled with *wh,* since this sound may be a *W,* a voiceless *W,* or an *HW. C* is not used, since it may have the sound of *S* or *K. Q* is not used, since its sound is *KW. X* is not used, since its sound is either *KS* or *GZ.*

In the chapter on *Articulation,* the symbol *TSH* is used in place of *TCH,* and the symbol *DZH* is used in place of *J.* There, TCHEEF is TSHEEF, and JAY is DZHAY.

Syllables. Syllables are separated by dashes: *finger* (FING-ger). It should be remembered that syllables can be indicated only roughly in English.

Accent. Only the primary accent of a word is given and this is indicated by capitals: *going* (GOH-ing), *demoniacal* (dee-mo-NY-a-kal). The secondary accent is not indicated because it usually does not present a problem.

Practice Exercise No. 82

Test yourself on the pronunciation of the following words.

WORD	SHOULD ONE SAY	OR
1. *women*	WIMM-in	WOH-men
2. *culinary*	KYOO-li-ner-ee	KULL-i-ner-ee
3. *awry*	a-RY	AW-ree
4. *faucet*	FAW-sit	FASS-it
5. *grievous*	GREEV-us	GREEV-ee-us
6. *ignoramus*	ig-no-RAY-mus	ig-no-RAM-us
7. *museum*	myoo-ZEE-um	MYOO-zee-um
8. *verbatim*	vur-BAY-tim	vur-BATT-im
9. *flaccid*	FLAKK-sid	FLASS-id
10. *suite*	SWEET	SOOT

COMMON MISTAKES IN PRONUNCIATION

Spelling Pronunciations

Certain mistakes in pronunciation are made because the speaker follows spellings too closely.

Sometimes there is good reason for this sort of mistake. Simple, old words may decline in use, or words common to one region may not be used in another. We may not have **heard** these words, and when we see them may consider them too simple to look up in a dictionary. These very ordinary words, however, deserve to be correctly pronounced:

WORD	SAY	NOT
ague	AY-gyoo	AYG
awry	a-RY	AW-ree
bade	BAD	BAYD
blackguard	BLAG-ard	BLAKK-GAHRD
breeches	BRITCH-iz	BREETCH-iz
comely	KUMM-lee	KOHM-lee
orgy	AWR-jee	AWR-guee
		(g as in get)
quay	KEE	KWAY
victuals	VITT-'lz	VIKK-tchoo-'lz

Sometimes the mispronounced words, while not literary, are a bit out of the ordinary. A careful speaker would have looked them up in a dictionary rather than guessed at their pronunciation from the spelling. In the word *misled,* the spelling pronunciation MIZZ-'ld probably occurs only when the word is read aloud.

WORD	SAY	NOT
comptroller	kon-TROH-ler	komp-TROH-ler
culinary	KYOO-li-ner-ee	KULL-i-ner-ee
disheveled	di-SHEVV-eld	diss-HEVV-eld
doughty	DOW-tee	DOH-tee
indict (to charge with a crime)	in-DYT	in-DIKT
longevity	lon-JEV-i-tee	long-GEV-i-tee
misled	miss-LED	MIZZ-'ld
parliamentary	pahr-li-MEN-ter-ee	pahr-lee-a-MEN-ter-ee
piquant	PEE-k'nt	PEE-kwant
solace	SOLL-iss	SOH-liss
subtle	SUTT-'l	SUBB-tel
vehement	VEE-e-mint	VEE-hem-ent
zoology	zoh-OLL-o-jee	ZOO-lo-jee

On the other hand, people occasionally mispronounce ordinary words that they must hear very frequently indeed. It is an extraordinary tribute to the power of the printed word that a warning must be issued about these curious spelling pronunciations.

WORD	SAY	NOT
comfort	KUMM-fort	KOMM-fort
cupboard	KUBB-'rd	KUPP-BOHRD
forehead	FORR-id, FOHR-, FAWR-	FOHR-HEDD
heroine	HERR-o-in	HERR-oyn
hiccough	HIK-up	HIK-koff
often	OFF-'n	OFF-ten
raspberry	RAZZ-berr-ee	RASP-berr-ee
said	SEDD	SAYD
says	SEZZ	SAYZ
whooping cough	HOOP-ing KOFF, KAWF	WOOP-ing KOFF
women	WIMM-in	WOH-men

The *spelling CH* so often has the sound of TCH, as in *chin,* that a common mistake is to tend to pronounce it always this way. But CH, especially in words taken from Greek, may also have the sound of K:

WORD	SAY	NOT
archives	AHR-kyvz	AHR-tchyvz
archipelago	ahr-ki-PELL-a-go	ahr-tchi-PELL-a-go
archangel	AHRK-ayn-jel	AHRTCH-ayn-jel
chasm	KAZZ-'m	TCHAZZ-'m
chimera	ky-MIRR-a, ki-	tchy-MIRR-a
chiropodist	ki-ROPP-o-dist	tchi-ROPP-o-dist
chiropractor	KY-ro-prak-tor	TCHY-ro-prak-tor
machinations	mak-i-NAY-sh'nz	match-i-NAY-sh'nz
schizophrenic	skizz-o-FRENN-ik	————

But notice:

WORD	SAY	NOT
archbishop	ahrtch-BISH-op	ahrk-BISH-op
archdeacon	ahrtch-DEE-k'n	ahrk-DEE-k'n
schism	SIZZ'm	SKIZZ-'m

The *spelling CH,* especially in words taken from French, may also have the sound of SH:

WORD	SAY	NOT
cache	KASH	KATCH
chaise	SHAYZ, or SHEZZ	TCHAYZ
chamois	SHAM-ee	TCHAM-ee
chassis	SHASS-ee	TCHASS-ee
chic	SHEEK	TCHIK
chicanery	shi-KAYN-er-ee	tchi-KAYN-er-ee

The *spelling G* is troublesome because it has three pronunciations. The hard G of *get,* the J of *jet,* and the ZH sound as in *pleasure* may be confused in the following words:

WORD	SAY	NOT
beige	BAYZH	BAYJ
garage	ga-RAHZH	ga-RAHJ
gesture	JESS-tcher	guess-tcher
gesticulate	jess-TIK-yoo-layt	guess-TIK-yoo-layt
gibbet	JIB-et	GIB-et
mirage	mi-RAHZH	mi-RAHJ
regime	re-ZHEEM	re-JEEM
rouge	ROOZH	ROOJ

WORD	SAY	NOT
mischievous	MISS-tchiv-us	miss-TCHEEV-ee-us
once	WUNSS	WUNST
streptomycin	strep-to-MY-sin	strep-to-MY-o-sin
wash	WAHSH, WAWSH	WAHRSH, WAWRSH
Washington	WAHSH-ing-ton, WAWSH-ing-ton	WAHRSH-ing-ton, WAWRSH-ing-ton

Reversing the Order of Sounds

If spelling is not looked at carefully enough, mispronunciations may occur because the order of certain sounds is reversed:

WORD	SAY	NOT
bronchial	BRONG-kee-al	BRONN-i-kal
cavalry	KAVV-al-ree	KAL-va-ree
irrelevant	ir-RELL-e-vant	ir-REVV-e-lant
larynx	LARR-ingks	LAHR-niks
pharynx	FARR-ingks	FAHR-niks
relevant	RELL-e-vant	REVV-e-lant

The sound R is particularly troublesome in this respect:

WORD	SAY	NOT
children	TCHILL-dren	TCHILL-dern
hundred	HUN-dred	HUN-derd
modern	MODD-ern	MODD-ren
incongruous	in-KONG-groo-us	in-KONG-ger-us
pattern	PATT-ern	PATT-ren
perspiration	pur-spir-AY-shun	press-pir-AY-shun

Added Sounds

In uneducated speech, sounds may be added to words because of their similarity to other words or because of a mistaken idea of their spelling. (Sounds added to ease the saying of difficult sound-combinations are discussed in the chapter on *Articulation*.)

WORD	SAY	NOT
across	a-KROSS	a-KROST
attack	a-TAKK	a-TAKT
attacked	a-TAKT	a-TAKK-ted
aureomycin	aw-ree-o-MY-sin	aw-ree-o-MY-o-sin
column	KOLL-um	KOLL-yum
drowned	DROWND	DROWN-ded
escape	es-KAYP	eks-KAYP
grievous	GREEV-us	GREEV-ee-us
height	HYT	HYT'TH

Sounds Left Out

Where two vowels occur together in a word, one is sometimes left out so that a syllable is lost. This sounds careless.

WORD	SAY	NOT
cruel	KROO-el	KROOL
diary	DY-a-ree	DY-ree
jewel	JOO-el	JOOL
poem	POH-em	POHM
ruin	ROO-in	ROON
violet	VY-o-let	VY-let

The mistake of leaving out a syllable may occur in other types of words:

WORD	SAY	NOT
president	PREZZ-i-dent	PREZZ-dent
probably	PROBB-a-blee	PROBB-lee
regularly	REGG-yoo-lar-lee	REGG-yu-lee
valuable	VALL-yoo-a-b'l	VALL-a-b'l

In careless speech, consonants are often left out. Be sure to say the consonants in these words:

WORD	SAY	NOT
all right	AWL RYT	AW RYT
Arctic	AHRK-tik	AHR-tik
district	DISS-trikt	DISS-trik
exactly	eg-ZAKT-lee	eg-ZAK-lee
flaccid	FLAKK-sid	FLASS-id
gentlemen	JENN-tel-man	JENN-l-man
help	HELP	HEPP
hound	HOWND	HOWN
hundred	HUNN-dred	HUNN-ed
recognize	REKK-og-nyz	REKK-o-nyz
succinct	sukk-SINGT	su-SINGT
thousand	THOW-zand	THOW-zan
told	TOHLD	TOHL

Substitution of One Sound for Another

One sound is sometimes mistakenly substituted for another. This may be a foreignism or a spelling pronunciation.

WORD	SAY	NOT
average	AVV-er-ij	AVV-er-itch
because	be-KAWZ	be-KOSS,
		be-KAWSS
college	KOLL-ej	KOLL-itch
electricity	e-lekk-TRISS-i-tee	e-lekk-TRIZZ-i-tee
gas	GASS	GAZZ

Sound-substitutions also occur in uneducated or provincial speech. Some of the pronunciations may once have been acceptable, but are now considered archaic.

WORD	SAY	NOT
deaf	DEFF	DEEF
drama	DRAH-ma,	DRAY-ma
	DRAMM-a	
faucet	FAW-sit	FASS-it
genuine	JENN-yoo-in	JENN-yoo-wyn
ignoramus	ig-no-RAY-mus	ig-no-RAM-us
length	LENGTH,	LENTH
	LENGKTH	
pincers	PINN-surz	PINCH-urz
radiator	RAY-dee-ay-tor	RADD-ee-ay-tor
radio	RAY-dee-o	RADD-ee-o
rather	RATH-er,	RUTH-er
	RAHTH-er	
rinse	RINSS	RENTCH
strength	STRENGTH,	STRENTH
	STRENGKTH	
tremendous	tre-MENN-dus	tre-MENN-jus
wrestle	RESS-'l	RASS-'l

The letter X may cause confusion because it has two pronunciations, KS and GZ. In words beginning with *ex-*, which have the accent on the first syllable, the *ex* is pronounced EKS (*exodus*, EKS-o-dus). This is also the case if the accent falls on the second syllable and the second syllable begins with a consonant (*expect*, eks-PEKT). But if the second and accented syllable begins with a vowel, the sound is either EGZ or IGZ, *exalt* (egz-AWLT, igz-AWLT). Note, however:

exit	either EKS-it or EGZ-it
exile	either EKS-yl or EGZ-yl
luxury	LUKK-shu-ree
luxurious	either lukk-SHUR-i-us or lugg-ZHUR-i-us

Confusing Words with Similar Spelling

Words of different meaning but similar spelling are sometimes confused in pronunciation:

WORD AND MEANING	SAY
adjoin, to lie next to	a-JOYN
adjourn, to suspend a session	a-JURN
aural, pertaining to the hearing or the ear	AW-ral
oral, pertaining to the spoken word or the mouth	OH-ral
coral, skeleton of a sea animal	KORR-al
corral, pen for horses	ko-RAL
crochet, kind of needlework	kro-SHAY
crotchet, a perverse fancy	KROTCH-et
croquet, a lawn game	kro-KAY
croquette, crumbed, fried minced meat	kro-KETT
era, period of time	EE-ra, IRR-a
err, to be mistaken	UR
error, a mistake	ERR-or, ERR-a
lineament, feature of the face	LINN-ee-a-ment
liniment, liquid for sprains	LINN-i-ment
precedence, priority in order or rank	pre-SEE-dens
precedents, cases which serve as examples	PRESS-e-dens
slough, a reedy or marshy pool	SLOO
slough, n., soft muddy place; condition of degradation; v., to plod through mud	SLOW (OW as in HOW)
slough, to cast off skin	SLUFF
viola, a stringed instrument	ve-OH-la, vy-OH-la
Viola	VY-o-la, VEE-o-la, ve-OH-la, vy-OH-la

Accenting the Wrong Syllable

The accenting of certain syllables is an important feature of English pronunciation. Mistakes in placing the accent are either wrong guesses made by persons who have not yet acquired the habit of looking up pronunciations in a dictionary, or are relics of older pronunciations now too infrequently used to be considered acceptable. The list below gives both the acceptable and the unacceptable forms of words in which the accent is frequently misplaced.

WORD	SAY	NOT
acumen	a-KYOO-men	AKK-yoo-men
alias	AY-lee-as	a-LY-as

WORD	SAY	NOT
brigand	BRIG-and	bri-GAND
cabal	ka-BAL (as in *cat*)	KABB-al
cement	si-MENT	SEE-ment
clematis	KLEMM-a-tiss	kle-MAT-iss
condolence	konn-DOH-lens	KONN-do-lens
contribute	konn-TRIBB-yoot	KONN-tri-byoot
decade	DEKK-ayd, DEKK-ad	de-KAYD
demonstrate	DEMM-on-strayt	de-MONN-strayt
disciple	di-SY-p'l	DISS-i-p'l
elixir	i-LIKK-sur	ELL-ik-sur
episcopal	e-PIS-ko-pal	ep-i-SKAH-pal
exigency	EKK-si-jen-see	ek-SIJJ-en-see
exponent	ek-SPOH-nent	EKS-poh-nent
gondola	GONN-do-la	gon-DOH-la
grimace	gri-MAYSS	GRIMM-as
horizon	ho-RY-z'n	HORR-i-zon
hyperbole	hy-PUR-bo-lee	HY-pur-bohl
incognito	in-KOGG-ni-toh	in-kogg-NEE-toh
influence	IN-floo-enss	in-FLOO-enss
integral	IN-te-gral	in-TEGG-ral
lyceum	ly-SEE-um	LY-see-um
municipal	myoo-NISS-a-p'l	myoo-ni-SIPP-'l
museum	myoo-ZEE-um	MYOO-zee-um
police	po-LEESS	POH-leess
robust	roh-BUST	ROH-bust
sepulchre	SEPP-ul-kur	se-PULL-kurr (as in *cut*)
theater	THEE-a-tur (*th* as in *thin*)	thi-YITT-ur, the-AY-tur
vagary	va-GAYR-ee	VAYG-a-ree

Notice that a root may cause a misplaced accent:

impious	IMM-pee-us	imm-PY-us
impotent	IMM-po-tent	imm-POH-tent

The four-syllable adjectives ending in *-able* (*admirable*) are frequently mispronounced. The mistaken tendency is to accent them on the second syllable, usually on the analogy of the word from which they have been formed (*admire*). These adjectives are correctly accented on the first syllable.

WORD	SAY	NOT
amicable	AMM-i-ka-b'l	a-MIKK-a-b'l
admirable	ADD-mir-a-b'l	ad-MY-ra-b'l
applicable	APP-li-ka-b'l	a-PLIKK-a-b'l
comparable	KOMM-pa-ra-b'l	komm-PAYR-a-b'l
despicable	DESS-pik-a-b'l	de-SPIKK-a-b'l
equitable	EKK-wit-a-b'l	e-KWITT-a-b'l
formidable	FAWR-mid-a-b'l	fawr-MIDD-a-b'l
hospitable	HOSS-pit-a-b'l	hoss-PITT-a-b'l
lamentable	LAMM-en-ta-b'l	la-MENT-a-b'l
preferable	PREFF-ur-a-b'l	pre-FUR-a-b'l
reputable	REPP-yoo-ta-b'l	re-PYOO-ta-b'l

Notice also:

indefatigable	in-de-FATT-i-ga-b'l	(do not accent the 2nd or 4th syllable)
irreparable	i-REPP-a-ra-b'l	i-re-PAYR-a-b'l
irrevocable	i-REVV-o-ka-b'l	i-re-VOH-ka-b'l

But **indisputable** may be said either as in-dis-PYOO-ta-b'l or in-DISS-pyoo-ta b'l.

Affectations

Certain persons go out of their way to pronounce words differently from their acquaintances or from the educated persons of their part of the country. They seek out Britishisms, or poetic or archaic pronunciations and seem to put quotes around each of these whenever they say them.

Avoid such affectation. Let the pronunciations of the educated people of your region be good enough for you.

WORD	SAY	NOT
aerial	AYR-ee-al	ay-IRR-ee-al
aeroplane	AYR-o-playn	AY-e-ro-playn
again	a-GENN	a-GAYN (unless you're coastal New England)
coupon	KOO-pon	KYOO-pon
either	EE-ther	Y-ther
hearth	HAHRTH	HURTH
hygiene	HY-jeen	HY-ji-een
issue	ISH-oo	ISS-yoo
laboratory	LABB-o-ra-toh-ree	LABB-ra-tree
nature	NAYTCH-er	NAYT-yoor
neither	NEE-ther	NY-ther
rabies	RAY-beez	RAY-bi-eez
stature	STATCH-er	STATT-yoor
vase	VAYSS, VAYZ	VAHZ (British pronunciation)

Some persons who are not trying to act superior but are merely trying to be careful, try **too** hard, and succeed in **sounding affected**. (See also *Articulation*.)

One instance of this is saying the ending *-ness* as if it were an accented syllable, NESS. The ending is always unaccented and should be said with an indeterminate vowel, resembling NISS.

EXAMPLE	SAY	NOT
madness	MADD-niss	MADD-ness

Another instance is saying the ending *-or* as AWR. This ending is also unaccented and should be said with an indeterminate vowel, resembling ER.

EXAMPLE	SAY	NOT
actor	AKK-ter	AKK-tawr

Practice Exercise No. 83

This quiz is based on the words in the preceding section, Common Mistakes in Pronunciation.

	WORD	SHOULD YOU SAY	OR
1.	*ague*	AY-gyoo	AYG
2.	*piquant*	PEE-kwant	PEE-k'nt
3.	*cupboard*	KUBB-'rd	KUPP-BOHRD
4.	*archangel*	AHRTCH-ayn-jel	AHRK-ayn-jel
5.	*gibbet*	GIB-et	JIB-et
6.	*poem*	POH-em	POHM
7.	*succinct*	su-SINGT	sukk-SINGT
8.	*luxury*	LUKK-shu-ree	LUGG-zhu-ree
9.	*era*	EE-ra, IRR-a	ERR-a
10.	*incognito*	in-KOGG-ni-toh	in-kogg-NEE-toh
11.	*formidable*	fawr-MIDD-a-b'l	FAWR-mid-a-b'l
12.	*coupon*	KYOO-pon	KOO-pon

HELPS TOWARD BETTER PRONUNCIATION

Influence of Part of Speech on Pronunciation

Certain words are accented on the first syllable when used as nouns or adjectives, on the second when used as verbs.

EXAMPLE	NOUN OR ADJ.	VERB
absent	ABB-sent	ab-SENT
addict	ADD-ikt	a-DIKT
annex	ANN-eks	a-NEKS
perfect	PUR-fekt	per-FEKT

Other words which shift accent in this way are:

collect	export	project
combat	import	rebel
combine	imprint	record
compound	incense	reject
conduct	increase	subject
contract	permit	survey
convert	prefix	suspect
desert	present	transfer
digest	produce	transport
escort	progress	

Notice, however:

WORD	NOUN OR ADJ.	VERB
attribute	ATT-ri-byoot	a-TRIBB-yoot
consummate	kon-SUMM-it	KONN-su-mayt
perfume	PUR-fyoom, per-FYOOM	per-FYOOM
refuse	REFF-yooss	re-FYOOZ

The word *adept* is pronounced ADD-ept when used as a noun, a-DEPT when used as an adjective.

The word *compact* is pronounced KOMM-pakt when used as a noun, kom-PAKT when used as a verb, and either KOMM-pakt or kom-PAKT when used as an adjective.

The word *cleanly* is pronounced KLENN-lee when used as an adjective, KLEEN-lee when used as an adverb.

When certain words ending in *-ate* are used as verbs, this last syllable is pronounced AYT. But when they are used as adjectives or nouns, the final vowel is indeterminate in quality and the syllable resembles -IT.

EXAMPLES	NOUN OR ADJ.	VERB
advocate	ADD-vel-it	ADD-vo-kayt
aggregate	AGG-re-git	AGG-re-gayt

Other words which shift pronunciation in this way are:

alternate	deliberate	intimate
appropriate	designate	moderate
approximate	desolate	predicate
associate	duplicate	separate
degenerate	estimate	
delegate	graduate	

Note, however, that *prostrate* is pronounced PROSS-trayt both as verb and as adjective.

Words We Read but Seldom Say

Writing tends to be formal, to use learned (LURN-ed) words. In talking, we try for informality, directness, simplicity.

Therefore, there are many words which we read and know the meaning of, but which we seldom hear and seldom say. And when we do have to say them, as when we read aloud to our family or friends from a newspaper or magazine, we are frequently at a loss as to how to pronounce them.

The list below contains a sampling of such words. Read them. Say them out loud. Memorize their pronunciation. Check them in your dictionary. Make a habit of looking up the pronunciation of other "hard" words when you come across them.

Only a few mispronunciations are given below, for the simple reason that the words are not said often enough to acquire any common mispronunciations.

WORD AND MEANING	PRONOUNCED
aborigines, primitive inhabitants	ab-o-RIJ-i-neez
abstemious, sparing in diet	ab-STEE-mee-us
aggrandizement, enlargement in size or power	a-GRANN-diz-ment
bestial, brutal, inhuman	BESS-tchel, BEST-yal
congeries, collection of particles in a mass	kon-JIRR-eez, kon-JIRR-i-eez
Deity, the; God	DEE-i-tee (not DAY-i-tee)
demise, death	di-MYZ
demoniacal, possessed by an evil spirit	dee-mo-NY-a-kal
egregious, remarkably flagrant: *an egregious lie*	e-GREE-jus, e-GREE-ji-us
epitome, a summary	e-PITT-o-mee (not EPP-i-tohm)
harbinger, a forerunner	HAHR-bin-jer
heinous, hateful, odious	HAY-nus
inveigle, to win over by guile	in-VEE-g'l, in-VAY-g'l
lugubrious, ridiculously mournful	loo-GYOO-bri-us
malinger, to feign sickness to avoid work	ma-LING-ger
phlegmatic, not easily excited	flegg-MATT-ik
promulgate, to proclaim formally	pro-MULL-gayt
recluse, a person who lives in seclusion	re-KLOOSS, REKK-looss
spontaneity, action proceeding from an inner impulse	spon-ta-NEE-i-tee (not NAY-i-tee)
squalor, foulness	SKWOLL-or
unguent, a salve or ointment	UNG-gwent
zealot, one showing excess of zeal	ZELL-ot

Choice of Pronunciation

Sometimes persons dispute about the pronunciation of a word, not realizing that two (or even more) pronunciations of that word are equally acceptable. The unabridge dictionaries carry a special section devoted to such words.

Below is a list of fairly common words for which a choice of pronunciation is allowed. Of the pronunciations given, plan to use the one you hear most frequently among your friends or in your part of the country. Follow the same practice when you find two or more pronunciations given in a dictionary.

WORD	SAY EITHER	OR
abdomen	ABB-do-men	ab-DOH-men
adult	a-DULT	ADD-ult
advertisement	ad-VUR-tiss-ment	ad-ver-TYZ-ment
almond	AMM-ond	AH-mond
alternate, n., adj.	AWL-ter-nit AL-ter-nit	awl-TUR-nit al-TUR-nit
alternate, v.	AWL-ter-nayt	AL-ter-nayt
amenable	a-MEE-na-b'l	a-MEN-a-b'l
apparatus	app-a-RAY-tus	app-a-RATT-us
aspirant	a-SPYR-ant	ASS-pi-rant
banal	BAY-nal, BANN-al	ba-NAL, ba-NAHL
betroth	be-TROTH	be-TROHTH
betrothal	be-TROTH-al	be-TROH-thal
brusque	BRUSK	BRUUSK (as in *look*)
calliope (steam organ)	KAL-ee-ohp	ka-LY-o-pee
cerebral	SERR-e-bral	se-REE-bral
chastisement	TCHASS-tiz-ment	tchass-TYZ-ment
chauffeur	SHOW-fer	sho-FUR
coadjutor	koh-a-JOO-tor	ko-AJJ-u-tor
combatant	KOMM-ba-tant	kom-BATT-ant
conduit	KONN-dit	KONN-doo-it
contractor	KONN-trak-tor	kon-TRAK-tor
dais	DAY-iss	DAYSS
decadent	de-KAY-dent	DEKK-a-dent
defect	di-FEKT	DEE-fekt
detail, n. *but* detail, v.	di-TAYL *only* di-TAYL	DEE-tayl
diocesan	dy-OSS-e-san	dy-o-SEE-san
exquisite	EKS-kwizz-it	(for special emphasis eks-KWIZZ-it)
extant	EKS-tant	eks-TANT
extraordinary	ek-STRAWR-di-nerr-ee	eks-tra-AWR-di-nerr-ee
finance	fi-NANS	FY-nans
financier	finn-an-SEER	fy-nan-SEER
gala	GAY-la	GAL-a
gladiolus	gladd-i-OH-lus (the plant)	gla-DY-o-lus (the genus)
grovel	GRUVV-'l	GROVV-'l
harass	HAR-is (as in *cat*)	ha-RASS
hovel	HUVV-'l	HOVV-'l
illustrate	ILL-u-strayt	i-LUSS-trayt

WORD	SAY EITHER	OR
indissolubly	in-DISS-o-lyoo-blee	in-di-SOLL-yoo-blee
inquiry	in-KWYR-ee	IN-kwi-ree
isolate	Y-so-layt	ISS-o-layt
jocund	JOKK-und	JOH-kund
obligatory	o-BLIGG-a-toh-ree	OBB-li-ga-toh-ree
patronize	PAY-tro-nyz	PATT-ron-yz
penalize	PEE-na-lyz	PENN-a-lyz
persist	pur-SIST	pur-ZIST
pianist	pi-ANN-ist	PEE-a-nist
quinine	KWY-nyn	kwi-NEEN
ration	RASH-on	RAY-shon
reservoir	REZZ-er-vawr	REZZ-er-vwahr
resource	re-SOHRS	REE-sohrs
route	ROOT	ROWT (as in how)
sacrilegious	sak-ri-LIJJ-us	sakk-ri-LEE-jus
vaudeville	VOHD-vill	VAW-di-vill
version	VURR-zhon	VURR-shon

Note that *provost* and *oblique* are pronounced PROVV-ost and o-BLEEK in civilian life, proh-VOH and o-BLYK in military life. *Carbine* is pronounced both KAHR-byn and KAHR-been.

Words ending in *-ile* present no definite pattern with regard to pronunciation, some taking -ILL, some -YL (as in *file*), and some either -ILL or -YL.

A choice of either -ILL or -YL is allowed in: **infantile, juvenile, senile, versatile.**

-ILL is preferred by Americans in: **agile, docile, futile, hostile, textile,** and **virile** (VIRR-ill or VY-ril). Britishers use -YL for these words.

But **sterile** takes only -ILL, and **exile, gentile** and **profile** take only -YL.

Practice Exercise No. 84

This quiz is based on the preceding section, Helps Toward Better Pronunciation.

WORD	SHOULD ONE SAY	OR
1. *consummate,* adj.	kon-SUMM-it	KONN-su-mayt
2. *consummate,* verb	kon-SUMM-it	KONN-su-mayt
3. *advocate,* noun	ADD-vo-kayt	ADD-vo-kit
4. *advocate,* verb	ADD-vo-kit	ADD-vo-kayt
5. *epitome*	e-PITT-o-mee	EPP-i-tohm
6. *inveigle*	in-VEE-g'l	in-VAY-g'l
7. *zealot*	ZEE-lot	ZELL-ot
8. *extant*	EKS-tant	eks-TANT
9. *patronize*	PAY-tro-nyz	PATT-ro-nyz
10. *profile*	PROH-fyl	PROH-fill

FOREIGN WORDS AND PHRASES

Latin Words and Phrases

The following words and phrases taken from Latin are fairly often encountered in English. They are heard in business, law, logic, politics, the arts, and in conversation generally.

A brief definition accompanies each entry.

WORD AND MEANING	SAY
a fortiori; with the greater force, said of one conclusion as compared with another	AY fawr-shi-AW-ry
ad infinitum; without limit	ADD in-fi-NY-tum
ad libitum (ad lib); as one wishes	ADD LIBB-i-tum
alma mater; fostering mother; hence, one's school	AHL-ma MAH-ter, AL-ma MAY-ter
alumnus, /i, /a, /ae; graduate of a school	masc. a-LUMM-nus, pl. -ny; fem. -na, pl. -nee
anno Domini; in the year of the Christian era	ANN-oh DOMM-i-nee
a posteriori; known afterwards; hence, through experience	AY poss-tirr-i-OH-ree
a priori; known beforehand; hence, through reasoning	AY pri-OH-ry, pry-OH-ry; AH pri-OH-ree
bona fide; in good faith	BOH-na FY-de; as adj., BOH-na FYD, BONN-a
carpe diem; enjoy the day	KAHR-pe DY-em
corpus delicti; in a murder case, the actual death of the one alleged to have been murdered	KAWR-pus di-LIKK-ty
data; things given, esp. facts on which an inference is based	DAY-ta, DATT-a
de facto; actually, in fact	DEE FAKK-toh
de jure; by right or lawful title	DEE JOO-ree
dramatis personae; characters in a drama	DRAMM-a-tiss pur-SOH-nee
ex cathedra; by virtue of one's office	EKS ka-THEE-dra
ex officio; by virtue of an office	EKS o-FISH-i-oh
ex post facto; done afterwards but retroactive	EKS POHST FAKK-toh
extempore; without preparation	eks-TEMM-po-ree
finis; end	FY-niss
gratis; for nothing	GRAY-tiss, GRATT-iss

WORD AND MEANING	SAY
habeus corpus; a writ to bring a person before a court	HAY-be-us KAWR-pus
imprimatur; license to publish a book	imm-pri-MAY-tur, -pry—
in absentia; in absence	IN abb-SENN-shee-a
in extremis; near death	IN eks TREE-miss
in toto; entirely	IN TOH-toh
non sequitur; a conclusion which does not follow from the premises	NONN SEKK-wi-tur, NAHN-
obiter dictum, -a; incidental remark or observation	OBB-i-ter DIKK-tum
per diem; by the day	PUR DY-em
persona non grata; an unacceptable person	pur-SOH-na NONN (NAHN) GRAY-ta
prima facie; at first view	PRY-ma FAY-shi-ee, FAY-shi
pro rata; according to share	PROH RAY-ta, RAH-ta
pro tempore (pro tem); for the time being	PROH TEMM-po-ree
quasi; as if, seeming	KWAY-sy, KWAH-see
re; with reference to	REE
sine die; without naming a day to meet again	SY-ni DY-ee
status; state of a person or affairs	STAY-tus, STATT-us
status quo; the state existing	STAY-tus KWOH, STATT-us
stratum, -a; a layer or level	STRAY-tum, STRATT-um, plur. -ta
subpoena; a writ commanding appearance in court	su-PEE-na, sub-
ultimatum; a final proposition	ull-ti-MAY-tum
verbatim; word for word	vur-BAY-tum
via; by way of	VY-a, VEE-a
viva voce; orally	VY-va VOH-see
vox populi; voice of the people	VOKKS POPP-yoo-ly

French Words and Phrases

The French words and phrases in the lists below occur fairly frequently in English. They have been grouped in several categories, but of course they may be used in other fields.

When we say these words and phrases we usually tend only to approximate the French pronunciation, to give them a slightly French flavor, as it were. Sometimes we Anglicize them entirely, saying them as if they were native words.

When an N is italicized below as in *en* (AH*N*), it means that the preceding vowel is nasalized (with the soft palate dropped slightly and the tone allowed to resonate in the nose) while the N itself is silent.

French syllables are more evenly stressed than English syllables, with a slight stress on the last syllable of the word or phrase. This is frequently carried over into English, as in **à la carte** (ah la KAHRT).

Food and Restaurant Words

WORD AND MEANING	SAY
à la carte; dish by dish, with a stated price for each	ah la KAHRT
à la mode; 1. dessert served with ice cream, 2. stewed or braised with vegetables and served with gravy, 3. fashionable	ah la MOHD, AL a mohd
cuisine; style of cooking	kwe-ZEEN
entrée; 1. main course of a meal, 2. the dish before the main course, 3. right of entry	AHN-tray
filet mignon; round fillet of beef	fee-lay-mee-NYAWN, fe-LAY-MEEN-yonn
garçon; waiter, boy	gahr-SAWN
gourmand; a lover of good eating	GOOR-mand, goor-MAHN
gourmet; one who shows taste in appreciating good food	GOOR-may, goor-MAY
hors-d'oeuvre; appetizer	AWR DU(R)VR (like an UR without R)
menu; bill of fare	MENN-yoo, MAY-nyoo
pièce de résistance; main dish	PYESS de ray-zees-TAHNSS
table d'hôte; meal for which one pays a fixed price	TAH-b'l DOHT, TABB-'l

Military Words

WORD AND MEANING	SAY
aide de camp; officer-assistant to a general	AYD de KAMP, EDD-de-KAHN
camouflage; disguise of a camp, and so any disguise expedient	KAMM-o-flahzh (zh, like s in pleasure)
corps; body of persons under common direction	KOHR (not KAWRPSS) plur. KOHRZ

WORD AND MEANING	SAY	WORD AND MEANING	SAY
coup de grâce; a finishing stroke	KOO de GRAHSS	cortège; 1. procession, 2. train of attendants	kahr-TEZH, -TAYZH
hors de combat; disabled and so out of the combat	awr de kaw*n*-BA (part-way between *c*at and *c*alm)	crèche; representation of the figures at Bethlehem	KRESH, KRAYSH
		cul-de-sac; a blind alley or deadlock	KULL de sakk (or *u* as in p*u*ll)
		début; entrance on a career or into society	DAY-byoo, de-BYOO

Words from the Arts

WORD AND MEANING	SAY	WORD AND MEANING	SAY
bas-relief; sculpture in low relief	bah re-LEEF, BAH re-leef, BASS (as in *c*at)	débutante; one making a début	debb-yoo-TAHNT, DEBB-yoo-tant
		⎧ deshabille; loose or careless style	dezz-a-BEEL
		⎩ dishabille; of dress	diss-a-BEEL
baton; conductor's stick, staff of office	ba-TONN, BATT-on	élite; the choice part, as of a group	i-LEET, ay-LEET
belles-lettres; aesthetic, rather than informational, literature	bell LETT'r	enfant terrible; child whose remarks cause embarrassment	ahn-fah*n* te-REEB'l
connoisseur; one competent as a critic of art	konn-i-SUR	en route; on the way	ahn ROOT
façade; face of a building, front of anything	fa-SAHD	faux pas; false step, offense against social convention	foh PAH, plur. PAHZ
nom de plume; pen name	NOMM de ploom	gauche; awkward	GOHSH
protégé; one under protection of another	PROH-te-zhay	gendarme; policeman	ZHAHN-dahrm
		joie de vivre; keen enjoyment of life	zhwa de VEE'vr (*a* between *c*at and *c*alm)
tour de force; feat of strength or skill	toor de FAWRSS	loge; box in a theatre	LOHZH
		mal-de-mer; seasickness	mal de MERR
		qui vive, on the; on the alert	kee VEEV

Political Words and Phrases

WORD AND MEANING	SAY	WORD AND MEANING	SAY
bourgeois; middle class	boor-ZHWAH, BOOR-zhwah	sang-froid; coolness in any circumstance	sah*n* FRWA
		savoir faire; social ease and grace	SAVV-wahr FAYR
bourgeoisie; people of the middle class	boor-zhwah-ZEE		
cause célèbre; legal case of great interest	kohz se-LEBB'r	suite; 1. set, 2. retinue, 3. instrumental composition	SWEET
entente cordiale; cordial understanding between two governments	ahn-TAHNT kawr-DYAL	tête-à-tête; conversation for two alone	tett a TETT, tayt a TAYT
laissez faire; non-interference	LESS-ay FAYR	vis-a-vis; face to face	vee-za-VEE

Social and General Words

German Words and Phrases

A few German words have gained acceptance in English speech.

WORD AND MEANING	SAY	WORD AND MEANING	SAY
au revoir; goodby till we meet again	oh re-VWAHR	auf Wiedersehen; till we meet again	owff VEE-der-ZAYN
beau geste; ingratiating act or gesture	boh ZHEST	ersatz; substitute	err-ZAHTSS
bête noire; bugbear	bett NWAHR, bayt	Gesundheit; to your health	ge-ZUUNT-hyt (UU as in p*u*t)
billet doux; love letter	BILL-i-doo, BILL-ay, plur. dooz	Lebensraum; territory desired by a nation for expansion	LAY-benss-ROWM (OW as in h*ow*)
bon vivant; lover of good living	bawn vee-VAH*N*	leitmotif; theme associated with a person or idea	LYT-moh-teef
carte blanche; unconditional power	KAHRT BLAHNSH	Reichstag; Germ. legislative assembly	RYKS-tahg
château; 1. castle, 2. large country house	sha-TOH		

WORD AND MEANING	SAY
verboten; forbidden	fer-BOH-ten
wanderlust; strong impulse to wander	WONN-der-lust, VAHN-der-lust
Weltanschauung; world-view	VELT AHN-show-ung (ow as in h*ow*)
Weltschmerz; sadness from a pessimistic world-view	VELT-shmerrts
Zeitgeist; spirit of the times	TSYT-gyst

Italian Words

A great many Italian words are used by musicians and artists. Below are a few words which present special pronunciation problems:

WORD AND MEANING	SAY
adagio; slowly	a-DAH-joh, -zhoh (*zh* like *s* in pleasure)
concerto; composition for one or several instruments and orchestra	kon-TCHERR-toh
crescendo; gradual increase in volume	kre-SHENN-doh
Fascisti; Ital. anti-socialism, anti-democracy followers of Mussolini	fa-SHISS-tee, -SHEESS-
piazza; veranda	pi-AZZ-a, Brit. pi-ATT-sa
pizzicato; plucked	pitt-si-KAH-toh
vivace; lively	vee-VAH-tchee

Practice Exercise No. 85

This quiz is based on the words in the preceding section, Foreign Words and Phrases.

WORD	SHOULD ONE SAY	OR
1. *finis*	FINN-is	FY-niss
2. *per diem*	pur DEE-em	pur DY-em
3. *ultimatum*	ull-ti-MATT-um	ull-ti-MAY-tum
4. *coup de grace*	KOO de GRAHSS	KOO de GRAYSS
5. *au revoir*	oh re-VWAHR	oh re-VAWR
6. *ersatz*	ERR-zahtss	err-ZAHTSS
7. *loge*	LOHZH	LOHJ
8. *pizzicato*	pitt-si-KAH-toh	pizz-i-KAH-toh
9. *baton*	ba-TONN	BATT-on
10. *gratis*	GRAY-tiss	GRATT-iss

NAMES OF PERSONS AND PLACES

Names of Persons

The names of persons are often a troublesome problem in pronunciation. For family names, the family itself decides how its name is to be pronounced.

The following lists contain examples of choices in the pronunciation of names, or of common mispronunciations.

Family Names

NAME	USUALLY PRONOUNCED
Beauchamp	BEE-tcham (not BOH-shahm)
Knopf	KNOPPF (not NOPPF)
MacLeod	ma-KLOWD (as in h*ow*)
McLean	ma-KLAYN (not mak-LEEN)
Monroe	munn-ROH (not MONN-roh)
Pierce	PIRRSS or PURRSS
Roosevelt	ROHZ-e-velt, or ROHZ-velt (not ROOZ-e-velt)
Van Wyck	vann WYK (not vann WIKK)
Xavier	ZAY-vi-er (not ekk-ZAY-vi-er)

Nationalities

Arab	AR-ab (not AY-rab)
Celtic	SELL-tik or KELL-tik
Czech	TCHEKK
Maori	MAH-o-ree, MOW-ree (ow as in h*ow*) MAH-ree
Italian	i-TAL-yan (not Y-TAL-yan)

Note also:

Magi	MAY-jy (not MAGG-y)

Composers

Bartok	BAHR-tokk, -tohk
Beethoven	BAY-toh-ven
Berlioz	BERR-li-ohz
Chopin	SHOH-pann, shoh-PA*NN*
Debussy	de-BYOO-see, or Fr. de-bu-SEE (u as a lip-rounded EE)
de Falla	de FAHL-ya
Dvorak	DVAWR-zhakk, -zhahk
Haydn	HY-d'n
Purcell	PUR-sel (not pur-SELL)
Saint-Saëns	san SAH*NS*
Shostakovitch	shoss-tah-KOH-vitch
Villa-Lobos	VEE-lah LOW-bawss
Wagner	VAHG-ner

Authors

Balzac	BAL-zakk or BAWL-zakk
Boccaccio	boh-KAH-tchi-o
Cellini	tche-LEE-nee
Cervantes	ser-VANN-teez, ser-VAHN-tayss
Dostoevsky	dawss-to-YEFF-skee
Dumas	DYOO-mah, DOO-mah

NAME	USUALLY PRONOUNCED
Goethe	GOE-tuh (for OE, lips rounded as for OH, while trying to say AY), GU(R)-tuh
Maeterlinck	MAY-ter-lingk
Maugham	MAWM
Pepys	PEEPS, PEPS, PEP-iss
Yeats	YAYTS

Characters

Adonis	a-DOH-niss, a-DONN-iss
Aeschylus	ESS-ki-lus, Brit. EES-
Don Juan	donn JOO-an, dahn; don HWAHN
Don Quixote	donn KWIKK-sit, don kee-HO-tay
Odysseus	oh-DISS-yoos, oh-DISS-i-us
Oedipus	EDD-i-pus, EE-di-pus

American Place Names

The pronunciation of American place names is usually determined by the locality itself. Interesting differences occur, and the pronunciations of one part of the country often surprises those living elsewhere. The following list contains examples of some of the more outstanding pronunciations, and also compares American with British examples. (In the *Foreign Place Names* list, compare the foreign and native pronunciations for *Cairo, Delhi, Lima.*)

NAME	SAY
Albuquerque	AL-bu-kurr-kee
Arkansas (the state)	AHR-kan-saw
Arkansas River	ahr-KANN-zas
Boise	BOY-zee, BOY-see
Butte	BYOOT
Cheyenne	shy-ENN
Chicago	shi-KAW-goh, -KAH- (not tchi-KAH-goh)
Chisholm	TCHIZZ-um
Des Moines	de MOYN, de MOYNZ
Derby	DUR-bee
(compare with *British*)	DAHR-bee
Greenwich Village, N.Y.	GRENN-itch
(compare with *Greenwich, Eng.*)	GRIN-ij, GRENN-itch
Houston, Tex.	HYOO-ston
Houston St., N.Y.C.	HOW-ston
Iowa	Y-o-way (locally); Y-o-wa
Los Angeles	loss ANG-ge-les, ANN-je-les, -leez
Missouri	mi-ZOOR-i, -ee, -a

NAME	SAY
Montana	monn-TANN-a, -TAH-na
St. Louis	saynt LOO-iss, LOO-ee
Schuyler	SKY-ler
Schuylkill	SKOOL-kill
Spokane	spo-KANN
Spuyten Duyvil	SPY-ten DY-vil
Terre Haute	TERR-e HOHT
Thames, U.S.	THAYMZ, TAYMZ, TEMMZ
(compare with *British*)	TEMMZ

Foreign Place Names

Foreign place names fall into two categories with regard to their pronunciation in English:

The names of the larger, better-known cities and towns are completely Anglicized. We say mi-LANN or MILL-an for Milan, as if it were a native word, and with no thought of the fact that Italians call the place mee-LAH-noh.

For the less well-known places, we tend to approximate the foreign pronunciation, partially Anglicizing it, and sometimes keeping only one element of the original pronunciation. *Nice* is said NEESS.

Choices are possible for fairly well-known places. Difficulties in pronunciation occur when, for some reason, places formerly obscure suddenly become well-known. The following list contains some interesting examples of the pronunciation of foreign place names.

NOTE: You may use the foreign pronunciation of a place name if you wish, but do so only if your command of the foreign language is good and if you find that your friends and acquaintances do not raise their eyebrows at such attempts. Of course, if you are going abroad, learn the foreign pronunciation of place names while you are studying the language.

NAME	SAY
Aix-la-Chapelle	AYKSS lah-shah-PELL, EKKS
Aachen (Germ. name of above)	AH-ken
Bayreuth	BY-royt
Buenos Aires	BWAY-nos Y-rizz, BOH-nos AYR-eez
Caen (compare with *Cannes*)	KAH*N* (nasalized AH)
Cairo, Egypt	KY-roh
(compare with *Cairo, Ill.*)	KAYR-oh

NAME	SAY
Calais	KAL-ay, KAL-is, ka-LAY
Cannes	KANN, KANNZ
Caribbean	kar-ii-BEE-an, ka-RIB-ee-an
Delhi, India	DELL-ee
(compare with *Delhi, U.S.*)	DELL-hy
Guadalajara	gwah-dah-lah-HAH-rah
Himalaya	he-MAHL-ya, him-a-LAY-a
Hiroshima	hir-o-SHEE-ma
Kiev	KEE-eff
Lima, Peru	LEE-ma
(compare with *Lima, Ohio*)	LY-ma
Lourdes	LOORD
Lyons	LY-onz, lee-AWN
Madras	ma-DRASS, ma-DRAHSS
Marseilles	mahr-SAY, older, -SAYLZ
Milan	mi-LANN, MILL-an
Monte Video	MONN-te vi-DAH-oh, MONN-te VIDD-i-oh
Moscow	MOSS-kow, MOSS-koh
Nice	NEESS
Peiping	BAY-PING, formerly PEE-PING
Prague	PRAHG, older, PRAYG
Rheims	REEMZ
Rio de Janeiro	REE-oh de zha-NAYR-oh
Transvaal	trans-VAHL, tranz-
Trieste	tre-EST
Versailles	vur-SAYLZ, vayr-SY
Ypres	EE-pr

Practice Exercise No. 86

This quiz is based on the preceding section, Names of Persons and Places.

	WORD	SHOULD ONE SAY	OR
1.	*Van Wyck*	vann WYK	vann-WIKK
2.	*Dvorak*	DVAWR-zhakk	DVAWR-zhahk
3.	*Boccaccio*	boh-KAH-tchi-o	boh-KASS-i-o
4.	*Oedipus*	EDD-i-pus	EE-di-pus
5.	*Spokane*	spo-KAYN	spo-KANN
6.	*Bayreuth*	BAY-rooth	BY-royt
7.	*Ypres*	EE-pr	Y-pres
8.	*Milan*	MILL-an	mi-LANN
9.	*Rheims*	REEMZ	RAMMZ
10.	*Cairo, Egypt*	KY-roh	KAYR-oh
11.	*Cairo, Ill.*	KY-roh	KAYR-oh

Practice Exercise No. 87

This is a general quiz, based on the preceding sections and also containing some words not considered there.

	WORD	SHOULD ONE SAY	OR
1.	*chiropodist*	ki-ROPP-o-dist	tchi-ROPP-o-dist
2.	*chaise*	SHAYZ, SHEZZ	TCHAYZ
3.	*lamentable*	LAMM-en-ta-b'l	la-MENT-a-b'l
4.	*aye,* meaning yes	Y	AY
5.	*ay,* meaning ever	Y	AY
6.	*cerebral*	SERR-e-bral	se-REE-bral
7.	*re*	RAY	REE
8.	*Magi*	MAGG-y	MAY-jy
9.	*Cannes*	KANN	KANNZ
10.	*bestial*	BESS-tchel	BEEST-yal
11.	*vagary*	VAYG-a-ree	va-GAYR-ee

CHAPTER IX

ARTICULATION

PRELIMINARY EXPLANATIONS

Articulation is the muscular process by means of which we modify voice or breath with tongue, teeth, lips, and other speech organs, to produce speech sounds.

Good articulation is important, first of all, because it enables you to speak with the least muscular effort. The people who are most skilled in any physical activity are those who have learned to use their muscles in so relaxed and efficient a manner that they do not tire quickly. If talking soon fatigues you physically, the likelihood is that you are not using your speech muscles efficiently. And the resulting drain on your energies impairs your total speech effectiveness.

Secondly, good articulation helps you to speak more distinctly. Better muscular skill in speaking means not only less exertion, but greater audibility. By producing the sounds of speech more accurately, it enables your listeners to hear you clearly even though you speak in quiet tones.

Thirdly, better articulation helps you to focus attention on your message. A manner of speaking which calls attention to itself is a serious obstacle to your speaking purpose. Sound-peculiarities like whistling S's will so distract some listeners that they do not get a word of what is being said. Good articulation lets your listeners concentrate on the substance of your speech.

Lastly, poor articulation may be the cause of other speech trouble. Artificial pronunciations and shrill or husky voice qualities are often due to misguided efforts to make poor articulation more audible. In such cases, better articulation may be an important key to the improvement of other aspects of your speech personality.

How Articulation Can Be Improved

The factors influencing our articulation are much the same as those which determine the kind of voice we have (discussed in *Chapter VII*). Most important are:

The physical make-up of our speech organs such as the tongue, teeth, and lips.

The social influence of those with whom we speak.

The speech habits we have formed earlier in life.

More can usually be done about the physical factors which affect articulation than about those which affect voice quality. An orthodontist can often straighten out tooth irregularities which interfere with such sounds as F, V, TH, S, and Z. Minor surgery can take care of the "tongue-tied" condition which distorts sounds like T, D, L, and R.

The services of specialists are of course necessary, but it is best to consult a general medical practitioner first. The same holds true of any other physiological impediment which seems to prevent you from forming speech sounds as described in this chapter.

Most of our articulation difficulties, however, are due to *muscular habits* formed under the *social influence* of those with whom we speak. Early in life we may have unconsciously imitated someone who mumbled his words, who spoke out of the corner of his mouth, who lisped, or who had a foreign accent.

More likely still, we may have been influenced by examples which were not so much harmful to our speech as un-helpful to it. A large number of people who are quite meticulous about their grooming and dress are astonishingly unaware that the frayed edges of their articulation "show" every time they talk. They may spend an hour before a mirror each morning deciding which tie or dress to wear. But they never give a moment's thought to the hand-me-down speech pattern which they keep "making-do" even though it never "does a thing for them."

The main tendency against which we have to work is just plain slovenliness in articulation.

And that takes more effort than is commonly realized.

To correct a pronunciation we need only to find out what the dictionary says about it. But to improve our articulation it is not enough merely to learn *what* should be done. We must also learn *how* to do it.

The difficulty is that our articulation is a set of habits so long established that we never give them conscious thought. Such habits can be changed only by *regular practice* over a considerable period of time.

Some people think they will improve their articulation merely by "taking more care when speaking." But that is as futile as it is absurd. To think about the movements of one's tongue while discussing the issues of the day or the affairs of one's friends, does not make for better speech any more than it makes for good conversation or naturalness of conduct.

The only effective care you can take is to take care to practice. The most important part of the rest of this chapter are the *exercises*. The *explanations* are mainly to help you practice these exercises in such a manner as to get the best result for the time spent.

There is little value in going through the motions of the drills. A ritualistic muttering of certain words to yourself may testify to your good intentions, but is not likely to do your articulation any good.

Notice that you are never advised in the exercises merely to say something "carefully." You are always given *specific suggestions as to what to be careful about in each particular case*. Even the order of the drills is based upon principles of effective practice. So it is important, as you work through them, to make sure you do your utmost to apply the principles explained.

Where wide opening of the mouth, or vigorous lip movement is recommended, do not be afraid to "make faces." That will be only temporary. A vigorous muscular approach is necessary from the beginning in order better to articulate the differences between similar speech sounds. It will also help to overcome any tendency toward the more common "frozen lip" appearance of many speakers. Once you are beyond the initial stages, you will find your facial appearance becoming one of natural expressiveness, with neither distortion nor the more common "dead pan" effect.

Social clowns may poke fun at an earnest individual repeating "How now brown cow" before a mirror. They may also jeer at an athlete jogging around a track, stopwatch in hand. But these are the training methods which produce results. More truly ludicrous is an articulation pattern which is muffled and blurred when it could be sharp and clear.

Let both the spirit and method of your articulation practice be athletic. Then, when you are later in a serious speaking situation, better muscular habits will help you. Your articulation will take care of itself, leaving you free to concentrate on the real issues of the occasion.

The Organs of Speech

It will be helpful in understanding many of the explanations in this chapter to study first the accompanying diagram of the speech tract.

Note that the **blade** of the **tongue** is the part just behind the **tip**.

The **palate** (PAL-et) is divided into two main parts—the **hard palate** which is forward toward the teeth, and the **soft palate** which is further back. By raising the tip of the tongue gradually up and back from the upper front teeth, you can feel that the roof of the mouth is hard, up to a point about midway, and softer from there back.

The **gum ridge**—also called the **alveolar** (al-VEE-o-lar) **ridge**—is that part of the hard palate which is about one quarter of an inch behind the upper front teeth. Hardly used at all for the articulation of many languages, it is the most important single reference point for the articulation of English.

The **uvula** (YOO-vyoo-la) may be seen in a mirror if you open your mouth toward a source of light. It is a small finger-like projection down from the center at the back of the mouth. Important in many languages for the articulation of the *R* sound, its use is to be wholly avoided in English.

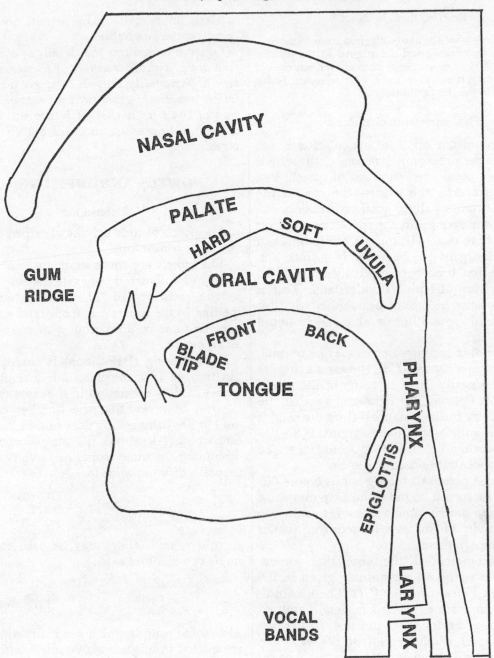

Fig. 5.
Diagram of the Speech Tract

Practice Exercise No. 88

Sketch and label the above diagram from memory. Check your work against the original in the text.

Prepare a clear correct copy on a convenient card or sheet and keep it as a place marker for reference during your work in the rest of this chapter.

The Importance of Listening

One important organ of articulation is not shown on the preceding diagram. Ordinarily it is not even considered an organ of speech. Yet, in some respects, this organ—the ear—is the most important of all for good articulation.

Have you ever heard the speech of a person who was born deaf? His tongue, teeth, lips, and other such organs may be perfectly normal. Yet, unless he has been very carefully trained, his speech is very difficult to understand. This is simply because he cannot hear either what his speech should sound like or what it does sound like.

Though our auditory nerves may be normal, all of us are partly "deaf" to the extent that we do not ordinarily listen to many of the things we are able to hear. The ticking of a watch, the hum of traffic in the distance—these are sounds which our minds habitually ignore. If we listened to them all the time we should never be able to concentrate on anything else.

But **if our present listening habits ignore differences in speech sounds, the first and most basic step in speech improvement is to cultivate the sensitivity of our ears in detecting shades of difference in them.**

It is recommended, therefore, that you review the exercises on ear-training given in the chapter on *Voice* (*Chapter VII*). Then, as individual sounds are explained in detail, and exercises are given for their practice, in the rest of this chapter, listen carefully to the way these sounds are articulated by others—your friends, people at work, speakers on radio and television programs.

Note how each of these sounds is articulated by persons whom you otherwise consider to be neat, pleasant, competent, well educated. Note also how the same sounds are articulated by persons whom you otherwise consider to be careless, unpleasant, incompetent, poorly educated, coarse, laughable.

Observe how often *the details of speech pattern are just another aspect of the same general type of personality*. But also observe how *articulation sometimes gives such a mistaken impression of the person that, if improved, it would allow him to present his other qualities to better advantage*.

VOWELS AND DIPHTHONGS

Definitions

All speech sounds may be classified as either **vowels** or **consonants.**

The **vowels** are those sounds which are relatively unobstructed in articulation by the tongue, teeth or lips. They are represented in spelling by the letters *a, e, i, o, u,* and sometimes *y,* or by some combination of these such as *ie, ei, ai, ou,* etc.

A **diphthong** (DIF-thong) is simply a combination of two vowel sounds articulated together in close succession in the same syllable.

NOTE, however, that the number of letters used in English spelling does not, in itself, indicate whether a sound is a simple vowel or a diphthong. In some words *two letters* are used to spell a *diphthong,* as in:

house	HOWSS
raise	RAYZ
point	POYNT

In others, *two letters* may be used to spell a *single vowel* sound as in:

said	SED
tough	TUF
sieve	SIV

Also, some sounds which are really *diphthongs* are spelled in English with a *single letter,* as in:

late	LAYT
go	GOH
I	Y = AH plus EE

(For an explanation of how pronunciations such as the above are to be read, see the general explanation at the beginning of the preceding chapter.)

Practice Exercise No. 89

Which of the following words contain single vowel sounds, and which contain diphthongs?

1. do	8. point
2. day	9. raise
3. dog	10. I
4. go	11. said
5. house	12. sieve
6. late	13. seek
7. lease	14. poet

The Special Role of Vowels in Speech

Although there are only five vowel letters in our alphabet, most Americans use at least fifteen different vowel *sounds* in their speech. And a large number of the words we most commonly use differ from each other in sound only by relatively small shades of distinction in this wide range of possible vowels.

Consider, for example, how many different words can be formed by putting different single vowels or diphthongs between the first two consonants of the alphabet, B and D. Some are:

bead	bad	buoyed	beard
bid	bide	bawd	bared
bayed	bud	bowed	bard
bed	bode	booed	bird

(NOTE: The *r* in a few of these words is, of course, optional as to pronunciation, and is generally left out in the Eastern and Southern parts of the United States.)

Here are sixteen different words all beginning with the same split-second explosive sound, *B*, and ending with the similar explosive sound, *D*. They are distinguishable by the ear only through a nuance of intervening vowel.

Practice Exercise No. 90

What similar lists of different words can you form simply by placing different vowels or diphthongs between the following other pairs of consonant sounds?

(a) *K* and *D*	(c) *M* and *N*
(b) *K* and *T*	(d) *T* and *N*

(NOTE that we refer here only to *sounds*, and *not* to the *letters of ordinary spelling* which sometimes have nothing to do with sounds. When we refer to words beginning with the sound *K*, we do not mean such words as "know" or "knight" even though their spelling begins with the alphabet letter, "k." But we do mean such words as "car" or "queen" even though there is no letter, "k," in their ordinary spelling.)

Vowel Production

It follows from the foregoing that, in order to speak distinctly, we must fully articulate all the many subtle nuances of difference among the vowel sounds.

Since a vowel is the physical result of modifying the basic sound of the voice by a particular shape in the opening of the mouth, *the difference between any two vowels is due to differences in the positions of the jaw, tongue, and lips.*

The **jaw** may be held relatively far *down* with the **mouth** more *open,* or relatively far *up* with the mouth more *closed.*

The arch of the **tongue** may be held in positions relatively far *front* or *back, high* or *low,* in the mouth cavity.

The **lips** may be held so as to form a *larger* or a *smaller* **opening** with different shaped **contours** and different degrees of *protrusion* or *retraction.*

How all these muscular adjustments are variously combined can be seen most clearly in the case of those sounds which require them in the most extreme degree.

The Extreme Vowels

Consider for a moment the vowels in the following four *B-D* words taken from the list above:

bead (B*EE*D)	booed (B*OO*D)
bad (B*A*D)	bawd (B*AW*D)

Notice that in order to enunciate the *EE* sound in *bead* (BEED) very distinctly, you tend to:

a. Drop the *jaw* so that the mouth is open

b. Arch the *front of the tongue to* a position *high* and *forward* in the mouth cavity, with the sides of the tongue touching the teeth or gums

c. Pull back the *lips* to a somewhat *retracted* position

For good clear enunciation of the *A* sound in *bad,* you tend to:

a. *Drop* the *jaw* much further so that the *mouth* is *wide open*

b. *Flatten* the arch of the *tongue* so that it is *low* and *forward* in the mouth cavity

c. Again pull the *lips* back to a somewhat *retracted* position close to the teeth

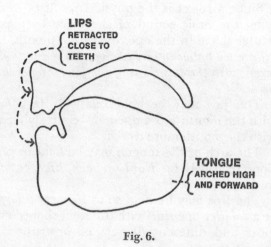

Fig. 6.

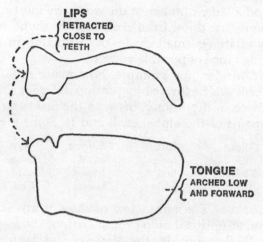

Fig. 8.

d. *Open* the lips to a *large circular contour.*

d. Broaden the *opening* of the lips to a *flat oval-shaped contour.*

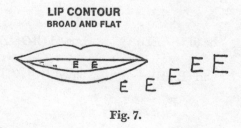

Fig. 7.

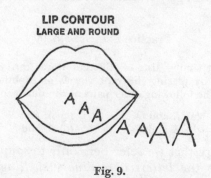

Fig. 9.

For the *AA* sound in *baad,* you tend to:

a. *Drop* the *jaw* way down so that the mouth is again *wide open*

b. *Flatten* the *tongue* so that its arch is *low* and *back* in the mouth cavity

c. *Protrude* the *lips* to a position somewhat forward from the teeth

For good clear enunciation of the *OO* sound in *booed,* finally, you tend to:

a. *Drop* the *jaw* somewhat less, as for *EE*

b. *Arch* the *back of the tongue* to a position *high* and *back* in the mouth cavity

c. Again *protrude* the *lips* to a position somewhat *forward* from the teeth

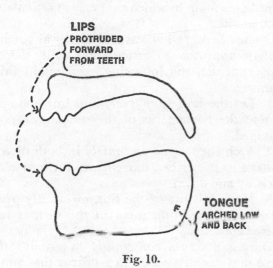

Fig. 10.

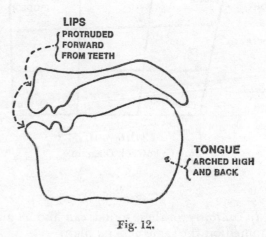

Fig. 12.

d. Narrow the *opening* of the *lips* to a *tall oval-shaped contour.*

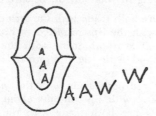

Fig. 11.

d. Round the *lips* to a *small circular contour.*

Fig. 13.

Consider now the following diagram (fig. 14) of possible placements of the arch of the tongue in the mouth. The divisions, *front, center,* and *back,* indicate how far forward or back in the mouth the tongue is arched. The divisions, *high, mid,* and *low,* indicate whether the tongue is arched very high with a relatively small jaw opening, moderately high with a medium jaw opening, or is allowed to drop very low with a wide jaw opening.

The four sounds we have just described are located at *the four extreme corners.*

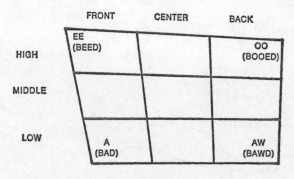

Fig. 14.
Tongue Position Diagram

Lip contours for these sounds can also be diagrammed on the same general plan:

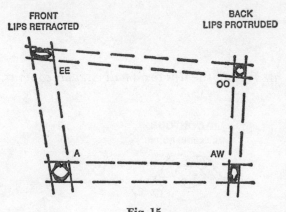

Fig. 15.
Lip Contour Diagram

Practice Exercise No. 91

Sketch the above *Tongue Position Diagram* and *Lip Contour Diagram* from memory.

Check your work against the originals in the text.

Prepare clear corrected copies to add to your placemarker for convenient reference during your work in the rest of this chapter.

Although everyone *tends* to make the above-described muscular adjustments in forming these vowels, many people do so only in a cramped, half-hearted way. With their jaw muscles too tense, their mouths too closed, or their lips held too rigid, they literally do not allow themselves room in which properly to articulate such sounds.

Remembering what was said earlier about an athletic approach to articulation drill, therefore, approach the following exercises in this manner:

1. Let the jaw drop *freely* and low enough so that the movements of the tongue are not cramped.

2. Arch the tongue *accurately* in both directions of its prescribed movements, forward and back, up and down.

3. Make full use of the lips, *vigorously* protruding or retracting them in the various required contours.

During practice, *consciously exaggerate* all these movements. Watch in a mirror that your mouth is really open wide enough, that your lips are really moving as you intend them to. The more accurately and energetically you go about it, the clearer your resulting articulation will be.

Practice Exercise No. 92

In the manner described in the text, practice making each vowel sound at the four corners of the above diagrams. Watching in your mirror, be sure that:

EE and *A* are both made with the arch of the tongue forward and with the lips retracted in broad contours.

AW and *OO* are both made with the arch of the tongue back and with the lips protruded in narrow contours.

A and *AW* are both made with the jaw down, the tongue low, and with lip contours about equally tall.

EE and *OO* are both made with the arch of the tongue high, and with lip contours about equally short in the vertical direction.

A and *OO* both have rounded lip contours.
EE and *AW* both have elongated lip contours.

Articulate the same four sounds, one after the other, in different sequences, prolonging each several seconds.

EXAMPLES

EE...A...AW...OO...
EE...OO...AW...A...
EE...A...EE...AW...EE...OO...
AA...EE...A...OO...A...AW..., etc.

With similar attention to the clear articulation of the vowels, practice each of the following columns of words separately several times:

(1) EE	(5) A	(9) AW	(12) OO
bead	bad	bawd	booed
heed	had	hawed	who'd
heel	Hal	hawl	who'll
heat	hat	haughty	hoot
Keats	cat	caught	coot
mead	mad	Maude	mood
geese	gas	Goss	goose
lead	lad	laud	looed
she	shall	shawl	shoe
deed	dad	Daw	do

With the same precautions, work back and forth across the lines in the above columns. Vary the sequence, prolonging each sound for several seconds.

The Front Vowels

Again from our original list of *B-D* words, consider now the following:

(1) *bead* (B*EE*D)

(2) *bid* (B*I*D)

(3) *bayed* (B*AY*D)

(4) *bed* (B*E*D)

(5) *bad* (B*A*D)

With the words so arranged, their vowels are approximately in the same relative places as the corresponding tongue positions required to articulate them. On the front part of the preceding *Tongue Position Diagram* for vowels, they would be placed as follows (fig. 16):

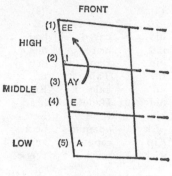

Fig. 16.

Since *AY* is a diphthong, only the first part of it is in the position indicated above. Its second part is usually somewhere between *I* and *EE*, and for its articulation the arch of the tongue moves as is shown approximately by the arrow.

The most important thing to note in the above diagram, however, is that *there are five distinct vowels to be articulated with the tongue at almost the same distance forward in the mouth.* The main difference in the production of all these sounds is in the dropping of the jaw, the height of the tongue positions, and the contours of the lips.

Obviously, if the jaw is held tight, the mouth nearly closed, and the lips rigid, all these sounds will be so "jammed down" upon each other that their differences will be difficult to hear distinctly.

Practice Exercise No. 93

With the same precautions as in the preceding exercise on the corner vowels, practice positioning each of the above front vowels. Using your mirror, see that your mouth opens successively wider as you work from (1) *EE*, through (2) *I*, (3) *AY*, and (4) *E*, to (5) *A*. Watch also that the contour of your lips begins broad for (1) *EE* and successively opens for each intermediate sound until it reaches a full rounded circle for (5) *A*.

Articulate all five sounds in varying sequences, prolonging each several seconds as in the preceding exercise, for *EE, A, AW* and *OO*.

Practice each of the following columns of words separately for distinct articulation of the vowels:

(1) EE	(2) I	(3) AY	(4) E	(5) A
bead	bid	bayed	bed	bad
meet	mit	mate	met	mat
dean	din	Dane	den	Dan
teen	tin	Taine	ten	tan
keel	kill	kale	Kell	Cal
heed	hid	Hade	head	had
keet	kit	Kate	Kett	cat
peek	pick	opaque	peck	pack
keep	Kip	cape	kept	cap
week	wick	wake	Weck	whack

Work back and forth across the lines of the above columns, emphasizing articulation of the differences between the vowels.

The Low Vowels

Also from the original list of *B-D* words, consider next:

		U (7) bud		**AW** (9) bawd
A (5) bad	**Y** (6) bide		**AH** (8) bard	

Once more, with the words so arranged, their vowels are approximately in the same relative places as the corresponding tongue positions required to articulate them. On the lower part of the *Tongue Position Diagram for Vowels,* they would fill in as follows (fig. 17):

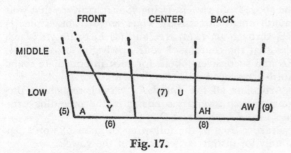

Fig. 17.

As in the preceding case of *AY*, only the first part of the *Y* sound is strictly in the position indicated above. The second part of this diphthong is in the area of *EE* or *I*, and for its articulation the tongue moves as shown by the arrow.

The most important thing to note here, however, is that *there are five different vowels to be articulated with the jaw down and the tongue arched at almost the same distance from the roof of the mouth.* The principal difference in the formation of these sounds is in the degree to which the tongue is pushed forward or pulled back, and in the corresponding contours of the lips.

Practice Exercise No. 94

Apply the routines of the first two parts of the preceding exercise to the low vowel sequence (5), *A,* through to (9), *AW.* Watch in your mirror that the lips gradually narrow their contour and protrude, in the movement from *A* to *AW,* and that the jaw remains down and relaxed for all of them.

As in the third part of the preceding exercise, practice the following, up and down the columns, and back and forth across the lines, emphasizing distinct articulation of the vowels.

(5) A	(6) I	(7) U	(8) AH	(9) AW
bad	bide	bud	bard	bawd
cat	kite	cut	cot	caught
tack	tike	tuck	tock	talk
Dan	dine	done	Don	dawn
hack	hike	Huck	hock	hawk
lack	like	luck	lock	law
gal	guile	gull	golly	gall
bat	bite	but	Bott	bought
sad	side	sud	sod	sawed
sat	site	Sutter	sot	sought

The Back Vowels

Again from the list of *B-D* words, plus the additional word "wood," consider the following:

(12) *booed (OO)*

(11) *wood (UU)*

(10) *bode (OH)*

(9) *bawd (AW)*

(8) *bard (AH)*

The arrangement is again one in which the vowels are approximately in the same relative places as the corresponding tongue positions required to form the sounds. At the back of the *Tongue Position Diagram for Vowels,* they would be placed as follows (fig. 18):

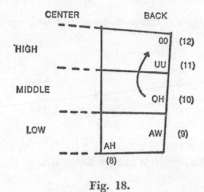

Fig. 18.

As in the preceding cases of *AY* and *Y,* only the first part of the diphthong *OU* is in the indicated position, the second being in the area to which the arrow points.

Note, however, that once again *there are five distinct vowels to be articulated with the tongue at almost the same distance from the front of the mouth.* As in the case of the front vowels, the main differences in the production of these sounds are in the dropping of the jaw, the height of the tongue positions, and the corresponding contours of the lips.

Once more your practice must emphasize the successively wider openings of the mouth from top to bottom of the chart, and the corresponding protruded formations of the lip contours.

Practice Exercise No. 95

Apply the routines of the preceding exercises to the back vowels and to the following columns:

(8) AH	(9) AW	(10) OH	(11) UU	(12) OO
bard	bawd	bode	wood	booed
hod	hawed	hoed	hood	who'd
tock	talk	toe	took	too
bock	balk	beau	book	boo
lock	law	low	look	Lou
shock	Shaw	show	shook	shoe
hock	hawk	hoe	hook	who
cod	cawed	code	could	cooed
cock	caulk	Coke	cook	coo
shod	pshaw	showed	should	shoo

The Central Vowels

Centered as to tongue position in the mouth are the vowels in the following words:

(13) bird (*UR*)

(14) *ago* (*a*)

(7) bud (*U*)

These are their relative places in the *Tongue Position Diagram* for the vowels (fig. 19):

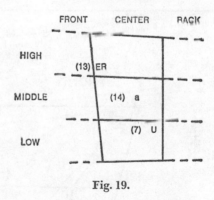

Fig. 19.

Possibly because of its less extreme tongue position, the vowel *UR* (13), is sometimes confused with *U* (7), as when *first* becomes FUSST. Thus we get the inelegant word, "bust," or "busted," from "burst."

The vowel, *UR,* is more commonly confused, however, with the diphthong *OY* which consists of *AW* followed by *I* or *EE.* Note that the movement of the tongue in saying *OY* must be from a position below and behind that of *UR* for *AW,* to one above and in front of it for *EE.*

The remaining vowel, a, is called the neutral vowel because, while articulating it, the tongue remains in a relaxed neutral position—neither high nor low, front nor back. It is used only in unaccented syllables and unstressed words (see *Over-Articulation,*

Practice Exercise No. 96

Pushing the tongue deliberately up and forward for *UR* and pulling it deliberately back and down for *U*, practice the following, reversing order, etc., with strong vowel distinctions:

(13)	(7)	(13)	(7)
UR	**U**	**U**	**UR**
bird	bud	turn	ton
curd	cud	burn	bun
third	thud	fern	fun
lurk	luck	burst	bust
Turk	tuck	curl	cull

Holding the tongue steadily as in the previous drill of this exercise for *UR,* and emphasizing the separate components *AW* and *EE* in the diphthong *OY,* practice, varying the order, etc.:

(13)	(15)	(13)	(15)
UR	**OY**	**UR**	**OY**
earl	oil	Berle	Boyle
bird	buoyed	hurl	Hoyle
curl	coil	learn	loin
furl	foil	Kern	coin
first	foist	adjourn	adjoin

Combine the two preceding drills with variations of:

(7)	(13)	(15)
U	**UR**	**OY**
cull	curl	coil
bud	bird	buoyed
tuck	Turk	toy
fun	fern	Foy
cud	curd	coy, etc.

All the vowel groups we have studied may be put together in a single diagram.

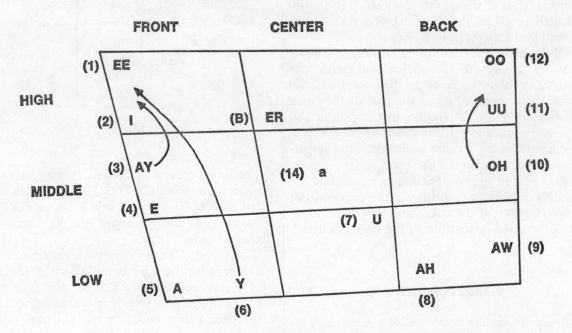

Fig. 20.

As before, arrows point to the second part of sounds which are usually diphthongized (fig. 20).

NOTE: There is still another vowel which could be placed in the lower right-hand corner of figure 20, but the sound does not occur at all in most American speech. In British English and in the speech of some parts of the northeastern United States, it is sometimes used for the *AH* or *AW* of General American English. When used, an expression like "The pot is not hot (the PAHT is NAHT HAHT)" sounds to the average American's ears more like "The PAWT is NAWT HAWT." Likewise, "The dog is in the office (the DAWG is in the AW-fice)" sounds more like "the DAHG is in the AH-fice." But this vowel is actually placed between *AH* and *AW*.

Practice Exercise No. 97

Sketch and label figure 20 from memory. Check your work against the original in the text. Then prepare a clean copy to add to your place marker for convenient reference elsewhere in this chapter.

Making a rough sketch of the nine-boxed plan of the above diagram, write in the *B . . . D* words "bead, bid, bad . . ." etc. so that their vowels are correctly placed as to tongue position. Do the same with the *K . . . D*, *K . . . T*, *M . . . N*, and *T . . . N* words given in answer to Practice Exercise No. 90. Put an X where no word is supplied, as in the following example (fig. 21).

	FRONT	CENTER	BACK
HIGH	KEYED KID	CURD	COOED COULD
MIDDLE	X KED	X	CODE
LOW	CAD X	CUD COD	CAWED

Fig. 21.

In the manner of previous drills on separate groups of vowels, practice distinguishing all the vowels on the above chart, varying sequence, etc.

Do the same for the word series used in the drill above on B . . . D, K . . . D, M . . . N and T . . . N words.

Do the same for the vowels in the following sentences:

(1) He meets Steve three times each week.
(2) Little Kit bit the pit in his mitt.
(3) Lane and Jane stayed away all May.
(4) Let them set the rest of the mess on the deck.
(5) Mack ran back after the bag and the basket.
(6) By and by the kite will fly high in the sky.
(7) The hunter cut up the unlucky duck for supper.
(8) Clark's dark pot is not on the hot spot.
(9) Claude sorted all, short and tall, along the wall.
(10) Going home slowly, Joe stole the whole show.
(11) By hook or by crook, get a look at that book.
(12) Who will do for you what you won't do for Lou?
(13) Her first words were pert, curt, and worldly.

Distortions

Now that the general pattern of all the basic vowels has been presented, we may conclude our drill on them with attention to distortions which cross lines of division between the groups thus far considered separately.

Ea for A. If the mouth has been habitually held too closed, the *A* sound in *bad* tends to become more like the diphthong in *bared*. Then a sentence like *The mAn put his hAnd in the bAsket* sounds like *The mEan put his hEand in the bEasket*.

A glance at the *Vowel Chart* (fig. 20) should suggest why this happens. With the jaw placement too tight for proper *A* tongue placement, the nearby *E* sound is articulated instead and glides off into a neutral vowel to complete the substitution.

OY for Y. A similar explanation may be given for the tendency of the diphthong *OY* sometimes to be substituted for (*EYE*). When *I'll have a fine time* sounds more like *OYll have a fOYn tOYm*, muscular tightness is probably keeping the back of the tongue humped too close to the roof of the mouth and the lips too close together.

AOW or EOW for OW. In the same type of tight-jawed articulation, *Brown is down town* sounds more like *BrAOWn is dAOWn tAOWn* or *BrEOWn is dEOWn tEOWn*.

Practice Exercise No. 98

Review the front-vowel drills (Practice Exercise No. 92). Then practice the words in the columns and lines below, reinforcing the distinction between the *A* in the first column and the *Ea* in the third column by means of the intermediate *E* in the second column.

A	E	Ea
bad	bed	bared
tan	ten	tear
can	ken	care
ban	Ben	bare
man	men	mare
cad	Ked	cared
fan	fen	fare
than	then	there
ran	wren	rare
barrow	berry	bearing

Review the low-vowel drills (Practice Exercise No. 93). Then practice the words below in the same manner as those above, ending with strong distinctions between the diphthongs in the first and last columns.

OY	AW	AH	Y
buoyed	bawd	bard	bide
soy	saw	Saar	sigh
toyed	tore	tar	tide
joy	jaw	jar	jibe
boy	bore	bar	by
Lloyd	law	lard	lied
poise	pause	pa's	pies
oil	all	Ollie	I'll
toil	tall	doll	tile
coy	caw	car	kite

Review the sound distinctions between *E, A,* and *AH* in the first three of the following columns. Then add practice of the fourth column, making sure the jaw is well down so that the first vowel in the diphthong is clearly the *AH* of the third column.

E	A	AH	OW
bed	bad	bard	bowed
den	Dan	Don	down
Ked	cad	cod	cowed
net	gnat	not	knout
led	lad	lard	loud
let	Latt	lot	lout
hell	Hal	holly	howl
sped	spat	spot	spout

Also:

How loud is the sound of mountain fountains!
Howard found no clowns in our sound town, etc.

THE CONSONANTS

Definition

Consonants are those speech sounds in which the voice or breath is partially hindered by some combination of the tongue, teeth, lips, or other organs of articulation. They include all speech sounds other than the *vowels*.

The various *kinds* of consonants will be defined as their articulation is discussed.

The Alveolars

We are easily amused at the innocence of the small boy who thought that "The people in China must be awfully smart to be able to speak so unusual a language as Chinese!" Yet, we are all a little like this lad.

We find it hard not to think of the language we have always spoken as "natural," and the other languages as somehow "out of the ordinary." However, in the general pattern of articulation, it is English which is exceptional.

In most languages, the group of sounds which include the *T, D, N, L, S,* and *Z,* are called **dentals,** or **linguo-dentals.** That is because they are actually articulated by placing the tongue (Latin: *lingua*) on the teeth (Latin: *dentis*). People who speak some of those languages normally let the tongue lie on the lower jaw with the tip behind the lower teeth. They sound their dentals by lifting the jaw so that the blade of the tongue touches the upper teeth. The movement is much like that of biting.

In English, however, the true linguo-dentals are the *TH*'s—sounds which do not occur at all in most other languages. We more properly call our *T, N, S,* group *alveolars* (al-VEE-o-lahrz) because they are articulated on the **alveolar,** or **gum, ridge.**

Moreover, although we have thus far worked only on the vowels, *we cannot altogether separate our articulation of the vowels from that of the consonants.* No matter how much we drill on such sounds as *E* or *AW* individually, we shall form them differently in words like "dead" or "taught" if our *D*'s and *T*'s are dentalized than if they are articulated on the alveolar ridge. In one respect, the vowels are merely voiced transitions from one consonant to another. As in the case of any other movement, that of the tongue in forming vowels depends partly on where it starts from and where it goes to.

Work on this group of consonants, therefore, involves much more than the improvement of a few individual sounds. *How we articulate the alveolars affects almost the entire structure of our speech pattern.* By starting our consonant work with them we can accomplish more, from the outset, than by any other means.

In order to improve any of the alveolars, however, we must first strengthen the tongue muscle for high placements independent of the lower jaw.

Practice Exercise No. 99

Watching in a mirror, open your mouth wide as for *A,* and raise the tip of the tongue to the upper teeth.

Then gradually draw the tip of the tongue up along the center of the hard palate as far as you can while keeping the jaw down and the lips in the rounded *A*-contour.

NOTE: You should be able to do this to a point at about the center of the roof of the mouth where the soft palate begins. But if your tongue has habitually been held too low, or left habitually lying on the lower jaw and lifted only with a biting motion of the jaw, you may not at first be able to reach so high. Do not, however, close the mouth in order to reach higher with the tongue. Keep the lower jaw down and proceed with the tongue tip at the highest point you can reach. As the tongue muscles become stronger and more flexible with repeated practice, you will be able gradually to raise the tip higher.

On the roof of the mouth, trace a small clockwise circle with the tip of the tongue. Then reverse direction to counter-clockwise, tracing numbers and other figures in the circle, etc.

CAUTION: Check in your mirror that the facial muscles are relaxed and that the jaw is not "wagging" with the above routine. Movement should be localized in the tongue itself.

Of course, no actual sounds are made with the tongue in the positions of the above exercise. It is a basic routine for limbering, stretching, and strengthening the tongue muscles. It cannot profitably be continued for more than a few minutes at a time. But you should return to it regularly at the beginning of each practice session.

The N Sound. The easiest to articulate of all the alveolars is the *N,* so we shall start with it in order to be able, later, to transfer its placement to the others in the group.

Practice Exercise No. 100

Opening the mouth wide, sound the vowel *A* for three beats. Then, watching in your mirror that the jaw and lips remain relaxed in the *A* position, raise the tip of the tongue to the alveolar ridge and continue without a pause, sounding *N* for three beats. Still without a pause, return to *A* for three beats, etc., thus:

A . . . N . . . A . . . N . . . A . . . N, etc.

Do the same for other low vowels:

AH . . . N . . . AH . . . N . . . AH . . . etc.

Watching in the mirror, practice each of the following columns with the mouth remaining open as for the vowels, and with both vowels and *N*'s prolonged:

-N	-N-	N-	N-N
an	Anna	knack	Nan
kine	Heine	nigh	nine
on	honor	knock	non-
own	owner	no	known
cane	caner	nay	inane
in	inner	nick	ninny

In the same manner, practice working across the lines in the above columns.

NOTE: Since *N* is a nasal sound, we do not actually need to have the mouth open wide to articulate it alone. But we recommend practicing it in this way because opening the mouth is relatively easy for the *N,* and because doing so *helps with the articulation of other sounds.*

The T and D Sounds. When the tongue has been strengthened for high positions, and when the *N* has been well placed, we can use its placement to help "anchor" other alveolars to the same ridge.

First will be the *T* and *D. Characteristically, in English these consonants have a light, delicately executed sound* which is difficult to obtain when the tongue gets on or near the teeth. Note the differences of tongue, jaw, and lip positions on the following diagrams:

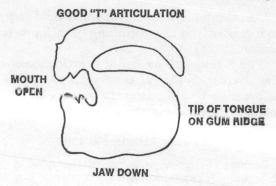

GOOD "T" ARTICULATION

MOUTH OPEN

TIP OF TONGUE ON GUM RIDGE

JAW DOWN

Fig. 22.

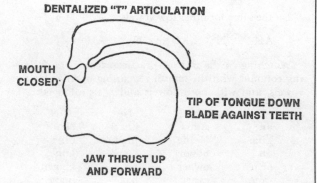

DENTALIZED "T" ARTICULATION

MOUTH CLOSED

TIP OF TONGUE DOWN BLADE AGAINST TEETH

JAW THRUST UP AND FORWARD

Fig. 23.

Practice Exercise No. 101

Practice the following columns as in the preceding exercises, but at the end of each *N*, well positioned on the gum ridge, allow the *T* or *D* to explode lightly and delicately with a quick flick of the tip of the tongue.

NOTE: Unless the tip of the tongue breaks its contact with the gum ridge sharply and abruptly, there is likely to be a noisy, scraping effect like *Tch*, even though the contact point is correct.

NT	ND	NT	ND
ant	and	went	wend
pint	pined	paint	pained
hunt	gunned	anti-	Andy
want	wand	hunter	under
haunt	yawned	Wanter	wander

Similarly practice expressions such as:

Untie Auntie.
The hunter wanted to hinder the panda.
Candy is dandy for Andy, etc.

After confirming that the *T* and *D* are well positioned by the *N* approach, exercise on these sounds separately in *tongue gymnastics*. Make sure that both tongue movements and sounds are executed lightly and delicately, thus:

T T T D D D T T T D D D, etc.
T T D D T T D D T T D D, etc.

Combine these tongue gymnastics with practice of the words in the following columns by preceding each with three practice sounds, thus:

T T T TAHK		D D D DAHK, etc.	
T	**D**	**T**	**D**
tock	dock	at	add
tuck	duck	height	hide
tore	door	Ott	odd
ten	den	net	Ned
tear	dare	ate	aid
Taine	Dane	cat	cad
tone	Doane	tot	Dodd
tent	denned	tight	died
tint	dinned	Tut	dud
taunt	dawned	tat	dad

Practice the following, watching that the *T*'s, in the middle position do not tend to become voiced as *D*'s.

attar	better	ability
otter	bitter	electricity
butter	batter	scarcity

Review all the above in practice of such phrases and sentences as:

Taunted tot.
Tinted tent.
Take a turn at tic tac toe.
Dad aided the dude.
The otter shuddered at the adder, etc.
Better butter makes better batter.
The bitter hatter's heart went pitter patter, etc.

The L Sound. *L* is also properly articulated with the tip of the tongue on the alveolar ridge, but the rest of the tongue is narrowed and lowered so that the sound of the voice escapes around it on both sides.

Some people say a sentence like *Please close the closet quietly* more like *PWease cWose the cWoset quietWy*. This is a major *speech defect* called **lallation** (la-LAY-shn). Its *W*-like substitution for *L* is due to failure to place the tip of the tongue *anywhere* on the roof of the mouth.

Weakness of distortion of the *L*, however, is more commonly due to failure to place the tip of the tongue high enough, or failure to bring the sides of the tongue low enough.

In the first case, the tip of the tongue is sometimes visible, protruding slightly under the biting edge of the upper teeth. The second case has no externally visible symptom, but the sound takes on the "Continental quality" of a French or German *L* which is easily detected by the ear.

Practice Exercise No. 102

Review the preceding *N*, *T*, and *D* exercises.

Practice the following slowly, being careful to place the *N*'s high on the alveolar ridge and to release only the sides of the tongue for the following *L*'s. Say the two-word expressions continuously as though they were one ("caN . . . L . . . , enil," etc.):

NL	NL	NL
only	can-lead	Dan-lied
unlike	none-lit	Nan-led
inlay	tin-lamp	one-land
in-law	tan-light	fine-lawn

Practice the following in a similar manner, using the *T* and *D* this time to anchor the *L* to the alveolar ridge.

TL	DL
neatly	oddly
nightly	madly
went-late	maudlin
out-lay	odd-lad

NOTE: When followed by an alveolar, the *T* and *D* should not be allowed to explode as when followed by a vowel. This muffling of the explosion in the next sound is called **implosion** and the *T* or *D* is said to be **imploded**.

To check that the *L* sound *remains* positioned on the alveolar ridge throughout its duration, practice the following, with attention to the placement of the *N*'s, *T*'s, and *D*'s.

LN	LT	LD
ill-now	all-tuned	all-day
all-night	I'll-talk	I'll-do
call-none	All-told	ill-done
I'll-need	ale-tank	tall-dam

The following is to help lower the sides of the tongue and so clarify the *L* sound. Sound a prolonged *A* vowel, watching jaw and lip positions in your mirror. Then alternate with prolonged *L*'s well positioned on the alveolar ridge. Do the same for all the other vowels on the vowel chart, beginning with the lower ones and working to the higher, thus:

A . . . L . . . A . . . L . . . ,
AH . . . L . . . AH . . . L . . . ,
E . . . L . . . E . . . L . . . , etc.

Apply the same precautions to practice of the following words:

-L	-L-	L-L
Al	alley	lall
aisle	tiling	lisle
owl	doweling	lull
ell	Ollie	loll
ill	tiller	Lil
Ole	holy	lowly

Since the *L* is more likely to cause difficulty after *P*, *B*, *K*, or *G*, practice the words in the following column in two stages, first without the preceding stopped sounds, then with them, thus:

L . . . ACK,   PL . . . ACK, etc.

PL	BL	KL	GL
plaque	black	clap	glass
ply	blithe	clam	glamour
pluck	blood	clot	glottis
plot	blot	clay	glaze
plea	bleed	clue	glue

Apply all the foregoing to practice of such expressions as:

Tra-la-la-la-la-la. Tra-la-la-la-la.
Lovely, lowly lily, etc.

The Sibilants. The last group of alveolars, *S, Z, SH,* and *ZH*, are commonly called **sibilants** because of their hissing sound. They are perhaps the most commonly mis-articulated sounds in speech.

S and Z. Properly to form the *S*, the tongue should seal off the escape of air along the gum ridge except at the very center where a single thin stream of air should be allowed to pass between the ridge and the tip of the tongue. If the lower lip is held a bit down, and the lower teeth are held slightly down and behind the upper teeth as when in position for a normal bite, there will be as little interference as possible with the escaping breath stream.

Sigmatism is a general name for the speech defects which occur when this is not properly done.

In the extreme case where the tongue is pushed forward very bluntly on to the biting edge of the teeth, there is a *TH*-like substitution, as when *Sister Suzie* is made to sound like *THiTHter THuTHie.* Sometimes the sound is also *faked,* however, by bringing the lower lip to the upper teeth with a result more like *FSiFSter FSuFSie,* with *FS* used here to indicate a sort of hissing *F*-like sound. Both of these cases are more commonly called **lisping.**

Faulty tooth alignment or spacing, especially if it dates from childhood, sometimes encourages habitual tongue placement which allows the breath to escape at one side rather than at the center of the tongue. This is technically known as **lateral emission.**

The most common trouble with *S* articulation, however, is due to low placement of the tongue. The resulting **low S,** as it is called, may be **whistling** if the sound is worked into the groove between the two upper front teeth; or, it may be **noisy** or **slushy** if the tongue placement is less firm and if too wide an opening is formed.

Practice Exercise No. 103

Review the *N* placement exercises and the *T* and *D* tongue gymnastics above.

As in the above exercises for *T* and *D,* make use of the easy placement of *N* to position *S* and *Z* in the following:

NSN	NZN
dance-now	Don's-not
once-new	one's-new
ounce-net	owns-none
tense-neck	Dane's-net
wince-not	wins-now

Ensnare one's net on snow.
He wins not who earns not, etc.

Make similar use of *N, T,* and *D* placements in practicing:

NTST	NDZD
wants-to	pond's-dry
can't-stay	lands-down
Aunt-Stella	ends-day
won't-stop	bends-down
bent-stick	finds-Dad

With no further help from preceding *N*'s now make use of *T, D,* and *L* placements alone to position *S* and *Z.* It is useful to combine this drill with tongue gymnastics in four steps as follows:

T T T HAT	D D D AD
T T T HATS	D D D ADZ
T T T . . . TAWR	D D D . . . DAUN
T T T HATSTAWR, etc.	D D D ADZDAUN, etc.

TST	DZD	ISL	IZL
hat-store	adds-down	will-slip	Will's-lap
hot-stove	kneads-dough	fill-slowly	fills-lamp
meat-stew	kid's-doll	call-slyly	calls-lad
neat-sty	bird's-dead	tell-Slim	tells-Linda
let-stay	lad's-day	cool-slate	cools-lips

To avoid contracting *STS* to a mere prolonged *S,* practice the following, holding the first *S* for a moment, then saying the *TS* quickly and lightly, almost as if saying one sound. EXAMPLE: *cas-ts*

casts	fists	coasts
lasts	mists	boasts, etc.

Apply all the above to step by step practice of such expressions as:

Suspicious circumstances
Lists of casts, etc., etc.

SH and ZH. Articulation of the *SH* and *ZH* sounds is much like that of the *S* and *Z* except that the tongue is pulled up and back slightly to form a somewhat broader, slit-like opening between the gum ridge and the blade of the tongue just behind the tip.

Because their placement is higher, these sounds are sometimes weak, or lispy, even when the *S* and *Z* are relatively well articulated. Sometimes, too, the *S* tends to sound more like the *SH* when it precedes a *T.*

Practice Exercise No. 104

To strengthen the *SH* and *ZH* sounds, practice them in their common combination with a preceding *T* or *D* as in *chat* (TSHATT) or *jaw* (DZHAW). Drill on the following columns may be combined with such tongue gymnastics as:

T T T TSH . . .   D D D DZH . . .
T T T TSHAT, etc.   D D D EDZH . . .

TSH-	DZH-	-TSH	-DZH
chat	jam	catch	badge
child	jibe	larch	large
chuck	jug	etch	edge
char	jar	"H"	age
Chet	jet	torch	George
chose	Joe's	church	judge

To sharpen the distinction between the *ST* and *SHT*, first practice the following three columns from left to right and from right to left. Then continue in a similar manner with the first and third, leaving out the center one.

SH-	S-	ST-
shy	sigh	stye
shock	sock	stock
shuck	suck	stuck
Shaw	saw	store
shed	said	steady
shirr	sir	stir
Shay	say	stay

Miss Shaw makes delicious fish-sticks.
She also sells seashells by the seashore, etc.

The Linguo-dentals

The *true linguo-dentals* of English are, as we have said, the *TH*'s—*voiced* as in "the," *unvoiced* as in "thing."

The main difficulty with their articulation is due to tendencies to blunt them as dentalized *T*- or *D*-like sounds, or to lisp them as *S*- or *Z*-like sounds.

In either case, these consonants are most troublesome when they occur in combination with the sounds with which they tend to be confused.

Practice Exercise No. 105

To strengthen the positioning of the *TH*'s, first *exaggerate* their articulation as follows: Protruding the tongue from the mouth, press the blade against the upper teeth and expel the breath while drawing the surface of the tongue slowly back until the tip is just under the biting edge of the teeth. Prolong the sound *in this final position* for several seconds. Then do the same for the corresponding voiced *TH*.

With preliminary *TH*'s articulated as above, practice each of the words in the second column of each of the two groups of columns below. Then practice the words across the page, emphasizing the differences in the key sounds.

T	TH	S
tie	thigh	sigh
tun	thunder	sunder
tore	thaw	saw
tin	thin	sin
tick	thick	sick
pat	path	pass
mat	math	mass
mit	myth	miss
mental	menthol	mensal
ought-to	author	hoarser

D	Th	S or Z
die	thy	sigh
Dow	thou	sough
den	then	Zenda
dough	though	Zoe
disc	this	Ziss
bade	bathe	bays
laid	lathe	lays
load	loathe	lows
muddy	mother	muzzle
weeder	either	easier

By breaking the articulation down into easy steps, practice the following until they can be said smoothly.

EXAMPLE: *Sixths*

  SIK
  SIKS
  SIKS-TH
  SIKS-THS

widths	depths	sixths
breadths	tenths	bathed
lengths	hundredths	loathed, etc.

Apply the same technique to such phrases and sentences as:

Hither and thither through thickets of thistles.
Neither their father nor mother was there.
They measured the depths in tenths and hundredths, etc.

The R Sound

Next to *S*, the *R* is perhaps the most commonly mis-articulated sound.

In other languages this consonant is a trilled or scraping sound made either with the tip of the tongue near the teeth or with the back of the tongue near the uvula. It is still another peculiarity of English, however, that its *R* is really a *semi-vowel* formed by placing sides of the tongue high against the gums at the sides of the mouth.

Most trouble with the sound is due to the high tongue position which it requires. Until their tongue muscles are strong enough and well enough under control to reach this position, most children tend to substitute a *W*-like lip movement for it. Thus, *railroad* becomes *Wail-Woad* or *rabbit* becomes *Wabbit* And the replacement often remains to a greater or lesser degree throughout life.

Some side-mouthed articulation is a one-sided lip substitution for the true *R*.

The sound is also sometimes faultily made by the teeth with a biting movement, or by the lower lip against the upper teeth. In the latter case the substitution may approach the *V*-sound after a *B*, as when *Bring brown bread* becomes more like *BVing, bVown, bVead.*

Practice Exercise No. 106

Watching in your mirror that the mouth is kept open as for *AH*, raise the sides of the tongue to a point of contact high on the gums of the back upper teeth, keeping the tip raised, and make a prolonged *R* sound. Then, without pausing between sounds, alternate *R*'s with *AH*'s, thus:

AH . . . R . . . AH . . . R . . . AH . . . , etc.

Do the same with the other vowel sounds in order, beginning with the lower ones. Check that your lips are not making movements as for *W*.

To emphasize tongue, rather than lip, movement, alternate the above exercise with *L*'s, thus:

AH . . . L . . . AH . . . R . . . AH . . . L, etc.

Practice the pairs of words in the following columns, emphasizing the above indicated difference in their articulation especially with regard to lip movement.

R-	W-
rag	wag
right	white
run	one
rod	wad
red	wed
ray	way
row	woe
reel	wheel
rue	woo
reêd	weed

To strengthen the tongue in articulating the *R* in the more difficult position after *B* or *P*, practice the following in two steps, thus:

ROW, PROW	ROW, BROW, etc.
PR	**BR**
prow	brow
pry	bright
pray	bray
probe	broke

Similarly, strengthen the first *R* in the following words of special difficulty:

lib*R*ary	(*not* li-herry)
lib*R*arian	(*not* li-berrian)
Feb*R*uary	(*not* Feb-you-ary)

Review the preceding by careful practice of such phrases and sentences as:

Hurry, Harry, hurry.
Broken railroad tracks.
The arena's a horridly arid area.
The present librarian presided in February, etc.

GENERAL ARTICULATION FAULTS

Omissions

If all the above discussed sounds are well formed, you are not likely to have much difficulty with the others.

There are some common omissions of vowels and consonants which should be given further attention, however, because they give an impression of carelessness and may even result in misunderstanding.

Practice Exercise No. 107

Practice each of the following words carefully as they are indicated in the second column, never as in the third. (The pronunciations are respelled only enough to indicate correction of the faults.)

WORD	SAY	NOT
acts	AKTS	AKS
adopts	a-DAHPTS	a-DAHPS
kept	KEPT	KEP
help	HELP	HEP
didn't	DID-nt	DINT
didn't you	DID-nt you	DIN-tsha
wouldn't	WUD-nt	WUNT
shouldn't	SHUD-nt	SHUNT
going to	GO-ing to	GAWN-a
want to	WAHN-to	WAHN-a
suggest	sug-DZHEST	su-DZHEST
picture	PIK-ture	PITSH-er
modern	MAH-dern	MAHD-n

WORD	SAY	NOT
secretary	SEK-retary	SEK-itary
geometry	jee-AHMetry	JAHN-etry
government	GUV-ernment	GUV-mint
subject	SUB-ject	SUB-zhect

Additions

Sometimes the improper addition of sounds in words is due more to difficulty with their articulation than to actual error in their intended pronunciation.

Extra vowels may be added to words like *athlete* or *film* to make them sound like *A-tha-leet* or *FIL-um,* because the tongue has difficulty passing from the *TH* to the *L,* or because it has difficulty holding the *L* until the lips form the *M.*

Intrusive R's, as they are called, may be inserted into words where they do not belong, as when *idea of drawing* becomes *i-DI-Ruv-DRAW-Ring.* This is usually due to tightness in the jaw muscles which so cramps the movement of the tongue from vowel position to vowel position that *R* is unintentionally sounded during the transition.

Likewise, **a G sound** may be added to the *NG* between two vowels, as when *singer* is said as *SING-Ger;* but additions of this sort are discussed in more detail in the next chapter.

Practice Exercise No. 108

Practice the following as indicated.

WORD	SAY	NOT
athlete	ATH-lete	A-tha-lete
elm	ELM	ELL-um
film	FILM	FILL-um
umbrella	um-BREL-a	um-ber-EL-a
modern	MAH-dern	MAH-der-en or MAH-dren
idea	i-DI-a	i-DIER
drawing	DRAW-ing	DRAW-Ring
law	LAW	LAWR
Asia	AY-zha	AY-zher
India	IN-dia	IN-dieR
Nebraska	ne-BRAS-ka	ne-BRAS-keR
Utah	YOO-tah	YOO-tahr

Over-Articulation

In most of this chapter we have stressed the need of clear, strong production of the sounds we have considered. That is because the more common faults are due to weakness or indistinctness of articulation.

At times, however, the opposite error is made. *Some people, in trying to make their speech more distinct, emphasize the wrong sounds.* This results in making their speech sound queer.

A common instance is the articulation of *a* and *the* always as *AY* and *THEE.* Take, for example, the sentence:

A man and a woman walked across the Plaza.

Normally, this would be said:

a MAN and a WUU-man WAWKT a-KRAWS the PLA-za.

Some misguided speech-improvers, however, deliberately try to say such a sentence as:

AY MAN AND AY WO-MAN WAWKT AY-KRAWS THEE PLA-ZUH.

This is no improvement, whatsoever. By reminding the listener of the stumbling of a child reading his first primer aloud, this sort of **artificial over-articulation** is more distracting than helpful. And it sometimes gives the mistaken notion that better articulation is not to be desired.

A similar fault is theatrical *over-explosion* of *stopped sounds—K, G, T, D, P,* and *B—*when they come at the end of a word. Consider the sentence:

Bert and Mag went back to the last stop.

Misguided attempts at speech improvement will sometimes deliberately make it sound like:

BerT anD MaG wenT bacK to the lasT stoP.

There is an excuse for something a *little* like this from an actor on the stage of a large theatre with such poor acoustics that it is hard to hear normal speech in the back rows of the balcony. But the actor does this only to make the final consonants sound *normal* in such an auditorium. The artificiality has no place in ordinary speech under ordinary conditions.

Finally, the vowels in unaccented syllables of long words are also sometimes overemphasized. Consider the expression:

Constitutional convention

This is reasonably well said as:

kahn-sti-TYOO-shn-l kn-VEN-shn

Over-articulated, with stress on every syllable, it may sound like:

KAHN-STI-TYOO-SHUN-AWL KUN-VEN-SHUN

But here again, *artificial additions to normal articulation distort, rather than improve it.*

Speech improvement does require regular, energetic practice. But at certain points it *also needs restraint and good judgment.*

CHAPTER X

FOREIGN ACCENT

This chapter is devoted to special problems of speech commonly called "foreign accent." Those who spoke another language before English should study first the sections on *Stress, Linking,* and *Falling and Rising Inflections.* They should then study the chapter on *ARTICULATION* in the light of the suggestions made in the remaining sections. The chapters on *DEVELOPING THE VOICE* and *PRONUNCIATION* should also be studied.

Anyone who feels that his speech contains foreignisms, should practice the exercises on those problems, such as the *NG click* or *cognate confusion,* which are particularly his.

A HEALTHY APPROACH

People with foreign accents sometimes try to *hide* faulty articulation rather than to *correct* it. They talk very softly, as if hoping that their mistakes will not be heard; or very fast, as if at such speed their mistakes will pass unnoticed; or very loud, as if the increase in volume will help them to be better understood.

Such notions and such devices will only make it harder for you to improve your speech.

Adopt a healthy approach. Talk slowly while you are learning, and neither louder nor softer than the people about you. You will make mistakes, of course, and people will notice them, but don't let this disturb you. Study the descriptions given here, practice the exercises, practice them many times, and your accent will gradually improve.

STRESS

Accent. English is a stress language. In words of two or more syllables, one is usually said *more loudly,* on a *higher pitch,* and is held a *longer time* than the other syllable or syllables. The stressed syllable is said to be **accented.**

Practice the following words, stressing or accenting the capitalized syllables. *Prolong* these syllables, lift your pitch *up* for them, say them *forcefully.* Make the other syllables *weaker, shorter,* and *lower* in pitch. (The words have not been re-spelled to indicate pronunciation. Concentrate on *stress,* and do not concern yourself, for the present, with correct individual sounds. The words have been re-spelled for pronunciation in Practice Exercise No. 112, but use that list only after you have practiced these exercises.)

DOLL-ar	de-CEIVE	HAPP-i-ness
COW-ard	com-MIT	COW-ar-dice
YEAR-ly	a-BOUT	PAL-a-ces
AL-tar	a-MUSE	ME-te-or
A-ble	de-NY	CHOC-o-late

be-GINN-er	U-su-al-ly	e-CON-o-my
ac-COM-plice	PER-son-al-ly	ex-EC-u-tive
con-SU-mer	OB-stin-a-cy	a-LU-mi-num
de-CI-sive	FOR-mid-a-ble	ma-CHI-ne-ry
com-MER-cial	MIN-i-a-ture	la-BOR-i-ous

me-CHAN-i-cal-ly	in-EV-it-a-ble	in-COM-par-a-ble

Secondary Accent. In certain three-, four-, and five-syllabled words, one syllable is stressed *strongly,* and a second is given a somewhat *lighter* stress or accent, being held a little less long and being said with a little less force. Syllables with such *moderate,* or **secondary** stress are printed in *italics* in the list below. The remaining syllables are weak and unstressed.

OR-ga-*nize*	*pi*-o-NEER	ME-di-*a*-tor
MI-cro-*phone*	*per*-son-NEL	DIC-tion-*ar*-y
HOL-i-*day*	*con*-tra-DICT	AR-chi-*tec*-ture
DY-na-*mite*	*un*-der-NEATH	LEG-is-*la*-tive
O-ver-*tone*	*o*-ver-TAKE	MEM-o-*ri*-zing

a-COMM-o-*date*	*lo*-co-MO-tive	de-CLAM-a-*tor*-y
e-CON-o-*mize*	*e*-co-NOM-ic	a-POTH-e-*car*-y
con-SOL-i-*date*	*det*-o-NA-tion	au-THOR-i-*ta*-tive
per-SON-i-*fied*	*im*-po-SI-tion	pre-DOM-i-*na*-ting
ca-TAS-tro-*phe*	*pen*-i-CILL-in	con-TAM-i-*na*-ted

in-ge-NU-i-ty
in-ter-ME-di-ate
en-to-MOL-o-gy
math-e-MAT-i-cal
ann-i-VER-sa-ry

com-*mu*-ni-CA-tion
de-*ter*-mi-NA-tion
pro-*nun*-ci-A-tion
e-*lim*-i-NA-tion
en-*cy*-clo-PE-dic

Unstressed Syllables. In weak, **unstressed syllables, the vowel usually** has no very definite quality. It is neutral, indeterminate, the sort of tone one would make if one were simply vocalizing without trying to produce any particular vowel. This sort of sound is used especially when the spelling is *a, o,* or *u.* When the spelling is *e* or *i,* the sound may be either the neutral voice murmur, or a weak EE or I. for -*y* and -*ly* endings, the sound is between EE and I, but closer to EE.

Practice Exercise No. 109

Say the lists above out loud once again, using indeterminate or only slightly definite vowels for the weak, unstressed syllables.

Stress in Speech. These stress patterns are part of the structure of the language. Thus, in the phrase, *the first of March,* if one wanted to emphasize the *day,* one would say:

FIRST
of
the   *March*

But if one wanted to emphasize the month:

MARCH
first
of
the

NOTE: See the section on *Intonation* in the chapter, *DEVELOPING YOUR VOICE.*

Strong and Weak Forms. The words that carry meaning—nouns, verbs, adjectives, and adverbs—may have one or more acceptable pronunciations. If English is not your native tongue, when using the dictionary it would be best for you to use the first form listed there. Whatever pronunciation you select, however, say it in approximately the same way no matter how important it is in the sentence, that is, no matter whether you stress it strongly or moderately or comparatively lightly. You will always say *offer* as OFF-er.

But the small, connecting words of the language, the pronouns, the prepositions, the conjunctions, the auxiliary verb forms, and the articles, have two pronunciations. One, the **strong form,** the dictionary pronunciation, is used when we say the word by itself or emphasize it in a sentence. The other, the weak form, is used in unstressed positions. The vowels of the weak forms will be neutral and indeterminate. Sometimes they may not even be said. Compare: *That is MY book,* with *THAT is my book,* and *THAT's my book.*

The following is a list of connectives which have two pronunciations, a **strong** and a **weak.** They are arranged according to their use as *parts of speech* and roughly according to their *frequency of occurrence* in English.

Articles: the, a, an

Prepositions: of, to, in, for, with, on, by, at, from, up, into, upon

Conjunctions: and, that, for, as, but, or, than, nor

Auxiliary and Connecting Verbs: is, be, was, have, are, will, had, has, been, were, do, can, must, come, shall, should, am, does, could, would

Pronouns: it, you, he, we, his, our, their, my, him, them, her, your, she, us, some

Adverb: there

Practice Exercise No. 110

Read aloud any paragraph or any group of selections in this book, using indeterminate vowels in all the weak, unstressed words and syllables.

Underline these words and syllables beforehand, if you wish, but—

WARNING: Do not re-stress the weak, unstressed syllables and words. That is, do *not* prolong the indeterminate vowels, do *not* say them forcefully or lift them in pitch. Say them weakly, quickly, blurringly.

Linking Syllables. In English, one sound is linked closely to the next. The two-syllable word *seeing* is said with no break between the syllables, the EE flowing smoothly into the I.

An important aspect of this linking is revealed in the way we say the word *feeling.* For spelling purposes we would call *feel-* the first syllable and *-ing* the second. But in talking, the syllables are so linked that it is impossible to tell exactly when the first syllable ends and the second begins. The *l* is as much a part of the one syllable as the other. It is a link between the two syllables.

Practice Exercise No. 111

Say aloud one or two words from each group in the preceding lists, trying to link the syllables. Keep on saying them until you can do so without breaking the tone. (There will be minor breaks, of course, for voiceless consonants.)

Linking Words. Words are linked together as well as syllables. In conversation, it is as difficult to say where one word ends and the next begins as it is to separate the syllables.

Link the words in the phrases below, just as you link the syllables in the words above them. Syllable markings have been left out to emphasize the linking.

WORD	SAY	WORD	SAY
dollar	DOLLar	amuse	aMUSE
He knows	HEknows	by land	byLAND
cowardice	COWardice	beginner	beGINNer
pulling it	PULLingit	to find him	toFINDhim
economy	eCONomy	organize	ORganize
The nerve of it!	theNERVE ofit	Jim is here	JIMis*here*
pioneer	*pio*NEER	mediator	MEdiator
Put it down	*putit*DOWN	Spring is coming	SPRINGis *coming*
economize	eCONo*mize*	economic	eco*NOMic*
I saw the boy	iSAWthe*boy*	I saw no one	isawNOone
declamatory	deCLAMa*tory*		
The horn is blowing	theHORNis *blowing*		
ingenuity	inge*NUity*		
Who is Sylvia?	*whois*SYLvia		
communication	commu*ni*CAtion		
They never caught him	they*never*CAUGHThim		

The tone is broken eventually, of course, at the ends of sentences and phrases, to permit us to take a breath or to separate ideas; occasionally, also, for emphasis. The principles underlying the grouping of words are discussed in the section on *Phrasing* in the chapter, *DEVELOPING YOUR VOICE.* For the present it is much more important for you to learn linking.

FALLING AND RISING INFLECTIONS

In most cases, English ends a statement with a falling inflection. The voice slides down from the original pitch of the last syllable of the sentence, becoming softer until the voice stops.

Sometimes these slides are short and swift, as in saying, *Yes.*\ Sometimes longer and more gradual, as in saying, *No.*\

But their movement is always straight and directly downward, and involves a gradual weakening of tone.

Foreigners sometimes say the falling inflection waveringly. The voice falls, but as if down a bumpy playground slide.

Another fault is to say the inflection with *two* chief tones, instead of *one.* The foreigner starts on C, slides down to G, pauses briefly, and then continues his slide down.

Be sure that the last syllable of a sentence ending with a falling inflection is said with only one peak, and that the voice slides down directly and unwaveringly from that tone.

Some words in which the slide would be short and swift are: *gift, bit, heat, type, lock.* Some words in which the slide would be slightly longer and more gradual are: *be, go, fall, tin, glad, now.* The difference depends on the *length of the vowel,* discussed in the section, *Vowels and Diphthongs,* below.

A rising inflection is used to connect ideas, and at the end of questions which do not have a question-word: *apples,/ peaches,/ bananas,/ . . . Has he gone?/* The important thing about this inflection is that the voice glides up in pitch from a point at or near the pitch of the preceding syllable.

One should not start the glide up from a pitch well above that of the preceding syllable. For example, instead of *apples* and *he gone* being inflected as ./ they are sometimes said with a leap in pitch./

In the following phrases, glide, do not raise pitch on the syllables before the commas:

"We service Fords, Plymouths, Chevrolets, . . ." "of the people, by the people, . . ."

"He heard the bell, went to the door, opened it, . . ."

In the following questions, before saying the rising inflection on the last syllable, think of the pitch of the syllable you have just said:

"Did he go?"

"Are they here?"

"Have you seen John's book?"

NOTE: See the section on *Inflections* in the chapter, *DEVELOPING YOUR VOICE*.

Practice Exercise No. 112

Practice the following list, which duplicates the material used in this and the preceding sections of this chapter, with proper stress, linking, and inflection, and with greater care as to pronunciation. The words have been respelled to indicate pronunciation according to the scheme used in the chapter on *PRONUNCIATION*.

Say some groups of words as single words with falling inflections. Say others as words in series, the first four of a group with rising inflections, the last with a falling inflection. Say words across the page as well as down.

Return to practice this list occasionally as you go through the chapters on *ARTICULATION* and *DEVELOPING YOUR VOICE*.

DOLL-ar	de-SEEV	HAPP-i-niss
KOW-ard	kom-MITT	KOW-ar-diss
YIRR-lee	a-BOWT	PAL-a-sizz
AWL-tar	a-MYOOZ	MEE-te-or
AY-b'l	de-NY	TCHOK-o-lit
be-GINN-er	YOO-zhoo-a-ly	e-KONN-o-mee
a-KOMM-pliss	PUR-son-a-lee	igg-ZEKK-yu-tiv
kon-SOO-mer	OBB-stin-a-see	a-LOO-mi-num
de-SY-siv	FAWR-mid-a-b'l	ma-SHEE-ne-ree
kom-MUR-shal	MINN-i-a-tcher	la-BAWR-i-us
me-KANN-i-ka-lee	in-EVV-it-a-b'l	in-KOMM-par-a-b'l
AWR-ga-*nyz*	*py*-o-NIRR (NEER)	MEE-di-*ay*-tor
MY-kro-*fohn*	*pur*-so-NELL	DIKK-shon-*ayr*-ee
HOLL-i-*day*	*konn*-tra-DIKT	AHR-ki-*tekk*-tcher
DY-na-*myt*	*unn*-der-NEETH	LEJ-iss-*lay*-tiv
OH-ver-*tohn*	*oh*-ver-TAYK	MEMM-o-*ry*-zing
a-KOMM-o-*dayt*	*loh*-ko-MOH-tiv	de-KLAMM-a-*tohr*-ee
e-KONN-o-*myz*	*e*-ko-NOMM-ik	a-POTH-e-*kayr*-ee
kon-SOLL-i-*dayt*	*det*-o-NAY-shun	aw-THORR-i-*tay*-tiv

pur-SONN-i-*fyd*   im-po-ZISH-on   pre-DOMM-i-*nay*-ting

ka-TASS-tro-*fee*   *pen*-i-SILL-in   kon-TAMM-i-*nay*-ted

in-je-NYOO-i-tee   kom-*myoo*-ni-KAY-shon

in-ter-MEE-di-et   de-*tur*-mi-NAY-shon

en-to-MOLL-o-jee   pro-*nun*-si-AY-shon

math-e-MATT-i-kal   e-*lim*-i-NAY-shon

ann-i-VURR-*sa*-ree   *en*-sy-klo-PEE-dik

the FURST ov *mahrtch*; the furst ov MAHRTCH that iz MY buuk; THAT iz my buuk; THATS my buuk

HEE nohz; by LANND; PUULL-ing it; to FYND'm; the NURV ov it; JIMM is *hirr; putt* it DOWN; SPRING iz *kumm*-ing; y SAW the boy; y saw NOH wunn; the HAWRN iz *bloh*-ing; *hoo* is SILL-vi-a; thay *nevv*-er KAWT him

GIFT, BITT, HEET, TYP, LOKK

BEE, GOH, FAWL, TINN, GLADD, NOW

APP-'lz, PEETCH-iz, ba-NAN-az, . . . ; hazz he GONN?

we *sur*-viss FAWRDZ, PLIMM-othss, *shevv*-ro-LAYZ.

UVV the *pee*-p'l, BY the pee-p'l, . . . ; he HURD the *bell*, . . . WENNT to the *dawr*, OH-pend it, . . .

did he GOH? ahr thay HIRR?; havv you *seen* jonnz BUUK?

VOWELS AND DIPHTHONGS

Production of Vowels. English has both vowels and diphthongs (blends of two vowels). But the foreigner must remember that the English vowels are not "pure" vowels, in the sense of staying *one* sound from beginning to end. Rather, all English vowels are slightly *diphthongized*, that is, we glide *into* the sound and *off* it. This gliding or diphthongizing cannot be indicated in spelling, but is, nevertheless, part of the essential character of English vowels.

In studying vowels in the chapter on *ARTICULATION*, the foreigner may practice individual vowels by holding them steadily for their entire length. But when he says the word lists, he should consciously try to glide *into* and *off* the vowel.

English vowels are squeezed into a narrower compass than those of many other languages. The foreigner has difficulty because some are so "close" to each other. Thus, French has an equivalent for both the English EE and AY, but no equivalent for the English I which lies between them.

Follow carefully the directions for the production of vowels in the chapter on *ARTICULATION,* listen to the quality of the vowels used by native-born speakers, and in your practice distinguish particularly between:

EE and I	OO and UU	A, E, and AH
AY and E	U and UU	U, AH, and AW
	A and AW	

Production of Diphthongs. Foreigners may think of diphthongs as two single vowels said separately, one after the other, with about equal value. But English diphthongs are not formed in this way. In English diphthongs, one vowel shades into the other, and the first vowel is said strongly and the second very lightly. As a matter of fact, the foreigner should practice diphthongs by saying the first vowel and then gliding *toward* the second.

Practice the diphthongs and the vowels of which they are composed in the chapter on *ARTICULATION,* keeping in mind the suggestion just made. Then strengthen your diphthongs by practicing the following exercises. Pay particular attention to *AY* and *OH,* for these are not diphthongs but "pure" or single vowels in the European languages.

Practice Exercise No. 113

The final sound in *AY, Y,* and *OY* should be close to that of *EE.* Read across the page.

EE	AY	Y	OY
he	hay	high	ahoy
be	bay	by	boy
Lee	lay	lie	alloy
see	say	sigh	soy
knee	nay	nigh	annoy

The final sound of *OH* and *OW* should be close to that of *OO.*

OO	OH	OW
who	hoe	how
do	dough	endow
to	toe	kowtow
Lou	low	allow
new	no	now

When followed by a consonant, the final sound in *AY, Y,* and *OY* may be closer to that of *I.* Read across the page.

EE	I	AY	Y	OY
heat	hit	hate	height	Hoyt
meat	mit	mate	mite	moist
leak	lick	lake	like	——
delete	lit	late	light	loiter
keen	kin	cane	kine	coin

When followed by a consonant, the final sound in *OH* and *OW* may be closer to that of *UU.*

OO	UU	OH	OW
fool	full	foal	fowl
boon	book	bone	hound
noon	nook	known	noun
repute	put	compote	pout
cooed	could	code	cowed

Length of Vowels and Diphthongs. All English vowels and diphthongs may be held for longer or shorter periods of time. Vowels and diphthongs are comparatively long when final or when followed by voiced consonants, such as *b, l, z.* They are comparatively short when followed by voiceless consonants, such as *p, f, s.* (See *Cognate Confusion* below.)

LONG	SHORT	LONG	SHORT
fee, feed	feet, feast	pull	put
bid	bit	rue, rude	root, roost
may, maze	make, mace	burr, bird	Bert, burst
led	let	cub	cup
tag, tanned	tack, tact	lie, lied	life
log, lard	lock	how, house, v.	house, n.
saw, sawed	sought	joy, joys	joist
roe, road	wrote, roast		

The vowel in such words as *half, past, laugh, dance, path* (most often an *A,* but also any one of a number of variants between *A* and the British AH) is usually long.

Vowels in unstressed syllables are, of course, extremely short. The diphthongs *OH* and *AY* are shortened to single vowels in *rotating, chaotic.*

NOTE: Final vowels and those followed by voiced consonants will take longer, more gradually falling inflections; vowels followed by voiceless consonants will have shorter, swifter-falling inflections.

CONSONANTS

The Alveolars—T, D, N, L, S, Z, etc. Begin your study of consonants in the chapter on *Articulation* by paying special attention to the explanations of the *Alveolars*, T, D, N, L, S, Z, etc.

The alveolar or upper gum ridge is the focal point for the articulation of English. When we fail properly to place the tongue there, the entire structure of our speech pattern is distorted.

In figure 24, the short distance between the teeth and the alveolar ridge may suggest that the difference is not important. But this is a serious mistake. Lifting the tongue to the upper gum for *T, D, N, L* will poise the tongue habitually higher for many other sounds, including the vowels; whereas dentalized articulation permits the tongue to lie, relatively inert, on the lower jaw. In your practice emphasize the exercise for stretching your tongue up to the gum for these alveolar consonants.

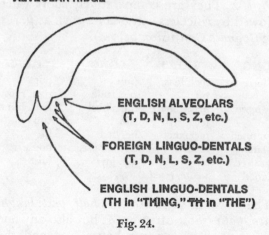

ALVEOLAR RIDGE

ENGLISH ALVEOLARS (T, D, N, L, S, Z, etc.)

FOREIGN LINGUO-DENTALS (T, D, N, L, S, Z, etc.)

ENGLISH LINGUO-DENTALS (TH in "THING," TH in "THE")

Fig. 24.

TH. Next study the linguo-dentals, the *TH*'s. These are included on the above diagram for purposes of contrast. You will improve your articulation of these consonants most if you practice *prolonging* them, and then practice sliding the tongue *easily* and *lightly* into position without any sudden, sharp contact. In fact, instead of thinking of touching the tongue to the edge of the teeth, think of keeping the tongue just *away* from the teeth.

R. In studying *R*, remember that you are trying to produce a sound which is probably quite different from your native sound. Avoid trilling it. Follow the directions in *Articulation* and use these special helps:

Say *TR-* words, such as *trip, tree,* lifting the tongue-tip somewhat higher than usual on the gum for the *T*, and then curling it up and back still higher for the *R*. Prolong the *R*, trying for a vowel-like and forward sound.

While prolonging *ZH*, drop the jaw slightly, then raise the point of the tongue toward the roof of the mouth. The resulting sound should be an *R*.

The foreigner must realize that learning to use an English *R* in conversation will take long practice. Begin your study of it early and come back to it from time to time as you go through the remaining consonants here and in the chapter on *ARTICULATION*.

W and V. The initial sounds of *will* (W) and *veal* (V) should be carefully distinguished. *V* is a friction-sound. The lower lip is raised to the upper teeth, and the voice is sent audibly between the lip and the edges of the teeth.

W is a glide or semi-vowel. To make it, quickly say the vowel *OO* with rounded, protruded lips, and then as quickly move into the following vowel. Practice:

W	V	V	W
way	vain	vote	woe
word	verb	voodoo	woo
wick	Vic	veal	wheel
why	vie	vigor	wig
was	vase	vim	whim
	(VAYS, VAYZ)		

NOTE: Many Americans use a voiceless W for "wh."

Y and J (DZH). Some foreigners confuse these sounds. The initial sound of *yes* (Y) is a glide or semi-vowel. For *Y*, quickly say the vowel *EE,* the tongue being arched high and front, and then as quickly move into the following vowel.

The initial sound of *jam* and *gem* is thought of as a *J* by Americans (*J* is used for the sound in the chapter on *PRONUNCIATION*). But foreigners will do better to think of it as a *D* plus a *ZH*, the two being said in very quick succession. See *DZH* in the chapter on *ARTICULATION*. Practice:

Y	DZH	DZH	Y
yam	jam	juice	use
yard	jarred	jeer	year
your	jaw	gyp	yip
yoke	joke	Joe-Joe	yo-yo
yarn	John	Japan	yap

COGNATE CONFUSION

Voiced and Voiceless Sounds. Most English consonants occur in pairs: the two consonants are identical in articulation except that one is made with the voice and the other with the breath. Such pairs are called **cognates**. The chapter on *ARTICULATION* discusses the cognates *T* and *D*, *S* and *Z*, *SH* and *ZH*, the *TH* in *thing* and the *TH* in *the*, and *TSH* and *DZH* (*TCH* and *J*). Other cognates are *P* and *B*, *K* and *G*, and *F* and *V*.

The foreigner probably has these cognates in his native tongue. But the difference between voiced and voiceless sounds may not be as important there as in English, or the rules for using them may be different. Again, the foreigner may tend to use only voiceless consonants at the ends of words. There is always, moreover, the problem of English spelling.

As a result, the foreigner frequently *confuses* cognates. Most often his error is to unvoice sounds which should be voiced. Thus, in the sentence, *He has no keys*, the foreigner may say, *He haSS no KeySS*, instead of *He haZ no keyZ*. Or in *The dog begs*, he may say, *The doK beKS*, instead of *The doG beGZ*. But he may also do the opposite. In the phrase, *The price of gasoline*, he may say *The pryZZ of gaZZoline* instead of *The prySS of gaSSoline*.

Although cognate confusions are among the most *conspicuous* traits of foreign accent, they are also among the *easiest to correct*. Time spent on the following special drills will bring quick improvement.

First, fix in mind the difference between sounds made with the voice and those made with the breath. Place your fingers on your Adam's apple and say the vowel *EE* very loudly. Prolong it and feel the vibration. Your vocal bands are vibrating, the sound is *voiced*. Still holding your fingers on your Adam's apple, *whisper* an *EE* and prolong the whisper. You will feel no vibration, for the vocal bands are not operating. A whisper is made with breath, and the sound is *voiceless*.

Now say a strong, prolonged *ZZZ*. You should feel as much vibration in your Adam's apple as when saying the *EE*. Keep on saying the *ZZZ* until the vibration-feeling *is* as strong. Now say a prolonged *SSS*. You should feel the same *lack of vibration* as when you whispered the *EE*. Keep on saying the *SSS* until you feel no vibration whatever. You will then have established the difference between voiced sounds, such as *Z*, and voiceless sounds, such as *S*.

Holding a finger in each ear while you say *ZZZ* and *SSS* will emphasize the difference between voiced and voiceless sounds.

Use the same techniques to point up the difference between the other cognates. Be sure to use the sound *itself*, however, not the *name* of the sound. Use *FFF*, not *EF*; use *VVV*, not *VEE*.

Practice Exercise No. 114

a. Practice the following words, preceding each *S* word with a prolonged *SSS* and each *Z* word with a fully-voiced, strong *ZZZ*.

S	Z	Z	S
ice	eyes	maze	mace
bus	buzz	phase	face
loose	lose	bays	base
cease	seize (SEEZ)	Lee's	lease
hearse	hers	lies	lice
hiss	his	cause	course

Note that these very common words are all said with Z: *as, was, has, these, those*.

Remember that vowels are shorter before the voiceless *S*, held longer before the voiced *Z*. When you are sure that you have learned to say the above list with *S* and *Z*, go over it again several times for proper vowel lengths as well as careful differentiation between the cognates.

b. Explode a *T* (the *sound*, not the *name TEE*) with a puff of breath. Say a strongly voiced *D*. Say three such aspirated *T*'s before each of the *T* words below, and three such strongly voiced *D*'s before each of the *D* words. Practice the words in pairs to emphasize their difference.

T	D	D	T
at	add	bowed	bout
height	hide	bud	but
cot	cod	bed	bet
cut	cud	heed	heat
heart	hard	ladder	latter
ate	aid	madder	matter

Note that these very common words have *T*: *it, that, what, not, sit, set, put, shut, first.*

Note that these very common words have *D*: *and, had, would, should, could, hand, second, third.*

c. Similarly practice:

TCH (TSH)	J (DZH)	J (DZH)	TCH (TSH)
batch	badge	ridge	rich
larch	large	urging	urchin
"H"	age	edging	etching
much	smudge	badger	catcher
etch	edge	margin	march in

d. Similarly practice:

F	V	V	F
half	have	believe	belief
safe	save	love	luff
life	alive	believes	beliefs
waif	wave	waves	waifs
leaf	leave	loaves	loafs

Pointers on P, T, K, B, D, G. The above are called **stops.** In making them the voice or breath is momentarily stopped and then released in any one of a variety of ways. *P* and *B* are stopped at the lips; *T* and *D* are stopped by the tongue on the upper gum ridge; *K* and *G* are stopped by the back of the tongue pressing against the soft palate. (*K* is stopped farther forward before front vowels.)

The following pointers should be of special help:

At the beginning of words or stressed syllables, as in *tea, attempt, pie, appear, key, recall,* the stops *P, T,* and *K* are released or exploded with a *puff of breath.* The sounds have an *H*-quality and are called *aspirated.*

But foreigners frequently explode these sounds in these positions *without aspirating* them. To American ears the *P* then sounds like a *B,* the *T* like a *D,* the *K* like a *G.* Though the foreigner is not actually confusing cognates, he *seems* to be doing so.

Practice *P, T,* and *K* by allowing air pressure to build up strongly behind the lips, tongue and gum, back of tongue and soft palate, respectively, and then releasing or exploding the air with a strong puffing out of the breath. Practice exploding *B, D,* and *G,* with strong voice (feel your Adam's apple), but with *no* puff of breath.

Practice these techniques in the following:

P	B	T	D	K	G
pea	bee	to	do	call	gall
pie	by	tame	dame	coal	goal
pen	Ben	ten	den	come	gum
impose	imbue	attune	produce	recall	against
repute	rebuke	attain	disdain	placate	regain
upon	abuse	return	redo	recur	ago

The above does not apply to *sp-, st-,* and *sk-* words. In these the *P, T,* and *K* are exploded but unaspirated, and have something of the quality of *B, D,* and *G.*

Distinguish between the aspirated and unaspirated stops in:

pill	spill	till	still	kill	skill
pie	spy	tie	sty	cane	skein
peak	speak	tier	steer	kin	skin

When two stops occur together in the same or consecutive words, the first is not exploded, but is held very briefly and then the second is exploded: *back door, big day, cupcake, rubdown, sitdown, bedclothes.*

The same is true for double stops: *hot tea, midday, bookcase, big gun, stop payment, tub bath.*

Foreigners should be especially careful to observe this rule where two stops occur together in the same syllable. Say the following words by not exploding the first stop, allowing a moment of silence, then exploding the second: *act, fact, licked* (LIKT), *nagged, lugged, apt, rapt, inept.*

When a stop occurs before *L, M,* or *N,* it is not exploded, and the air is released on the *L, M,* or *N*: *sudden, mitten, little, ladle, at night, midnight, at last, odd lot, Buckley, Bagley, rack man, ragman, acknowledge, ignoble.*

Distinguish carefully between the voiced and unvoiced stops in the above words, even though they are not exploded.

Final stops, if they follow a consonant, are exploded only very lightly: *crisp, bulb, mist, Lent, mind.*

The foreigner with an acute ear will have noticed that final stops which follow a vowel are frequently not exploded at all: *lap, lit, leak, lob, lid, leg.* Whether these stops are exploded or not is not very important for the foreigner.

In any case he should refrain from trying this method of articulation until he has learned extremely well how to explode aspirated initial stops.

The Endings -d and -ed. The endings -d and -ed of the past tense and past participle of regular verbs are pronounced:

T if the verb ends in a voiceless sound: *seeped* (SEEPT), *lacked, coughed* (KAWFT), *missed.*

D if the verb ends in a voiced sound: *seemed* (SEEMD), *failed, loved.*

ID if the verb ends in a *d* or *t: fainted* (FAYN-tid), *raided* (RAYD-id).

The Endings -s and -es. The endings -s and -es of the regular plurals and possessives of nouns, and of the third person singular of the present indicative of verbs are pronounced:

S if the preceding sound is voiceless: *lights* (LYTS), *makes, sips, laughs, Kate's.*

Z if the preceding sound is voiced: *needs* (NEEDZ), *John's, calls, seems, goes, legs, cabs.*

IZ if the preceding sound is an *S, Z, SH, ZH: mazes* (MAYZ-iz), *faces, losses, wishes, pitches, colleges.*

NG CLICKS AND CONFUSION

The words *finger* and *singer* look as if they should rhyme. Yet the first is said (FING-Ger) and the second (SING-er). Similarly *linger* and *flinger* are pronounced (LING-Ger, FLING-er).

To avoid *confusion* in pronouncing these and similar words, the foreigner should memorize the following simple rule for the pronunciation of the spelling "ng":

The spelling "ng" is pronounced NG-G when it occurs in the middle of a root. Otherwise it is pronounced NG.

The **root** is that basic part of a word from which all related words are formed. Thus, the roots of *singer* and *flinger* above are *sing* and *fling*. A *singer* is "one who sings" and a *flinger* is "one who flings." But a *finger* is not "something that fings," nor does *linger* mean "one who lings." The roots of the latter two are the entire words. The *ng* occurs in the middle of each and so, by the rule, is pronounced NG-G.

The only important exceptions to this rule are the words *younger, youngest, stronger, strongest, longer,* and *longest*. We say YUNG-Ger, STRAWNG-Gest, etc. by exception.

Learning this rule will help the foreigner to avoid confusion in pronouncing *ng* words. But he may also have to improve his *articulation* of the *NG* sound. For his native language either:

May not have the *NG* sound at all,

    or

May always have the *NG* followed by *G* or *K*.

In the first case he will tend to substitute a sort of *N* for *NG*. *Coming* will sound like *KUMM-in* or *KUMM-een.*

In the second, he will tend to add a *G* or *K* to *NG*. *Going out on Long Island* will be said as *GOH-ing GOWT on long GY-land* or *GOH-ing KOWT on long KY-land*. This is called an NG click. It is an unmistakable trait of a foreign accent, and the student should work hard to correct it.

Correcting the Substitution of N for NG. With the mouth slightly open, close the mouth cavity by lifting the tongue to the gum ridge, and let your voice resonate in the nose. This is an *N*.

With the mouth open, close the mouth cavity by raising the back of the tongue against the soft palate as if to make a *G*. Allow the voice to resonate in the nose. This is the *NG* sound.

Practice Exercise No. 115

Say several strong *N*'s before saying each *N* word below, several strong *NG*'s before saying each *NG* word. First read down each column, then read the words in pairs.

N	NG	NG	N
sin	sing	singer	sinner
win	wing	winging	winning
pin	ping	pinging	pinning
thin	thing	thinggumabob	thinner
kin	king	kingly	kinship
hand	hang	hanger	Hannah
tan	tang	tang-y	tanner
Lon	long	longing	clonic
Hun	hung	hung out	Hunnish

Correcting the NG Click. To eliminate the *NG* click at the ends of words:

Prolong an *NG*, beginning very loudly and gradually letting the sound die away. Do not move tongue or jaw until the sound has died away completely. Then slowly relax the tongue to a rest position, being careful to avoid even the smallest clicking noise.

Gradually shorten the time spent in letting the sound die away. Then apply the same method to the words in the first *NG* column in the list above. Prolong the *NG* in these words, letting it die away gradually; shorten the time spent in letting it die away; relax from the *NG* position gently and without any click.

To eliminate the *NG* click in the middle of words:

a. Emphasize or sharpen the distinction between *NG* and *NG-G*. Say *FING-GER* loudly, stressing *both* syllables, and even saying the second syllable with more stress than the first. Use a strong, voiced *G* to begin the second syllable.

Now say *SING-er* (or *SING-ing,* if you have eliminated the click at the end of words). Say the first syllable loudly and strongly; say the second lightly and weakly, "tossing it away" so that it is almost unheard.

Using the above technique, say *SINGerSING-erSINGerSINGer* very rapidly, hardly moving the back of the tongue at all.

Contrast *longer* and *hanger* in the same way, "LONG-GER" and "HANG-er," "HANGer-HANGerHANGerHANGer." **Feel** as well as **hear** the difference between *NG* and *NG-G*.

Read the words in the second *NG* column above, saying them as you said *singer* and *hanger*.

REMEMBER: In *NG* words, say the syllable which follows the *NG* fairly lightly; in *NG-G* words, say the syllable which begins with *G* fairly heavily.

b. Notice that the nasal *M* and the stops *B* and *P* are made with the lips; that the nasal *N* and the stops *D* and *T* are made with the tongue and upper gum; that the nasal *NG* and the stops *K* and *G* are made with the back of tongue and the soft palate.

If, in some foreign language, *M* were always followed by *B* or *P*, and *N* were always followed by *D* or *T*, anyone who used that language as his native tongue would tend to say the English sentences *Jim came home, John ran in,* as:

| JimB camB homB | Or: | JimP camP homP |
| JohnD ranD inD | Or: | JohnT ranT inT |

This may seem fantastic, yet the *NG* click is precisely the same sort of articulation effect. And the foreigner can learn to say *NG* properly by comparing it with the way he says *M* and *N*. Consider the words:

simmer	SIM-er	(*Not:* SIM-Ber)
sinner	SIN-er	(*Not:* SIN-Der)
singer	SING-er	(*Not:* SING-Ger)

In *simmer,* the lips part **gradually** from the closed position for *M*. In *sinner,* the tip of the tongue is released **gradually** from its contact with the gum ridge as one moves from the *N* to the vowel. If, in either case, the release is sudden or abrupt, like that of a faulty automobile clutch, the articulation result is an unintended stopsound, *B* or *D*.

Likewise with *NG*. The back of the tongue must be released **gradually** from its contact with the soft palate, as in the proper operation of a smoothly functioning car clutch. Otherwise, just as the car will jolt, so will an unintended *G* or *K* be interjected.

Practice Exercise No. 116

a. Establish the muscular feeling of easy, **gradual** release of the tongue from the *NG* sound. Practice the words below, prolonging the nasals as follows: DIMM . . . , DIMM . . . er; DINNN . . . , DINNN . . . er; DINNNG . . . , DINNNG . . . er.

dim	dimmer	Sim	simmer
din	dinner	sin	sinner
ding	dinger	sing	singer
whim	shimmer	ham	hammer
win	winner	Han	Hannah
wing	winger	hang	hanger
clam	clammer	Tam	Tammer
clan	clanner	tan	tanner
clang	clanger	tang	tang-y

b. Practice the following for the avoidance of *N* substitutions and for eliminating *NG* click.

Coming and going.
Eating and drinking.
Working and playing.
Coming in and going out.
Climbing up and falling off.
Swinging along.
Singing a song of longing.

c. Practice the following for a strong *NG-G.*

English language.
Anglican Englishman.
Single angler.
Singular angle.
Strongest finger.
Younger wrangler.
Longest tango.

d. Review by practicing the following sentences with their mixed *NG* and *NG-G* sounds:

The youngest of the English singers was fingering his song book longingly.

The seemingly longer was stronger and the seemingly stronger was longer.

The youngish angler lingered along with the angry stranger.

KEY: (Only exploded *g*'s are capitalized: G)

The young-Gest of the Eng-Glish singers was fing-Gering his song book longingly.

The seemingly long-Ger was strong-Ger and the seemingly strong-Ger was long-Ger.

The youngish ang-Gler ling-Gered along with the ang-Gry stranger (STRAYN-dzher).

NOTE 1. Words like *stranger* do not come under the above rule or discussion because the *n* in such words has a true *N* sound made with the tip of the tongue. *Range* is said RAYNDZH, and *astringent,* a-STRINN-dzhent. Other words of this type are: *singe, mange, strange, danger, manger, dingy, fungi, longevity, harbinger, laryngeal, laryngitis, pharyngeal, pharyngitis.*

NOTE 2. Once having learned to make *NG* without an *NG* click, be careful not to introduce this sound into words which take *NG-G.* If you find this happening, review the rule for pronouncing *ng* and practice the last two exercises above.

CONSONANT COMBINATIONS

When two consonants occur together in the same syllable in English, as in *play,* some foreigners will say these consonants as distinctly separate sounds. Americans tend, however, to run the sounds together more. The second sound follows the first, of course, but the succession is a very rapid one.

The foreigner will be helped if he adopts the concept that he should be preparing for the second consonant while saying the first.

In saying *play,* have the tongue in position for *L* before actually saying the *P.* Use the same technique for *blow, clay, glow,* and other words with the same consonant combinations.

In *crawl, green, pray, brown, free* and similar words, have the tongue in position for *R* before saying the initial consonants.

In *play, clay, crawl, pray, free* and similar words the puff of air from the initial consonant carries over into the second so that the *L* and *R* are half voiceless, half voiced.

In *tree, draw,* etc., the *T* and *D* are made somewhat higher than usual on the gum ridge to ease the upward movement of the tongue-tip for *R.* In *width, breadth, eighth* (AYTTH), the *D* and *T* are made somewhat lower than usual to ease the movement of the tongue downward for the *TH.*

When three or four consonants occur together, as in *fists, sixths* (SIKSTHS), careless speakers eliminate sounds, using for these words a prolonged *SSS* (FISSS, SIKSSS). Careful speakers will split the combination up into two parts, pausing slightly between the parts (FIS-TS, SIKS-THS).

Foreigners, of course, will want to follow the example of careful speakers of English.

(Practice material will be found in the sections entitled *Linguo-dentals* and *Omissions* in the chapter on *ARTICULATION.*)

ANSWERS

CHAPTER V

Practice Exercise No. 28

Question	Answer
a	Reports, Treasurer's
b	New Business
c	Reports, Committee
d	Unfinished Business
e	Reports, Officers'
f	Minutes, Correction of
g	New Business
h	Reports, Committee
i	General Orders

CHAPTER VII

Practice Exercise No. 61

KEY: In *a*, emphasize *bury, praise*.
In *b*, emphasize *Cowards, many, valiant, once*.
In *c*, emphasize *sleep, forgetting*.
In *d*, emphasize the words italicized below:

He who *knows*, and *knows* he knows,
He is *wise—follow* him.
He who *knows*, and knows *not* he knows,
He is *asleep—wake* him.
He who knows *not*, and knows *not* he knows not,
He is a *fool—shun* him.
He who knows *not*, and *knows* he knows not,
He is a *child—teach* him.

CHAPTER VIII

Practice Exercise No. 82

The pronunciations in the first column are the correct, that is, the acceptable ones.

Practice Exercise No. 83

1, 3, 6, 8, 9, 10 are right in the first column;
2, 4, 5, 7, 11, 12 are right in the second column.

Practice Exercise No. 84

1, 5, 10 are right in the first column;
2, 3, 4, 7 are right in the second column;
for 6, 8, 9, both columns are correct.

Practice Exercise No. 85

4, 5, 7, 8 are right in the first column;
1, 2, 3, 6 are right in the second column;
9, 10 are right in both columns.

Practice Exercise No. 86

1, 3, 7, 9, 10 are right in the first column;
5, 6, 11 are right in the second column;
2, 4, 8 are right in both columns.

Practice Exercise No. 87

1, 2, 3, 4, 10 are right in the first column;
5, 7, 8, 11 are right in the second column;
6, 9 are right in both columns.

CHAPTER IX

Practice Exercise No. 89

Single Vowels: 1, 3, 7, 11, 12, 13, 14.
Diphthongs: 2, 4, 5, 6, 8, 9, 10, 14.

Note: The last word, *poet*, has two syllables. The first contains a diphthong, the second a single vowel, thus: POH-et.

Practice Exercise No. 90

a: keyed, kid, Ked, cad, cud, cod, cawed, code, could, cooed, cued, cared, curd, etc.
b: kit, cat, Kate, kite, cot, cut, caught, coat, cute, coot, curt, etc.
c: mean, Min, main, men, man, mine, moan, moon, Marne, mourn, etc.
d: teen, tin, Taine, ten, tan, Tyne, ton, town, tone, tune, torn, turn, etc.

INDEX

Accent, 142, 177–178
Accenting wrong syllables, 145–146
Acceptable pronunciation, 140
Added sounds, 144, 175
Adjournment, parliamentary
  as an order of business, 86
  motion for, 88, 94
Affectations, 31, 146–147
Agenda, 83, 119–122
Alveolar ridge, 156, 157
Alveolars, 168–173, 181–183
American place names, 153
Analyzing a company, 33–34
Analyzing a job, 34, 39
Analyzing your voice, 124–125
Anecdotes, use of, 72–73
Application letter, 35–36
Applying for a position, 33–38
Approach, the sales, 43–44
Argumentation, 73–77, 112–116
Articulation
  artificial, 175–176
  as muscular habit, 155–156
  foreign influence on, 155, 176
  general faults of, 174–176
  importance of, 155
  of consonants, 168–172, 181–187
  of vowels, 158–168, 180–181
  social influences on, 155
Attitudes in conversation, 24–26
Audience analysis, 58–59
Audiences, typical examples of, 75–77
Authority, citing of, 77
Authority to interrupt, parliamentary,
  86

"Big Lie," theory of the, 73–74
Body of a speech, 61–63, 68–69, 72, 74
  77, 78
Breathiness, 129
Breathing
  controlled, 130–131
  mechanism, 127
Business, parliamentary
  new, 85, 95–96, 100–101
  order of, 83–86
  unfinished, 85, 95–96
Bylaws, 111–112

Chair, the
  appeal from decision of, 97
  rules concerning, 80–81

Chairmanship, 80–81, 95–96, 97, 104–
  105, 106, 107, 108, 109, 118, 121–122
Children, speaking to, 24
Choice of pronunciation, 148–149
Choosing a subject, 54–56
Circumflex inflection, 134
Close, the sales, 45
Cognate confusion, 183–185
Composition, speech
  as feeling for form, 77–78
  elements of, 61–67
  types of, 67–77
Conclusion of a speech, 61, 66–67, 69,
  77–78
Confusing similar words, 144–145
Consideration *in toto* or *seriatim*, 89,
  97–98
Consonant sounds
  alveolar, 169–173, 182–183
  cognate, 183–185
  combinations, 187
  linguo-dental, 168, 173, 182
  NG, 185–187
  R, 173 174
  stop, 184
  voiced and voiceless, 183
  W and *V*, 182
  Y and *J*, 182–183
Constitutions, 111–112
Controlled breathing, 130–131
Conversation
  defined, 19
  faults of, 30–32
  faulty attitudes in, 25–26
  getting started in, 26–28
  good attitudes in, 25
  keeping going in, 27–29
  misconceptions about, 20
  taboos in, 21
  topics for, 20–22
Conversion, remarkable because rare,
  75
Convince, the speech to, 57
Cooperative discussion, requirements
  for, 118–119
Cross-Questioning technique, 115–116

Data sheet, 34–35
Debate
  motions regulating, 92–94
  program types of, 112–116
Delivery, types of, 52–54

Denasalization, 137
Dentals, 169
Dewey, John, cited, 74–75
Dictionary, how to use a, 141
Diphthongs, 158–159, 180–181
Discussion
  informal group, 117–122
  parliamentary, 104–112
  program forms of, 112–116
Division of the assembly, 89, 99–100
Dress, 52
Duration, 123–124

Ear training, 123–124
Einstein, Albert, cited, 72
Eisenhower, Dwight, quoted, 65, 67, 72
Employment interviews, 33–41
Ethics
  of argumentation, 73–74
  of parliamentary strategy, 105–106
Evidence, 73–74, 76–77, 113–114, 120–
  121
Exhalation, 131
Exposition, 70–73
"Extemporaneous" speech, the, 54
Eye-contact, 52

Fad words, 31
Falling inflection, 134, 179
Feeling at ease, 47–48
Flash back technique, 68
Floor, having the, 82
Focus tone, to, 136
Foreign accent, 177 *ff*
Foreign place names, 153–154
Foreign words, 149–152
Forgetting names, 31–32
Forums, 116–117
Fosdick, Harry E., quoted, 65
French words, 150–151

German words, 151–152
Gesture, 51–52
Glottal shock, 129
Glottis, 126–127
Group dynamics theory, 117–118

"Hand me down" speech patterns, 155
Hitler, Adolph, cited, 73, 74
Hoarseness, 130
Humor, 64–65
Huskiness, 129–130

Impromptu talk, 52–53
Inflections, 134, 179–180
Inform, the speech to, 56
Inhalation, 131
Interest
  arousing, 64–66
  the speech to, 56
Interviews
  applicant, the, 33–38
  employer, the, 38–41
  planning, 40–41
  questions in, 36–37
  sales, 42–46
Intonation, 133
Introduction of a speech, 61, 64–66, 67–68, 70–73, 78
Introductions, 26–27
Inventory, personal, 35
Italian words, 152

Jargon, 50
Job analysis, 34, 39
Jungle view of human nature, 74

Key to pronunciation, 142

Larynx, 157
Lateral emission, 172
Latin words, 149–150
Learned words, 147–148
length of vowels, 181
Letter of application, 35–36
Lincoln, Abraham, quoted, 74
Linguo-dentals, 168, 173
Linking, 178–179
Lip contours in vowel production, 159–162
Lisping, 172–173
Listening
  importance of, 158
  in conversation, 28
  training, 124
"Loading the question," 112
Logic, 74–75, 113–114
Loudness, 134–136

Memorized speech, the, 53
Microphone, the, 60
Minutes of a meeting, 83–84
Mispronunciations, common, 142–146
Motions, parliamentary
  TABLE of, 88–89
  appendage, 91
  classes of, 90–96
  considered by parts, 99–100
  debatable, 87, 88
  incidental, 88, 96–100
  leave to withdraw, 100
  main, 85, 88, 100–101
  making of, 82–83, 85
  objection to considering, 99
  precedence of, 87, 88
  privileged, 88, 94–95, 96

reconsideration of, 101
renewable, 87, 88, 103
repeal of, 102
required votes for, 87–88
review, 88, 101–103
seconding, 83, 87, 88
strategic, 93–94, 105–107
subsidiary, 88, 90–94, 96
tabling, 92–94, 102–103, 105, 106
Mouth opening in vowel production, 159–162
Movement, 51
Musical composition, compared to that of speech, 77–78

Names of persons and places, 152–154
Names, ways to remember, 31–32
Narration, 67–70
Nasal resonance, 136
"Nasal" twang, 137
Nasality, 136–137
NG clicks and confusion, 185–187
Notes
  need for, 63
  preparation of, 52, 61–63

Objections, overcoming, 45
Older people, speaking to, 23–24
Omitted sounds, 144, 174–175
Oral resonance, 137
Order, parliamentary
  call to, 83
  motions in, 82, 86
  motion to suspend rules of, 98–99
  points of, 93
  rules of, 79–80
  standing rules of, 111–112
Orders, parliamentary
  general, 84–85
  of the day, 95–96
  special, 85
Oregon style debates, 114–116
Organizing a parliamentary group, 107–110
Organs of speech, 156–157
Orthodontia and articulation, 155
Over-articulation, 175–176
Overcoming objections, 45
Oxford style debates, 112–114

Pace, Frank Jr., quoted, 64
Palate, 156–157
Parliamentary procedure
  defined, 79
  formal and informal, 104–105
  inquiries concerning, 96–97
  points of, 96
  strategy of, 93–94, 105–107
Personal experiences, telling, 31
Personal privilege, questions of, 95
Persons, names of, 152–153
Pet words, 32
Pharyngeal resonance, 137–138

Pharynx, 157
Phonation
  breathing and, 131
  faulty, 129–130
  good, 127–129
Phrasing, 138–139
Pinched tone, 130
Pitch, 123, 132–134
Pitch level
  habitual, 132
  optimum, 132
  varied, 132–133
Posture, 51
Practice, athletic approach to, 155–156
Pre-approach, the, 43
Presentation, debate, 112–113
Presentation, the sales, 44–45
Previous question, call for, 89–92
Pronunciation
  acceptable, 140
  choices of, 148–149
  common mistakes, 142–146
  helps to better, 147–149
  key, 142
Propositions, debate, 112
Propriety of speech, 64, 82
Public speaking
  audience analysis, 58–59
  basic concepts, 48–50
  beginners' faults, 50
  choosing a subject, 54–56
  composing the speech, 61 ff
  visual factors, 50–52
Purpose of a talk
  general, 56–57
  specific, 57–58

Quality, 123, 136–138
Quibbling, 120

Radio and TV, 59–60
Rate, 124, 138–139
Rating sheets, 39–40
Rebuttal, 113
Recess, parliamentary, 86
Refutation, 113–114
Rejoinder, 113
Relaxation, achieving, 128
Relevance, parliamentary, 82
Reports of officers and committees, 84
Resonance, 127, 136–138
Reversing order of sounds, 144
Rising inflection, 134, 179–180
Rising to be recognized, 31
Robert's *Rules of Order*, 79

Sales interview, 42
Salesman, the good, 42–43
Secondary accent, 142, 177–178
Spelling
  faults in, 46
  steps in, 43–46
Semantics, 116

Shifting the grounds
    of consideration, 74, 116
Sibilants, 171–173
Sigmatism, 172
Slang, 31
Sophistry, 73–74
Speaking occasion, formalities of, 65
Speech impediments, 155
Spelling pronunciations, 142–144
Stage fright, 47–48
Statistics, 72–73, 77, 114, 115–116, 120–
    121
Stevenson, Adlai, quoted, 64, 67
Stimulate, the speech to, 56–57
Stock questions in interviews, 36
Stop consonants, 184
Story telling
    awkward, 31
    narration as, 67
    to children, 69–70
Strangers, adjusting to, 23
Strategy, parliamentary, 105–107
Stress, 177–178
Stridency, 130, 138
Strong forms, 178
Structure, speech
    chronological in narratives, 67–68
    logical in argumentation, 75
Substitution of sounds, 144–145

Subversive teachers, argument
    concerning, 115–116, 144
Summarizing
    a group discussion, 122
    a speech, 67
Surveying the facts, 73–74, 120–121
Symposia, 116

Taboos in conversation, 21
Telephone, on the, 30
Television, talking on, 59–60
Throat resonance, 137–138
Timbre, 123, 136–138
Tongue, the, 156, 157, 159, 162
Toning sluggish muscles, 128–129
Topics, discovering, 21
Transitions
    in conversation, 29
    in speeches, 66
Trick questions in interviews, 37

Unstressed syllables, 178
Uvula, 156–157

Variety in pitch, 132–134
Visual aids, 52
Visual art composition,
    compared to that of speech, 77–78
Visual factors, 50–52

Vocal bands, 126–127, 157
Voice, developing your
    basic concepts, 125–126
    pitch, 132–134
    quality, 136–138
    rate, 138–139
    volume, 134–136
Voice mechanism, 126–127
Voiced and voiceless sounds, 183
Volume, 123, 134–136
Vote
    call for count of, 97–98
    required, 87, 88
Vowel sounds
    and diphthongs, 158–159, 180–181
    back, 164–165
    central, 165–167
    defined, 158
    distortions of, 167–168
    extreme, 159–163
    front, 163–164
    low, 164
    production of, 159
    special role of, in speech, 159

Weak forms, 178
Weak voice, to strengthen, 135
Wilson, Charles E., quoted, 72–73
Written speech, the, 53–54